Censorship in Theatre and Cinema

Censorship in Theatre and Cinema

Anthony Aldgate

James C. Re

Edinburgh University Press

For Owen Dudley Edwards and Jeffrey Richards

© Anthony Aldgate and James C. Robertson, 2005

Edinburgh University Press Ltd
22 George Square, Edinburgh

Typeset in Monotype Ehrhardt by
Servis Filmsetting Ltd, Manchester and
printed and bound in Great Britain by
Antony Rowe Ltd, Chippenham

A CIP record for this book is available from the British Library

ISBN 0 7486 1960 7 (hardback)
ISBN 0 7486 1961 5 (paperback)

Contents

Illustrations

Acknowledgements

We are indebted to Kathryn Johnson of the British Library's Manuscripts Department, who was especially helpful. At the British Board of Film Classification (BBFC) we have to thank the late James Ferman, the Director from 1975 to 1998, and his successor, Robin Duval, for allowing us access to BBFC records. In addition Craig Lapper and Dave Barrett saw to it that we were provided with the BBFC files we needed. The staffs of the British Film Institute (BFI) National Library, the BBC Written Archives Centre at Caversham, the British Library's Manuscripts Room, the National Archives at Kew and the Theatre Museum in Covent Garden gave indispensable assistance. Finally, we greatly appreciate the co-operation and support of Sarah Edwards, our editor at Edinburgh University Press.

We have endeavoured to trace all copyright holders, but where we proved unsuccessful, if they will contact us at the publishers, we shall ensure that the necessary acknowledgements will appear in future editions. We thank the publishers of our previously published work for their permission to use this material: Cambridge University Press, Croom Helm, Flicks Books, Manchester University Press, Oxford University Press and Routledge. Above all, we are grateful to the British Library and the BBFC for their permission to quote from material in their possession, which forms the bulk of this book.

Abbreviations

BBFC	British Board of Film Censors/Classification
BFI	British Film Institute
GLC	Greater London Council
LCO	Lord Chamberlain's Office
MGM	Metro-Goldwyn-Mayer

CHAPTER 1

Introduction

Theatre censorship laid down by law lasted in Britain from 1737 to 1968, during which time no performance on a public stage could legally take place without the prior blessing of the Lord Chamberlain, an eminent royal official, and there was no provision for any appeal against a Lord Chamberlain's decision to ban or amend a play. Neither the 1737 statute nor the amending 1843 Theatres Act provided any criteria for the Lord Chamberlain to apply in making his decisions, but in 1909, following public protests from eminent dramatists over some of the Lord Chamberlain's recent bans, the Liberal government of the day established a Joint Parliamentary Select Committee on theatre censorship. Its sessions took place between July and November 1909, but the government knew from the outset that King Edward VII was opposed to the surrender of the Lord Chamberlain's power to censor plays.[1] The committee thus recommended the retention of the existing system but attached certain conditions. These were a presumption that any play would receive a licence unless it (1) was considered indecent, (2) contained the portrayal of offensive personalities, (3) depicted living people or people who had died only recently, (4) violated religious reverence, (5) encouraged crime or vice, (6) impaired relations with any foreign power, or (7) was calculated to cause or bring about a breach of the peace.

No legislation along these lines resulted, but this was the first time that a parliamentary body had defined how the Lord Chamberlain's theatre censorship should function, and in 1910 the Lord Chamberlain adopted the committee's findings as official theatre censorship policy.[2] These became the rules the Lord Chamberlain applied to submitted plays until Parliament abolished theatre censorship. In addition an Advisory Board of five members prominent in public life, which the Lord Chamberlain might consult in doubtful cases, was appointed. In the first instance submitted plays were read and reported on by a Reader of Plays, who was supervised by the Assistant Comptroller and then the Comptroller before the play was passed on to the Lord Chamberlain for the final decision. The 1909 committee recommendations and the Lord Chamberlain's acceptance of these were published at the time, but the names of the Advisory Board members were withheld.

However, by 1910 the cinema was well on the way to superseding the music hall and the theatre as the chief entertainment medium among the general population. As purpose-built cinemas rapidly mushroomed after 1906, pressure mounted for control over both the cinemas and the films shown therein. The outcome was the 1909 Cinematograph Act, the passage of which through Parliament ran more or less concurrently with the Joint Parliamentary Select Committee theatre censorship deliberations. The 1909 Act was concerned solely with safety regulations, but local authorities were soon exploiting their new powers to grant licences to cinemas also to control film content. The film industry found this development most unwelcome and contested it at law, but through a series of court cases from 1910 to 1921, it became legally established that only local licensing authorities possessed the power to allow, cut or ban films.

Meanwhile, facing the threat of an imposed central government censorship, the film industry set up early in 1912, with Home Office approval, its own voluntary censorship body, the British Board of Film Censors (BBFC), which commenced operations in January 1913. Under its first President, George (G. A.) Redford who had been a Reader of Plays at the Lord Chamberlain's Office (LCO) from 1895 to 1911, the BBFC bore a marked structural resemblance to the Lord Chamberlain's theatre censorship, with the President as the BBFC equivalent of the Lord Chamberlain and a full-time Secretary, Joseph Brooke Wilkinson, as the counterpart of the Comptroller. Nevertheless there were important differences between the two censorship agencies. First was the basic fact that the Lord Chamberlain's decisions carried the force of law. In the last resort he could thus take a firmer line with playwrights and theatre managements than the BBFC could take with film production companies, since the BBFC was a purely advisory organisation to local licensing authorities. Second, the Lord Chamberlain handled only home-grown productions, even when the material had emanated from overseas, while for the BBFC external, already completed films comprised the bulk of its work. The former always had the opportunity to shape any play to his requirements at its formative stage, but the BBFC was afforded the same opportunity mostly only with films made in Britain, a minority of those films it received. Even then, BBFC decisions required local authority support to be effective, and this was not always forthcoming. Britain was Hollywood's principal external market, American films forming about 60 per cent of films shown in Britain from as early as 1914, but only now and again was British censorship a factor influencing the initial production of an American film. Finally, the BBFC published annual reports from 1913 to the mid-1930s, with the exception of the last three years of the First World War. In these reports films were seldom mentioned by title, but at least for a time the British public was allowed a chance to glimpse into BBFC policies in detail as well as into its general *modus operandi*. There was never any Lord Chamberlain's equivalent of the BBFC annual report, so that the ordinary man or woman in the street languished in ignorance of what was carried out in his or her name over theatre censorship unless relevant reports appeared in the national press.

Important studies in both cinema and theatre censorship have appeared, but each realm has usually been treated in isolation, with scant regard to a possible interaction between the two media. Film has commanded most attention, but surveys of the BBFC's evolution down the years since 1913 drew mainly on secondary sources and journalistic material until the mid-1980s, and even the most notable recent addition has done little more than rework what was already known, at least for the BBFC up to 1975.[3] By contrast theatre censorship monographs have had the enormous benefit since the early 1990s of the public release of the Lord Chamberlain's censorship correspondence. However, the authors using this have to date concentrated on outstanding instances of censorship intervention over renowned playwrights or particular themes, especially homosexuality.[4] While based upon original research from primary sources, these books have also served to focus on gender at the expense of wider issues.

While this work is not a comprehensive study of either British film or stage censorship, it breaks new ground by, first, marrying scrutiny of cinema and theatre within a comparative framework. Second, it highlights key American and British plays which were often adapted into films. Third, in concentrating upon both American and British stage and screen properties, the book redresses what has of late developed into too much of a national, even parochial, concern with censorship. The detailed analyses of various noteworthy case histories will exemplify the censorship procedures in action, while, in keeping with the authors' previous censorship monographs, the studies are based upon the Lord Chamberlain's correspondence and BBFC files.[5]

Notes

1. Philip Magnus, *King Edward the Seventh* (London: John Murray, 1964), p. 439.
2. For a more detailed discussion of these developments, see John Johnston, *The Lord Chamberlain's Blue Pencil* (London: Hodder and Stoughton, 1990), pp. 23–8.
3. Tom Dewe Mathews, *Censored* (London: Chatto and Windus, 1994).

4. Nicholas De Jongh, *Politics, Prudery and Perversions* (London: Methuen, 2000) simply follows up the homosexual thematic approach of his 1992 *Not in Front of the Audience* (London: Routledge); while Adam Sinfield, *Out on Stage* (New Haven, CT and London: Yale University Press, 1999), singles out for special attention homosexual playwrights such as Noel Coward, Terence Rattigan and Tennessee Williams.

5. James C. Robertson, *The British Board of Film Censors: Film Censorship in Britain, 1896–1950* (London: Croom Helm, 1985). James C. Robertson, *The Hidden Cinema: British Film Censorship in Action, 1913–1972* (London: Routledge, 1989). Anthony Aldgate, *Censorship and the Permissive Society: British Cinema and Theatre, 1955–1965* (Oxford: Clarendon Press, 1995) was a seminal study, combining and comparing coverage of British stage and screen censorship during a vital period of social change.

CHAPTER 2

Sex Matters

The Lord Chamberlain banned any play that he considered indecent. Indecency in the context of upper-class sexual values in late Victorian and Edwardian Britain covered any sexual activity outside marriage, and for many years after 1910 successive Lord Chamberlains interpreted indecency in this fashion. The BBFC on the other hand did not restrict itself so severely when it began operations in 1913, regarding only nudity as a reason for rejecting a film. However, by the end of that year, presumably under the influence of George (G. A.) Redford, the President from 1913 to 1916, the BBFC had decided that 'indelicate sexual situations', 'scenes suggestive of immorality' and 'situations accentuating delicate marital relations', to cite the BBFC annual report for 1913, would be either reduced or removed altogether. The following examples show how all this functioned in practice at the two censorship agencies, both before and after the change in British sexual attitudes of the 1950s and early 1960s.

Damaged Goods

This was a French social drama dealing with venereal disease among sexually active young people. Written in 1902 by Eugene de Brieux, it had at once fallen foul of French theatre censorship, but when this was abolished just before the First World War, the play was performed not only in France but also in Germany and the United States. It even appeared at a London private theatre, not subject to censorship, during the early part of 1914 before an English-language scenario was submitted to the Lord Chamberlain's Office (LCO) in the following April.

In this form the play consisted of three acts, the first of which is a lengthy interview between patient Georges Dupont, a syphilis sufferer, and his doctor, who warns him against a forthcoming marriage and advises him to postpone this for at least three years. Dupont rejects this advice, and in the second act he is seen as a married man and the father of a three-year-old girl who has symptoms of a mysterious illness. Dupont summons the same doctor, who examines the girl and then strongly rebukes Dupont for his irresponsible conduct. Moreover, the family nurse in charge of the daughter suspects that she herself and her own family might be infected. However, she rebuffs Dupont's attempts to bribe her into silence, the act ending with the nurse leaving her employment in the Dupont household. Before she does so, she blurts out the truth, which Madame Dupont over-hears and then plunges into a hysterical rage at her husband. The final act is primarily a medical discourse via a dispute in a hospital between the doctor and Dupont's father-in-law, a deputy in the lower chamber of the French Parliament. The latter is intent upon a divorce for his daughter but calms down when he sees the doctor treating a number of syphilitic patients. After this the deputy decides to introduce legislation in the French Parliament to prevent such tragedies.

Ernest Bendall, the LCO Reader of Plays from 1913 to 1920, commented that no amount of detailed amendments to the dialogue would change the significance of this didactic drama. He felt that venereal disease was a sub-ject unfit for a description or a discussion on the public stage, no matter how worthy a playwright's motives.[1] Bendall declined to recommend a licence to Lord Sandhurst, the Lord Chamberlain from 1912 to 1921, but before the latter made a decision, he first consulted the five members of his Advisory Board, four of whom actually read the play and agreed with Bendall. Accordingly *Damaged Goods* was banned in May 1914.

Three months later war broke out with Germany. Over the next few years this led to a breakdown in pre-war sexual conventions, and as early as 1915 the BBFC rejected a film dealing with venereal disease. As the war continued, many men became afflicted with this and had to be discharged from, or refused entry to, the armed forces, a development of much concern at the War Office as casualties mounted in the military stalemate with Germany along the Western Front. At home in Britain, too, there arose civilian and religious dissatisfaction with a perceived moral decline in sexual relations. Consequently the National Council for Combatting Venereal Disease, an organisation supported by many prominent people in public life, placed pressure upon Sandhurst to allow *Damaged Goods*. In February 1917 the council resubmitted the play, but Sandhurst decided to grant a licence only after King George V himself had agreed. It was extremely unusual for the monarch to be involved in person with theatre censorship, which shows how important the matter of venereal disease pre-sented on a public stage was regarded.

The play ran at the St Martin's Theatre in London from March to October 1917 and was later shown extensively in the provinces, Ireland, Scotland and Wales. The success of the London run led the War Office to urge the Samuelson Film Company to produce a film along the same lines as the play to serve as a warning to both sexes against promiscuity. While the play was still running in London, the Samuelson company tackled the BBFC about its willingness to pass a film on such a theme. As a result, C. Hubert Husey, the BBFC's chief examiner from 1913 to 1930, went to see the play, reported to the company that no film based upon it would be allowed without considerable modification to both story and subject, and so informed the Home Office.[2] The BBFC's negative reaction evidently killed off the project for the duration of the war, but in 1919 the company revived the idea in the light of the continued publicly expressed anxiety about pre-marital sex among British youth.

Directed by Alexander Butler, the film of *Damaged Goods* made virtually no concession to the BBFC objections, the Samuelson company seemingly depending upon the film's warning message and high moral tone to surmount censorship obstacles. The film was based upon de Brieux's play, but the story was given a British dimension and also expanded to enhance its dramatic impact. It centred upon Edith Wray (Vivian Reece), newly arrived in London, who becomes a dress-shop saleswoman. Meanwhile French law student Georges Dupont (Campbell Gullan) and Henrietta Louches (Marjorie Day) become engaged in France before he returns to London to complete his degree. Edith is seduced by her landlord, has a child, loses her job, fails to obtain another and finally leaves her baby in a convent while she turns to prostitution in order to live. Georges passes his final law examination, and while celebrating that same evening, he meets Edith and sleeps with her. He then discovers he has contracted venereal disease and is advised by his doctor not to marry for several years. He ignores this advice, and when Henrietta bears their baby, the child is found to be infected. Consequently the marriage founders, after which the child is sent to a foster mother, but the child's health does not improve until a specialist takes over her treatment. Under the influence of her father (J. Fisher White), Henrietta sues for a divorce, but the specialist introduces her father to Edith, who tells him her story, as shown in flashback. The divorce proceedings are shelved, three years later the daughter is cured, Henrietta forgives Georges and the marriage is restored.

The unconvincing happy ending, absent from the play, the cautionary approach and the final emphasis on the sanctity of marriage were not sufficient to satisfy the BBFC. On 25 November 1919 the film was rejected on the ground that it was a propaganda vehicle, which the BBFC at that time defined as any film seeking to influence public opinion. However, the Samuelson company resolved to put up a fight, for in mid-December it arranged a private London viewing for high clergymen and Members of Parliament. The outcome was an alliance of liberal prelates and parliamentarians to mobilise public backing for a reversal of the BBFC's decision.

This campaign was taken up by some local authorities, but nonetheless the BBFC would not budge and no local authority was courageous enough to award the film a certificate on its own initiative. *Damaged Goods* has never been shown publicly anywhere in Britain.

In 1938 the film was remade in the United States. The treatment of the theme was even starker than in the 1919 version, but sensationalism for its own sake was avoided. Even so, in the light of the 1919 events, the distributors bypassed the BBFC and instead submitted the film, retitled in Britain *Marriage Forbidden*, to the London County Council, which allowed it with an 'A' (adults only) certificate. It opened at the Rialto cinema in the West End in January 1939 under the auspices of the British Social Hygiene Council, but later, doubtless for commercial reasons, it did not appear widely in London, nor apparently at all elsewhere in Britain. Even in London, once it had moved away from the Rialto, it was restricted to screenings before invited audiences in specially hired premises.

Following the outbreak of the Second World War and American involvement in this from December 1941, the arrival of American servicemen in Britain from 1942 onwards saw venereal disease once again become a major British social concern. In consequence the play *Damaged Goods* was revived in a slightly amended form compared to 1917. The Lord Chamberlain passed it without demur late in 1942, and it was performed at provincial theatres, beginning at the Empire Theatre in Leeds during January 1943.

Desire Under the Elms

Set on a New England farmstead in 1850, this Eugene O'Neill drama deals with Ephraim Cabot, a farmer in his mid-seventies who is ruthless in his treatment of other people even though he regards himself as solemnly religious. Ephraim has two sons, Peter and Simeon, by his first wife and another son, Eben, by his second wife. Both wives have died, leaving Eben to hate his father for having worked his mother to death and to believe that the farm rightly belonged to her and should now be his. Ephraim stores away a cash hoard, but Eben discovers this without his father's knowledge and uses the money to buy his two stepbrothers' shares in the farm. When Ephraim returns to the farm after a journey, he brings with him a new wife, Abbie, and family tensions swiftly emerge. Peter and Simeon become drunk, defy their father's authority and depart for California, where gold has recently been discovered, while Abbie has grown to dislike Ephraim, whom she had married merely to obtain the farm when he died. A sexual attraction develops between Abbie and Eben, but he is resistant to her advances and in the meantime Ephraim promises her the farm, provided that before he dies she bears him a son. Partly for this reason and partly from physical desire, Abbie becomes determined to bear Eben's child. Through her sheer physical beauty and her suggestion that by this means he can revenge himself upon Ephraim on his dead mother's behalf, she manages to seduce him.

The following year she gives birth to a son, but at the resulting celebration neighbours openly joke about Eben being the boy's real father. The incensed Ephraim informs Eben of his promise to Abbie, whereupon Eben's love for her is transformed into hatred. Once she realises the reason behind his altered attitude towards her, she murders the child. This act causes Eben to summon the sheriff, but before he arrives at the farm, Eben's love for Abbie has returned and he is ready to share the blame for what has happened. Having at last learned about Eben's theft of his savings, Ephraim mocks them both as he turns them over to the law.

In itself this gloomy theme was strong meat for the 1920s British theatre, but when this was combined with incest and infanticide, the likelihood of the play surviving the Lord Chamberlain's scrutiny was remote. However, the St Martin's Theatre, acting for producer Basil Dean, submitted *Desire Under the Elms* to the LCO in March 1925, when George Street, Reader of Plays since 1914 and Senior Reader from 1920 until his death in 1936, believed it was simply too horrible for a public performance in Britain.[3] He recommended a ban but went on to state that this should not be decided purely on the basis of his report. Lord Cromer, the Lord Chamberlain from 1922 to 1938, agreed with Street about a ban, noting that he was not prepared to sanction a play with such a horrible theme and observing, 'It is in fact typical of the sort of American play against which there is a growing resentment.' A month later Cromer met Dean, when the former explained that he himself had not read the play but would do so and would circulate it to his Advisory Board when it was submitted officially. Dean thereupon pressed his case in writing, but the play was not formally presented to the LCO until 1 July 1925, after which Cromer carried out his promise to Dean, although his covering letter to the five Advisory Board members strongly emphasised his personal opposition to any British public performance. The Advisory Board unanimously backed him, but when this decision was conveyed to Dean, the latter unsuccessfully sought Cromer's permission to publish the correspondence on the play. Nevertheless Dean notified the press about the fact of the ban, but this brought him no significant support either in Parliament or among the general public. Ironically the only three letters on the play which Cromer received – two from Britons living in New York City and one from a British resident in France – all congratulated him upon his stand. In August 1927 a forthcoming private production of the play at the Arts Theatre Club was announced but seems not to have taken place, while in January 1934 another intending producer enquired as to whether the ban might be reconsidered, only to be informed that it remained in force.

However, in mid-September 1937 the Westminster Theatre in London submitted a script for O'Neill's *Mourning Becomes Electra*, the story of Mannon family tensions at the end of the American Civil War. This included references to adultery, an attempt to induce a heart attack through physical sexual submission, murder, suggested but unfulfilled incest, and finally a double suicide. Despite the depressing atmosphere, Henry Game, Reader of Plays since 1930 and Street's successor as Senior Reader in 1936, recommended that the play should be allowed but with several dialogue cuts involving the use of 'God', 'Christ' and two references to a woman offering herself physically to her husband. In Game's view the incest proposal was allowable, partly because the incest did not actually occur and partly because it was dramatically justified within the context of the plot.[4] Cromer commented that the play was more to American tastes than British and questioned whether British audiences would accept such a long play, although he expressly endorsed Game's recommendation that the incest suggestion should be retained. In the event the play lasted for only two months at the Westminster Theatre, from mid-November 1937 to mid-January 1938, and it was not until 1947 that RKO Radio filmed it, a turgid version which the BBFC allowed uncut in June 1948, by which time the Board had relaxed its pre-1939 sexual standards.

Cromer's decision to grant a licence to *Mourning Becomes Electra*, which encountered no public criticism, encouraged the Westminster Theatre to try its luck with *Desire Under the Elms* in 1938. By then Cromer had been succeeded as Lord Chamberlain by Lord Clarendon, who held this post until 1952, and Game reported as follows:

> Perhaps a refusal was justified in 1925, but I hold very strongly to the opinion that it is no longer justified now.
>
> The potential audience for serious plays has very much increased during the intervening years, thanks to the work of the Sunday-producing societies and such theatres as the Westminster, and because of the great increase in the number of published plays, the Censorship, recognising this development in public taste, no longer treats the Theatre audience as if it was entirely composed of children: and the Theatre is now in process of attaining at long last a reasonable amount of freedom.
>
> At the Westminster, where the play is to be staged, the management has built up a numerous audience which wishes to see serious drama; and which by no conceivable flight of imagination can possibly derive any moral harm from the work of a man who is undeniably a poet and an artist.
>
> It is to me a humiliating thought to think of all the comedies of adultery and fornication which we have passed . . . while a work of art such as this lies under our ban,

just because it treats of the primal passions of a rude society . . . And finally I would ask upon what grounds can the play be forbidden? It would be difficult to substantiate a claim that it is morally harmful, or to forbid a play because some people prefer drawing-room drama or comedies is quite indefensible.[5]

Lord Clarendon concurred with Game, so that this time *Desire Under the Elms* was allowed in full despite the addition of a final scene showing Abbie and Eben ascending the gallows. However, the Westminster Theatre did not perform the play until January 1940 with Beatrix Lehmann as Abbie, Mark Dignam as Ephraim and Stephen Murray as Eben. It ran for approximately ten weeks, during which time there was no adverse press comment and the LCO did not receive a single public complaint.

Hollywood did not turn its attention to *Desire Under the Elms* until 1957, when the 1930s-style, Roman Catholic-dominated Production Code Administration in the United States had come under a strong challenge. Then Delbert Mann directed the film for Paramount with Sophia Loren, fundamentally miscast, as Abbie (renamed Anna), Burl Ives as Ephraim and Anthony Perkins as Eben. In essence O'Neill's plot remained, but a few episodes were added, including an unlikely one in which Eben comes close to murdering his father. By late 1950s British screen standards this was tame, and in December 1957 the BBFC passed the film uncut with the 'X' certificate, which had restricted audiences to those aged 16 and over with effect from 1 January 1951. Since its British release in April 1958 the film has plunged into an obscurity from which it appears unlikely to recover in Britain, and most British cinemagoers who saw it in 1958 were doubtless unaware of the near fourteen-year theatre ban between the two world wars.

The Shanghai Gesture

This American play by John Colton, notorious during the 1920s, is set in a Shanghai brothel managed by a Chinese woman known as Mother God Damn. Prince Oshima, a Japanese, brings his British mistress, Poppy, to the brothel, activities in which include young girls imprisoned in cages. Prince Oshima and Poppy arrange to meet again at the brothel that same evening, but meantime it becomes clear that Mother God Damn is a refined woman with a polished bearing and a command of languages, whose power derives from a knowledge of secrets about people who wished to keep these hidden. Her power extends to Shanghai high society and is so strong that even the heads of famous European firms operating in Shanghai cannot decline invitations to dinner at her brothel. One such dinner includes the wives of prominent European businessmen, and one of these, Sir Guy Charteris, puts himself forward as Mother God Damn's prospective lover in order that, as he puts it, he might experience 'strange, unholy delights'. However, her response is to present a British girl in a very large urn to be auctioned. Mother God Damn explains that she herself came from a Manchu noble family, which banished her after she had been seduced by an Englishman. The auction of the girl is intended to be her revenge upon the Englishman concerned, Charteris, who no longer recognises her, because the girl for sale is his legitimate daughter by his British wife. He had married her soon after his seduction of Mother God Damn, but the girl had been given to Mother God Damn in exchange for her own illegitimate daughter when the two girls were babies. The illegitimate daughter turns out to be Poppy, and when Mother God Damn discovers her real identity, she strangles Poppy out of shame at Poppy's behaviour and returns Charteris's legitimate daughter to her father.

This sordid tale of revenge going awry was very controversial during the inter-war period. Early in 1926 it was first submitted to the LCO, where George Street reported that it was impossible for the play to be staged in public, and that this was so obvious he was surprised the Adelphi Theatre had even bothered to send it. He continued that some scenes were revolting, while the play in general was full of coarseness. An extra reason for a ban was the display of important Europeans in the power of a Chinese.[6] Lord Cromer, the Lord Chamberlain, added that it was a most disgusting play, which the Adelphi Theatre ought to have been ashamed to submit. Of course he banned the drama, and in March 1927 A. H. Woods, the American theatrical producer who owned the British rights to the play, sought an interview with Cromer, who however declined to meet him.

Just over two years later, with *The Shanghai Gesture* having in the interim had a long Broadway run, Cromer received an invitation to attend a private performance of the play, the script supposedly having been considerably revised since the 1926 ban. Cromer was unenthusiastic, noting in May 1929 that he remained opposed to the play's entire ethos and theme, and that the producers should be given no encouragement to believe he would grant it a licence. All the same he sent Street and another senior member of his staff to the performance on Sunday evening, 12 May 1929, at the Scala Theatre in Charlotte Street, where the Venturers' Society presented it with Cathleen Nesbitt as Mother Goddam – a slight change of name, presumably to forestall accusations of blasphemy – Hermione Baddeley as Poppy, Lester Matthews as Oshima and S. J. Warmington as Charteris. Street and the other LCO member present did not alter their opinions, so that Cromer's ban remained valid, Cromer optimistically asserting that this should be the last he would hear of this horrible play.[7]

However, reviews appeared in six national newspapers, including *The Times*, and while none was keen on the play as drama and none called directly for Cromer to lift the ban, the esteemed critic of the *Daily Telegraph*, W. A. Darlington, came close to doing so when he claimed the play was outspoken rather than indecent. The Scala performance also attracted the attention of arch reactionary Conservative Home Secretary Sir William Joynson-Hicks, who was prepared to take up with Cromer the question of whether a banned play should even be privately staged on a Sunday, but before he could do so, a general election took place and the Conservatives lost office. In the event the Scala production was not followed up with another official submission until long afterwards, so that Cromer himself did indeed hear no more about the play while he remained Lord Chamberlain.

Meanwhile Hollywood had been interested in filming *The Shanghai Gesture* during the late 1920s, but many attempts to do so, reportedly more than thirty, had all been blocked by the American censors headed since 1922 by Will H. Hays. However, in the late 1930s Arnold Pressburger, a Hungarian producer who had worked in Germany and Britain before making his way to Hollywood, bought the play's screen rights and wrote an outline script which he believed would satisfy the Hays Office. At the time Pressburger was experiencing difficulty in securing work in Hollywood, but in 1940 he approached a fellow émigré, Josef von Sternberg, whose health and career were in decline, with his outline script. Von Sternberg and three other minor writers expanded and rounded this off, with the result that this time the Hays Office allowed the script during 1941, by which time it had undergone extensive revision by comparison with the play.[8]

First and foremost, the brothel setting was replaced by that of a spectacular, three-tiered casino. Mother God Damn was changed to Mother Gin Sling (Ona Munson), while Prince Oshima was renamed Dr Omar (Victor Mature), a hedonistic, womanising Eurasian clad in a cape, fez and tuxedo. Charteris's daughter by his British wife now became Dixie Pomeroy (Phyllis Brooks), a penniless American chorus girl whom Omar rescues from the clutches of the Shanghai police at the beginning of the film and then takes to the casino as one of his intended conquests. However, after she arrives there she is employed by Mother Gin Sling while Omar's attention is diverted to Victoria Charteris (Gene Tierney), alias Poppy Smith, on her first visit to the casino. Poppy's later degradation therein is depicted as the result of alcoholism, an infatuation with Omar and jealousy over Dixie, who, she mistakenly believes, is Omar's mistress. Poppy herself was now converted into the offspring of a short-lived marriage between Charteris (Walter Huston), calling himself at the time Victor Dawson, and Mother Gin Sling rather than of an affair between them. In the climax Mother Gin Sling shoots Poppy instead of strangling her after Charteris informs the former that Poppy is her daughter as well as his, for she had deliberately brought about Poppy's degradation as her planned revenge on Charteris on the assumption that Poppy was his daughter by his British wife.

Despite the numerous detailed changes from the play, which included the addition of both Asian and European acolytes of Mother Gin Sling, its decadent atmosphere remains, strongly aided by von Sternberg's striking visuals. In the casino the camera dwells upon many unescorted young women, while outside a well-dressed man is shown talking to a street girl. These shots alone make it plain that the casino, at the very least, serves as a pick-up point for casual liaisons, while Poppy on her first visit observes that anything could happen in the casino. Her subsequent trance-like behaviour hints at drug addiction, and at Mother Gin Sling's Chinese New Year dinner three girls appear in cages as the lots at a fake auction. She informs Charteris that such auctions really do occur in China, but, as in the play, the time of the story is not given, although the film begins with a notice on the screen stating that the setting is not contemporary, presumably to avert possible protests from the Chinese government.

In spite of the amendments, there remained sufficient in the film to have seriously concerned the BBFC if it had been submitted before the Second World War, for, quite apart from the sexual implications, the BBFC's rules for rejection had included 'equivocal situations between white girls and men of other races' and 'white men in a state of degradation amidst native surroundings'. However, by the time the film reached the BBFC early in April 1942, Britain, China and the United States were all allies fighting against Japan, while in any case the war itself had virtually compelled the Board to relax its pre-war sexual standards.[9] Accordingly the film was allowed uncut, a decision which neither the critics nor the public took amiss.

This development would have undermined the Lord Chamberlain's ban on *The Shanghai Gesture* if the play had been resubmitted to the LCO during the war or in the immediate post-war years, but in fact it was not forwarded to the LCO until November 1956, when times had drastically changed from the 1920s. Lieutenant-Colonel Sir Thomas St Vincent Troubridge, Reader of Plays at the LCO between 1952 and 1963, was moved to remark that the play was now merely a rather old-fashioned melodrama with nothing in it to shock a tolerably sophisticated schoolgirl.[10]

The plot was basically the same as thirty years earlier but was embellished
with extra detail, on which basis the play was granted a licence without any
disagreement at the LCO. It was performed without any vestige of public
controversy by Harry Branson's Court Players at the Princes Theatre in
Bradford during September 1957. This was a very far cry indeed from Lord
Cromer's ban in 1926.

Tobacco Road

Based upon an Erskine Caldwell novel, *Tobacco Road* was a play by Jack
Kirkland. It was produced on Broadway in 1933 and ran for several years
afterwards in defiance of critical revilement. Kirkland wrote his play at the
height of the 1930s great depression, and it deals with a once prosperous
but now derelict farm in a remote area of Georgia, where, because of the
Lester family's refusal to move, it has been reduced to squalor, misery and
resulting degeneracy. In Britain it was first performed privately with a
little-known cast in May 1937 at the Gate Theatre in Villiers Street, where
Cromer saw it and notified the theatre management that it would be point-
less to submit the play for a public audience.[11] However, in 1941 Hollywood
director John Ford, who at this stage of his career was interested in portraying lower-class life in the wake of his hugely impressive *The Grapes of
Wrath* (1940), made the film from Nunnally Johnson's script, a bowd-
lerised and much toned-down version of the play. The BBFC allowed this
uncut in April 1941, by which time the war had considerably reduced eco-
nomic hardship in Britain, and its release aroused no public disquiet.

In this way the path was apparently smoothed for a British public stage
production, the Playhouse Theatre in the West End duly forwarding a
script to the LCO in January 1946. Henry Game had not seen the pre-war
version at the Gate Theatre, but he believed that if the chief female character's erotic antics and dialogue were to be watered down to something
'more like the glad eye', if she was transformed into a reasonable human
being and if her part was reduced, then the play might be passed, although
other bawdy and irreligious dialogue would also have to be removed.

However, Lord Clarendon, the Lord Chamberlain, would have none of
this and instead decided upon a ban. In mid-July 1947 the private New
Lindsey Theatre at Notting Hill tried again with a slightly amended
version, but Clarendon confirmed the ban. American theatre director
Robert Henderson thereupon made representations to the LCO and even
offered to stage a special rehearsal performance for Clarendon in person.
Clarendon declined the invitation but sent R. J. Hill, the LCO Secretary, to
attend a routine rehearsal performance on 15 August. Hill reported that the

production was allowable with certain amendments, but he feared that producers and directors of other theatres would be less scrupulous than
Henderson and recommended a continued ban for this reason, a decision
that received some support in the national press.[12] The ban remained, but
Henderson did not give up easily and replied that no other version of the
play could be performed in Britain, since Kirkland had stipulated this in
his contract with Henderson. Brigadier Sir Norman Gwatkin DSO, the
recently appointed Assistant Comptroller at the LCO who went on to
become Comptroller from 1960 to 1964, was not convinced by Henderson's
case. Thinking that Clarendon might allow the play after all, Gwatkin
asked, 'Is this legal? And what happens in the unfortunate event of
Mr Kirkland's demise?' Despite his reservations, Gwatkin saw the play on
16 October and thought it a great improvement on the pre-war version,
which he had also seen. He still regarded the play as remarkably sordid, but
morally 'it hasn't got much on a lot of West End productions', and his
inclination was to pass it but with such sweeping amendments that he
hoped the author would be disinclined to carry them out.

Clarendon, though, would not be moved from his earlier ban, but
Henderson persevered and in December 1947 Gwatkin went to see Ford's
film of *Tobacco Road*, which had just been reissued. He thought that if the
characters of the two female leads were diluted along the lines of Nunnally
Johnson's script in Ford's film, the play could be allowed, and on this basis
Clarendon at last relented. Even so, the play was not publicly presented
until August 1949, when it opened at the Embassy Theatre in Swiss
Cottage to none too enthusiastic reviews. Following a three-week run
there, it was transferred to the Playhouse Theatre, and after several more
weeks the Playhouse production led to a protest to Clarendon from the
Public Morality Council on the grounds that religion was caricatured, and
that some sexual scenes were grossly offensive. The council sought the
removal of all this material, but Clarendon stood firm, pointing out that
the play, which featured Edie Martin, Thora Hird and Mervyn Johns, had
already been cut, and that to cut it further would alter the nature of the
entire play. The West End run continued without incident, and when it was
over at the very end of 1949, it toured the provinces, where, it appears,
Henderson sometimes delegated the direction to others.

In August 1950 the play arrived at the Empire Theatre in Oldham,
where salacious pre-publicity in the form of handbills reached the attention of the local police. As a result, an inspector and a police constable
attended the play on its first night, 28 August, and reported to the Chief
Constable that although the dialogue had adhered to the script approved
by Clarendon, there had been a departure from this through the players'

physical actions, 'stage business'. The Oldham police took up the matter with Sir Terence Nugent, the Lord Chamberlain's Comptroller from 1936 to 1960, who afterwards informed the office of the Director of Public Prosecutions that an offence had been committed. However, the office responded by telling Nugent that a prosecution would not be sanctioned because the chances of success were very low, to judge from previous prosecutions over 'stage business'. Although Nugent made personal representations on 12 September in an effort to reverse this decision, doubtless with Clarendon's authority, these failed and Nugent had to content himself with a warning to Henderson against future transgressions of this sort. In reply Henderson maintained that the 'stage business' objected to had occurred without his knowledge. In future the offending handbills would be withdrawn from circulation, and he would take personal charge of planned runs in London, Manchester and Scotland. In the light of these assurances Clarendon endorsed the licence for *Tobacco Road* on condition that the approved script would be followed faithfully. The play continued its tour until the end of 1950 without further mishap.

No Orchids for Miss Blandish

This was published in 1939 as an American gangster novel by British author James Hadley Chase. It sold well and was different from most of this genre up to that time in that it dwells upon gangster life from the inside and combines violence with abduction, murder and sex within a fast-moving action framework. It is set in 1936 Kansas City, where a gang of petty crooks kidnap heiress Miss Blandish and in the process murder her boyfriend. This gang is then itself destroyed by the more powerful Grisson mob, nominally under the control of Slim Grisson, but in fact led by his fearsome mother, a character probably based upon the notorious 1930s real-life American gang leader Ma Barker. Ma Grisson wishes to extract a large ransom from Miss Blandish's rich father, but Slim, sexually repressed and mentally semi-retarded, becomes besotted with his prey. Accordingly he loses interest in the ransom money and kills his mother when she tries to have Miss Blandish murdered in order to shake off the police from the gang's trail. Slim is ultimately killed, along with the remainder of the gang, by private detective and former newspaper reporter Dave Fenner. Finally, following her rescue, Miss Blandish commits suicide because she considers herself irredeemably polluted by her sexual relationship with Slim, enacted while she was drugged.[13]

Chase's tale provoked no real public concern, and his book continued to sell well during the early war years. On 19 November 1941 the author made an impact upon the theatre world when impresario George Black presented his *Get a Load of This* at the Hippodrome in London's West End. This play is set in New York City, and the audience is in effect invited to pretend that it was locked up inside a theatre staging a Park Avenue floor show while the police investigate a murder. The cast was largely unknown but was headed by celebrated comedian Vic Oliver, the players descending from the stage on occasions to mingle with the audience. This crime story, wrapped within a musical formula, lacks the sex and violence of *No Orchids* and presented no problems for the Lord Chamberlain. Perhaps due to its novel form of presentation, *Get a Load of This* proved sufficiently popular for its Hippodrome run to last almost a year, until the end of October 1942.

The success of this venture prompted Black to test out the LCO over a stage version of *No Orchids* in March 1942 without a scheduled opening theatre date. The submitted scenario was close to the book except that it is Miss Blandish herself rather than Fenner who shoots Slim Grisson down when the police arrive. Geoffrey Dearmer, the Assistant Reader of Plays since 1936 and Senior Reader from 1953 to 1958, commented, 'There is no cause to ban gangster muck of this kind . . . The language isn't too bad and love making may be said to be absent altogether . . . [14] The play was allowed with two dialogue cuts, accompanied by a general warning that the violence must be kept in check. The dialogue cuts were: (1) 'Know what happened when he got her on the bank? A rat ran out of her dress. The copper spewed', and (2) 'Listen, I once saw a fella burn.' The latter formed a part of Ma Grisson's description to her son of an electric-chair execution, and Black's proposed substitution of 'turn red as you burn' encountered Chase's objection. He argued that his original words were a graphic description of what actually happened at an electric-chair execution. These were very important to the play because Ma Grisson had vainly attempted to persuade Slim to kill Miss Blandish. Instead, Chase continued, she sets out to frighten him with the threat of the electric chair if he kills another gang member who is about to murder the heiress. Chase maintained that the details of electric-chair deaths were already known to the British public through the press and crime fiction. He won the argument, but in the following month, when Chase submitted his slightly revised script, Dearmer drily remarked that although the dialogue had been rearranged, this was no worse than before.

Shortly afterwards the play opened at the Grand Theatre in Blackpool, but on 18 and 19 May 1942, Chase appeared at the Old Bailey under his real name of René Raymond charged with obscenity in connection with another of his novels, *Miss Callaghan Comes to Grief.* He denied that this was obscene, but the jury read the book and decided otherwise, the judge

awarding him a hefty fine. Moreover, simultaneous prosecutions were
taken out against two similar books by Harold Ernest Kelly, *Road Floozie*
and *Lady Don't Turn Over*, with much the same result.[15] This crackdown
on perceived salacious pulp fiction caused the LCO to send an official
named Tomlinson to a performance of *No Orchids* in Blackpool during
mid-June 1942. Tomlinson's report was satisfactory, and for the moment
the LCO could relax, but Black apparently saw in Chase's obscenity conviction and the resulting publicity an unexpected opportunity to transfer
No Orchids to the West End with another revised script and a superior cast
headed by Robert Newton as Slim, Mary Clare as Ma, Linden Travers as
Miss Blandish and Hartley Power as Fenner. Clarendon allowed this
version a week after Tomlinson's report but cut two snatches of suggestive
dialogue – 'Not me. I was once chased up an alley by a sailor' and 'You've
got hot pants for that Blandish dame.'

The announcement of a West End run for *No Orchids* prompted an
unofficial cautionary letter to Clarendon from a Public Morality Council
committee member even before the play had opened in London. This drew
Clarendon's attention to Chase's recent court case and its outcome and
went on to state that the council's secretary had seen *No Orchids* in
Blackpool and regarded it as degenerate. Furthermore, the letter continued, in London it was more likely to be seen by the nationals of Britain's
wartime allies, who might take serious exception to its general ethos and
violent setting. This reference to possible American sensitivities did not
move Clarendon, whose reply signalled no retreat, but he was sufficiently
concerned to send Henry Game and Geoffrey Dearmer to the Prince of
Wales Theatre on 30 July, the day after its opening. The two Readers of
Plays gave it a clean bill of health, reporting that 'Those people who have
read the book and expect to see the same details on the stage will be disappointed.' The reviews were mixed, but by October, Clarendon had
received several protests from individual members of the general public, to
all of whom he yielded no ground. When in 1943 the London run ended
at the Lyric Theatre in Hammersmith, to which it had been transferred at
the end of October 1942 with a slightly different cast, a reduced and
peripherally amended version was allowed and performed at the Brighton
Hippodrome from 9 August 1943.

The first indication of a possible film version occurred early in June
1944, when a pre-production scenario was submitted to the BBFC with
minor differences in the plot. These included the murdered boyfriend of
Miss Blandish becoming her fiancé, his unintended murder then com-
pelling the petty crooks to kidnap her when their original motive had been
merely robbery. In addition it was now Fenner rather than Miss Blandish

who shoots Slim while the police look on with indifference. The BBFC proved unenthusiastic, to put it mildly. Colonel John Hanna, the BBFC chief examiner from 1930 to 1947, rejected the whole theme, although a more junior examiner, Mrs N. Crouzet, accepted it with modifications. These duly arrived at the BBFC in October 1944, when Hanna's reaction remained unchanged, while Mrs Crouzet found them acceptable except for one minor piece of dialogue. At this stage the amendments took on an added significance because some of them were featured in the eventual film. This time Miss Blandish actually falls in love with Slim, who is now portrayed as a reformed gangster trying, not very successfully, to go straight, and physically submits to him voluntarily before committing suicide following Slim's death.[16]

However, this project was shelved and might have remained at best a footnote in British cinema history but for the post-1945 British crime wave and the consequent emergence of British gangland films during the immediate post-war years. This development in censorship history has been traced in detail elsewhere.[17] Here it will suffice to note that the BBFC crossed the point of no return with Alberto Cavalcanti's *They Made Me a Fugitive*, passed uncut on 19 June 1947, and John Boulting's *Brighton Rock*, also passed uncut on 23 September 1947. Both contain more brutal sequences than the BBFC had ever previously countenanced in British films with a domestic gangland setting, but on the other hand there was no general firearms culture among British hoodlums, either in reality or on screen, and the violence in the two films was tepid compared with the 1930s American gangster classics. It was in this context that the small Renown company in late 1947 and early 1948 made *No Orchids*. This was based to some extent on the revised 1944 scenario, although the 1944 notion of a reformed Slim Grisson was abandoned, and he was depicted as an irredeemable monster, with whom Miss Blandish had inexplicably fallen in love. Uninspiringly directed by St John L. Clowes with Linden Travers repeating her stage role as Miss Blandish, the American actor Jack La Rue as Slim and the unknown Lilly Molnar as Ma, the film reached the BBFC on 23 February 1948, when no serious problems were anticipated, since both *They Made Me a Fugitive* and *Brighton Rock* had attracted relatively slight press criticism which found no echo elsewhere. The BBFC modified two reels of *No Orchids*, amounting to cuts of approximately one minute and twenty seconds, before allowing it on 12 March. Unfortunately, as the full version appears to be no longer extant and the BBFC records of its treatment are incomplete, it is at present impossible to reconstruct the deleted material, but to judge from its small running time, it was probably insignificant within the framework of the entire plot.

The film opened at the Plaza cinema in the West End on 15 April, after which it immediately encountered a hail of adverse criticism from many, but not all, critics. These attacks derived from a combination of, first, middle-class cultural prejudice against genres popular with the masses; second, too blatant a sexuality, for a refined Beauty falling for a low-class Beast and then willingly submitting herself to him provided a new twist in gangster dramas; and, finally, an anti-Americanism based upon a fear that the Americans might come to dominate the British film industry, as Brian McFarlane has shown.[18] At the time, in the wake of Britain's *ad valorem* tax upon all imported films from August 1947 to March 1948, the American major studios were at loggerheads with the largest single force in the British industry, the Rank Organisation, over the distribution of new American features in Rank-owned cinemas. However, although none of the *No Orchids* transgressions was new, it was probably the first time they had all been lumped together in one film. This might well explain, as McFarlane suggests, the ferocity of the critical broadsides, but perceptive as his analysis is, it contains no political dimension and it was in fact politicians who took action against the film, although doubtless there was some interaction between unfavourable critical comment and political events in regard to the film.

The political campaign against the film originated from inside Clement Attlee's Labour administration when junior minister Dr Edith Summerskill deprecated it while speaking at a private function. Her speech was delivered only a few days after the film's release, and it is unclear whether or not she had actually seen it. She appeared to advocate a ban, a stance taken up in the Commons by Labour backbencher Tom Driberg several days later. However, the government refused to intervene or change the film censorship structure. By then the Labour-controlled London County Council had already taken action, cutting the released version by a further two minutes. Other local authorities followed the London lead, yet others went along with the BBFC-authorised version, while a few, the most important of which was Surrey County Council, banned the film altogether. The politicians involved might have acted solely from a concern for established conventional sexual morality, but it is equally likely that other motives were at work. On the day before the London premiere of *No Orchids*, the Commons had voted by 245 votes against 222 to abolish capital punishment on a five-year trial basis against the advice of Home Secretary Chuter Ede, but the government was rescued from having to carry out this policy on 2 June, when the House of Lords removed that particular clause from a Criminal Justice bill by 181 votes to 28 after an impassioned speech in support of capital punishment by Lord Chief Justice Goddard. Significantly, it was during the interval between these two parliamentary votes when the uproar over *No Orchids* was at its zenith and local political steps against the film were sometimes taken. With a general election little more than two years away at the most and local elections also due before then, politicians of all parties wished to be seen taking action to combat crime, for many voters were believed to feel that crime films encouraged criminal behaviour, especially by the young. The campaign against *No Orchids* was a complex event with multifarious causes.

The attack upon the film was so strong that the BBFC felt driven only six days after its release to deliver an abject apology to the Home Office but a few days later to defend in public its decision to allow the film. As so often with British film censorship controversies, the episode proved to be a passing storm which largely bypassed British cinemagoers. Since 1948 *No Orchids* has plunged into a prolonged cinematic backwater, due less to the surrounding furore than to the basic fact that it is a poor film.

No Room at the Inn

The problem of British evacuee children billeted in unsuitable homes, uncared for and sometimes ill-fed as well as maltreated into the bargain, was not one that attracted the attention of either playwrights or film-makers while the Second World War was in progress. However, only two days after the cessation of European hostilities, the Embassy Theatre forwarded to the LCO a Joan Temple drama entitled *Weep for Tomorrow*, which with a modified script was retitled *No Room at the Inn*. This begins with the discovery of Mrs Voray's body on her bed in an upstairs room of her slum-like house. When policemen arrive, they are faced with five sullen, unkempt evacuee children who are all reluctant to talk until one of them, Mary O'Rane, at last breaks the wall of silence and reveals what has happened. The main story then unfolds.

Mary's mother had died suddenly. Her father, a merchant seaman, is at sea, and the local billeting officer is finding it difficult to secure accommodation for her. As a last resort he leaves her with Mrs Voray, who is a slut, drinks too much and is not averse to part-time prostitution. She is interested only in the allowance she will receive for Mary, while the responsible local authority is none too searching in its enquiries about Mrs Voray, who already has four other evacuees, including the cheeky and outspoken but essentially good-hearted Cockney girl Norma Bates. Mary soon discovers that Mrs Voray has no intention of looking after the children properly, but she is frightened of Mrs Voray, as are the other children, and fails to confide in anyone. Kate Grant comes to suspect what Mrs Voray is up to, but on account of the children's continuing silence there is little effective action she can take, although she does bring the matter to the attention of the local vicar, who, however, is all for letting sleeping dogs lie.

Mary's greatest hope is her father, but when he is on leave and visits Mrs Voray's home, she succeeds in first deceiving him over her treatment of the children and then seducing him. When he departs, he leaves her with money and a letter stating that Mary should remain at the house. This letter renders it difficult for the local authority to intervene, but when Kate Grant finds alternative accommodation for Mary, she refuses to go because of the other children, particularly one small boy she has taken under her wing. Inadvertently he spoils Mrs Voray's new hat, and as a punishment she locks him up in her damp coal cellar, but Mary and Norma, fearful that he will catch pneumonia, decide to steal the cellar key. This lies in Mrs Voray's handbag, and while she is lying on her bed in a drunken stupor, Mary places a pillow over her head to prevent her from waking. Unfortunately, Mary presses the pillow too hard and Mrs Voray suffocates. The policemen decide to turn a blind eye to what has occurred for the sake of the children who, the audience is left to surmise, will now face a brighter future.

As much an attack upon neglectful local authorities as upon those who mistreat evacuee children, the play caused Lord Clarendon no problems, and it opened at the Embassy Theatre on 10 July 1945 with Freda Jackson as Mrs Voray, Joan Dowling as Norma, Ruth Dunning as Kate Grant and Christopher Steele as the pusillanimous vicar. Well reviewed, it was transferred in May 1946 to the Winter Garden Theatre in the West End, where it was so successful that it ran until the end of May 1947. By that time the problem of maltreated wartime evacuee children had disappeared, but cruelty to children remained much in the news, while the play was also broadcast. To cash in on all this, as well as on the current fashion for 'realism' in British films, British National prepared a pre-production scenario, which spiced up the play, and submitted this to the BBFC at the end of 1947. Mrs Voray's occasional whoring was now developed into the conversion of her home into a brothel, a notion to which BBFC examiner Madge Kitchener was vehemently opposed even though she approved of the general theme, which she hoped might spearhead a national crusade for child welfare. Arthur Watkins, then being groomed for the BBFC Secretaryship in succession to the 77-year-old Brooke Wilkinson, agreed with her about the introduction of a brothel and prostitution into the story. He sought the removal of this material even though this idea permeated the entire scenario and was indeed integral to the story. Watkins was also critical of various pieces of dialogue, the most important of which was Mrs Voray's unfavourable view of approved schools for young criminals.[19]

Despite the BBFC's negative reaction, British National went ahead and retained the central brothel theme in the completed film. However, the BBFC might have been instrumental in a changed ending from the play, incorporated into the pre-production scenario, in that Mrs Voray meets her death by falling through a rotten handrail on a staircase and plunging headlong down the stairs. Since the BBFC has not preserved its file on *No Room at the Inn*, one cannot be certain that the BBFC was responsible, directly or indirectly, for this change, but it might well have been, for it is improbable that a child's smothering to death an adult with a pillow, however unintentionally, would have proved acceptable, if only because this was too easily capable of imitation. One review positively attributed this alteration to censorship considerations.[20] Scripted by Dylan Thomas and Ivan Foxwell, the film features Freda Jackson and Joan Dowling in their stage roles, Ann Stephens as Mary, Joy Shelton as crusading young teacher Juliet Drave (in place of Kate Grant), Harcourt Williams as the vicar, Hermione Baddeley as an elderly trollop friend of Mrs Voray, Niall MacGinnis as Mary's father, and James Hayter and Wylie Watson as two local councillors who oppose an investigation into Mrs Voray's activities because they are two of her clients.

These amendments in combination supplied the story with a sexier emphasis than in the play, but the BBFC nevertheless allowed the film with only minor cuts on 19 August 1948, by which time it was morally mild by comparison with the already passed *Brighton Rock*, *They Made Me a Fugitive* and *No Orchids for Miss Blandish*. When *No Room at the Inn* was released in October 1948, most critics were unimpressed and regarded Dan Birt's direction as more suited to the theatre than the screen. Since its initial release, it had not been publicly exhibited in Britain until the National Film Theatre revived it on 21 and 23 January 2002.

Pick-Up Girl/Good Time Girl

Elsa Shelley's 1944 American play *Pick-Up Girl* is set in a New York City juvenile court hearing the case of 15-year-old Elizabeth Collins, who has suffered from parental neglect and been found in bed with a middle-aged man. She had fallen into bad company and been led into semi-prostitution, as a result of which she has had an abortion and contracted venereal disease. All the same she is not yet totally beyond redemption, for she has gained the love of Peter, a 16-year-old boy who wishes to marry her despite his awareness of her sexually transmitted disease. This drives all thoughts of flight from Elizabeth's mind, and to make herself worthy of Peter's devotion, she resolves to accept and serve out without rebellion her inevitable reform school sentence.

Pick-Up Girl was sent to the LCO in May 1946, Lord Clarendon observing that while the story was sordid, it was also sincere and stressed the vital importance of parental responsibility. He granted it a licence subject to certain cuts.[21] In the light of the perceived juvenile crime eruption then current in Britain, Clarendon's decision was understandable, the required dialogue cuts being minor, although one involved a reference to the abortion, then a taboo topic for the Lord Chamberlain. However, shortly afterwards a private performance of the uncut script opened at the New Lindsey Theatre at Notting Hill, where it was seen and praised by both Queen Mary, the dowager queen, and Home Secretary Chuter Ede. This influential support was published in *The Star* of 5 June 1946, whereupon the play's director, Peter Cotes, appealed to Clarendon for the restoration of the deleted dialogue. Consequently Assistant Comptroller Brigadier Sir Norman Gwatkin attended a New Lindsey performance and reported that the cuts were unnecessary. In this way *Pick-Up Girl* survived the stage censorship intact and was transferred to the Prince of Wales Theatre on 23 July with Patricia Plunkett as Elizabeth, Joan Miller as her mother, David Markham as Peter and Ernest Jay as the juvenile court judge. The reviews praised the acting more than the play, and the run lasted approximately three months before the play was moved to the Casino Theatre, where it closed at the end of December 1946.

While the West End performances were coming to an end, indications of film interest emerged when early in October 1946 the BBFC was presented with a pre-production scenario. However, this received short shrift and was rejected out of hand on account of its prostitution and venereal-disease content.[22] The film was never made, but towards the end of 1946 David MacDonald directed *Good Time Girl* for Gainsborough from a script by Sydney Box, Muriel Box and Ted Willis. According to its credits, the film was based upon Arthur La Bern's novel *Night Darkens the Street*, which covers a notorious murder case of 1944, but in fact much of the film deals with the events leading up to the murder. These focus upon Gwen Rawlings (Jean Kent) who, like Elizabeth Collins in *Pick-Up Girl*, leaves home as the result of parental treatment. As a teenager she settles in a drab boarding house, where a fellow lodger, Jimmy Rosso (Peter Glenville), gets her a job at a London night club. The boss, Max (Herbert Lom), quarrels with Rosso, who quits the club but first persuades Gwen to pawn jewellery on his behalf. Unaware that the jewels are stolen, she is arrested in the home of a friend, Red Farrell (Dennis Price), found guilty of theft by a juvenile court and is sentenced to three years in an approved school. In the school she falls in with a group of hardened offenders and manages to escape. She finds Max, now running a new night club in Brighton, where she meets Danny (Griffith Jones), a playboy in whose company she attends a wild party. The worse for drink, she leaves the party by car when she has no driving licence, knocking down and killing a policeman. On the run in a train to London, she meets two American deserters (Bonar Colleano, Hugh McDermott), who go on to mug passers-by, hijack taxis and finally murder a car driver, none other than Red Farrell. Gwen is caught and sentenced to fifteen years in jail as an accomplice to murder.

All this bears a superficial resemblance to the real life of Welsh teenager Mrs Betty Jones, who had teamed up with American deserter Karl Hulten, an association resulting in the so-called 'cleft chin' murder. At their trial in January 1945 both were found guilty of murder, but whereas Hulten was hanged, Betty Jones was reprieved and detained indefinitely before being quietly released in 1953. However, much of *Good Time Girl* up to Gwen's escape from the approved school lies very close to the plot of *Pick-Up Girl*, too close to be sheer coincidence. As first filmed before the additions explained later in this section, *Good Time Girl* contained no moral element, while the 'crime does not pay' idea was introduced almost as an after-thought at the end with Gwen's fifteen-year sentence. However, the film showed much rich detail of unsavoury Soho night-club and gang activity, including razor slashing and vitriol throwing. This, coupled with the fact that the film was based upon a real, relatively recent murder case, was always likely to make the film a target for censorship troubles and press criticism, especially as one of the parties responsible for the murder remained alive. Doubtless for a combination of these reasons, Gainsborough early in January 1947 arranged a showing for Home Office representatives at its Shepherd's Bush studio.[23] The precise outcome is unclear, but the Home Office probably either sought the inclusion of extra material to provide the story with a moral dimension, which the BBFC might well have done anyway, or satisfied itself that the character of Gwen Rawlings was not too blatant a portrayal of Betty Jones. There was then a delay of more than six months before the film was completed and ready for BBFC inspection. The additional material, likely to have been instigated by Gainsborough under Home Office or BBFC pressure, assumed the form of two juvenile court scenes, one at the very beginning, causing the main story to be narrated in flashback, and one at the very end. The former sees the juvenile court chairman (Flora Robson) relating Gwen's story to a young girl (Diana Dors), who has been brought informally before her by the police, while the latter shows the young girl deciding to go home and mend her errant ways before she turns to crime and ends up like Gwen. The belated insertion of these two scenes gives the final version a structural similarity to *Pick-Up Girl* that was surely not accidental.

Lacking the abortion and prostitution content which had initially perturbed Lord Clarendon over *Pick-Up Girl*, *Good Time Girl* arrived at the BBFC on 15 July 1947. Unfortunately the BBFC file on the film is no longer extant, while the BBFC register entry shows only the final release version of 8,331 feet or 93 minutes' running time rather than the submitted footage. It is thus impossible to ascertain the extent of the BBFC cuts or what was cut or why. However, to judge by the time it took to satisfy the BBFC – the final version was not passed until 26 September 1947, a period of more than three months scrutiny – the cuts were likely to have been extensive. This speculation was reinforced by the personal testimony of Jean Kent herself when she introduced the film at the National Film Theatre in January 1983 and by references to censorship influence upon the completed film in the variable reviews it received after its very tardy release at the end of April 1948. Then the recent echoes of the *No Orchids for Miss Blandish* affair were still reverberating, and one local authority, Hertfordshire County Council, even went so far as to ban *Good Time Girl*, which has been scarcely seen since 1948.

The Moon is Blue

This 1950 F. Hugh Herbert play is a pleasant, occasionally whimsical and nowadays very dated American sexual comedy. It opens when rising young architect Don Gresham picks up Patty O'Neill at the Empire State Building observation tower and invites her to dinner at his apartment. She accepts on condition that he will do no more than try to kiss her. He agrees, and in Don's apartment she learns that he had split up from his girl friend, Cynthia Slater, just the previous evening. When Don leaves the apartment to buy their meal, a caller arrives who turns out to be David Slater, Cynthia's father and a habitual womaniser. He is attracted to Patty, who invites him to stay to dinner with herself and Don, much to the latter's disapproval when he returns. After the meal David proves reluctant to depart despite Don's persistent pressure for him to do so, and instead it is an exasperated Don himself who leaves. While he is absent from the apartment, David proposes to Patty, who turns him down flat but naively accepts his gift of 600 dollars because she is a none too successful model and an aspiring actress. When Don returns, he finds Patty embracing David in gratitude for her present, but Don jumps to the wrong conclusion before David at last departs. Don and Patty quarrel about David, but just as she too is about to leave, her irate father, a policeman, arrives at the apartment and knocks Don unconscious. Her father takes Patty home, but she returns to Don's apartment in the middle of the night. They fail to patch up their differences but agree to meet again next day, again at the Empire State Building observation tower, where he proposes and she accepts.

This simple tale of a girl's resistance to attempted seductions was unremarkable for its time, except for the use in the dialogue of words such as 'virgin', 'mistress', 'sex' and 'seduce'. Spoken by Patty as well as the men, they constituted an unusually frank contemporary discussion of physical sex between men and women within the framework of a highly conventional moral comedy. Nevertheless, when the play opened on Broadway on 8 March 1951 with Barbara Bel Geddes as Patty, Barry Nelson as Don, veteran Donald Cook as David and Ralph Dunn as Patty's father – the only four characters – there was no criticism from either critics or public figures. The play proved to be extremely popular, and by the end of May 1951 plans were afoot for a London production at the St James's Theatre, which forwarded Herbert's script to the LCO, where Charles Heriot, Assistant Reader of Plays since 1937 and Senior Reader from 1958 to 1968, regarded it as 'a completely adult little comedy' and gave it the go-ahead in entirety.[24] However, no immediate production followed, probably because the Broadway run lasted until May 1953, when impresario Jack Hylton took up the project with a view to an opening at the Theatre Royal in Birmingham at the end of June prior to a swift transfer to the West End. As in 1951, the Lord Chamberlain allowed the play without amendment. It opened at the Duke of York's Theatre in St Martin's Lane on 8 July to reasonably favourable reviews, although the critics were more taken with the acting, especially that of Diana Lynn as Patty, than by the play itself. This ran until 6 December with Biff McGuire as Don and Robert Flemyng as David, and, as in the United States, it drew no hostile reception from any quarter.

Meanwhile in the United States the play's producer, Otto Preminger, film director turned independent film-maker, had made a film version of the play between February and May 1953. Scripted by Herbert, doubtless in collaboration with co-producer Preminger, the film contained extra characters Cynthia Slater (Dawn Addams), a taxi driver (Gregory Ratoff), an actor in a television commercial (Fortunio Bonanova) and a couple with one short line of dialogue between them in the final scene on the Empire State Building observation tower (Hardy Kruger, Johanna Matz, both uncredited, who starred in the German language version, *Die Jungfrau auf dem Dach*, which Preminger filmed simultaneously). For box-office reasons Preminger replaced the New York stage cast with established screen stars William Holden as Don and David Niven as David to offset the inexperience of the unknown Maggie McNamara, who played Patty in her first film. The additional characters were relatively inconsequential, the dialogue and the plot retaining the sexual flavour of the play.

Figure 1 David Niven flirts with Maggie McNamara in *The Moon is Blue* (USA, 1953). United Artists/The Kobal Collection

Since the play had proved to be uncontroversial, despite its outspoken sexual dialogue, Preminger almost certainly did not anticipate the rejection of his film by the Production Code Administration, now headed by Joseph Breen in succession to Will H. Hays. When it was rejected, the large American cinema chains became reluctant to book it, but distributors United Artists declared it would no longer abide by the code and the film's American release took place on 3 June 1953. This struggle developed into the first round of a censorship clash which Preminger eventually won over the next nine months, during which time the film in theory could be shown only in cities or states where the local censors had sanctioned it. On 25 June, Cardinal Francis Spellman, the Roman Catholic Archbishop of New York, launched a broadside against the film when he advised Catholics in his archdiocese to boycott it, describing it as an occasion of sin. However, as David Niven retorted when he was told of the cardinal's outburst during an interview in Britain:

> Why didn't the Cardinal complain when it opened as a play on Broadway? It has been running there long enough. It's true that in the film I keep chasing the girl in the flat downstairs. But she's an inexperienced girl in reel one, and she's still inexperienced fourteen reels later. I can't see any 'occasion of sin' in that.[25]

It is unclear whether Spellman had actually seen *The Moon is Blue*, either as a play or a film, before he denounced it, but when the opening of the film in New York City was announced for 9 July 1953, he reportedly sent a latter to every pastor in his archdiocese, again denouncing it and alleging it violated 'standards of morality and decency'. His letter urged Catholics to avoid the film and was read in the city's Catholic churches on 28 June.[26] What effect it had is difficult to know, but elsewhere American cinemas continued to screen it, and during the early months of 1954 the police confiscated prints during performances in New Jersey and Kansas City.[27]

This conflict proved to be but one battle in the 1950s censorship struggle between Hollywood and the Catholic-dominated Legion of Decency which, in accordance with Spellman's wishes, condemned *The Moon is Blue*.[28] Eventually the 1930s film censorship structure collapsed, but this lay in the future and in 1953 the American events in relation to the film were noted at the BBFC, where it had arrived not long after the play began its London run. It was initially viewed by Sir Sidney Harris, the BBFC President from 1947 to 1960, Arthur Watkins, the Secretary since mid-1948, and two examiners, one male and one female. Differences evidently surfaced, for all four subsequently saw the play together, after which it was agreed that the entire censorship team should view the film together. This viewing took place on 28 July, when it was decided upon cuts and the 'X' certificate, intended by Harris and Watkins to promote the production of films of 'good adult entertainment' value by restricting audiences to those sixteen years old and over. In fact *The Moon is Blue* was a good example of the difficulties in defining 'good adult entertainment', and Watkins on 29 July explained to distributors United Artists that only the 'X' certificate was possible, whether or not cuts were carried out. However, the dialogue cuts the BBFC wanted did not involve the use of 'virgin' or 'mistress' but instead comprised the following: 'After all, there are lots of girls who don't mind being seduced. Why pick on those who do?', 'Is she pregnant?', 'Steaks, liquor and sex. In that order', 'Suspicion. The most powerful aphrodisiac in the world', 'There is no closed season for seducers', 'There is more joy in heaven over one sinner that repenteth', 'What's wrong with adultery?', and 'If you seriously plan to embark on a life of sin, I would not attempt to dissuade you'.[29] United Artists was slow to respond because consultation with Preminger was necessary, while in the interval John Trevelyan, a part-time examiner from 1951 who was to become BBFC Secretary between 1958 and 1971, saw the play. On 30 July he wrote,

> I was sure that we were right in our choice of lines to be cut. There are some lines that go beyond what can reasonably be allowed, and I was somewhat surprised at the Lord

Chamberlain's tolerance. I think that with these cuts we shall have a good 'X' film, good in the sense that it is definitely adult and not in any way unpleasant for anyone to see. There will be objections of course, but they should not be difficult to overcome.

On 10 August two representatives from United Artists saw Watkins in an effort to reverse at least some of the BBFC decisions, but Watkins remained adamant about the deletion of 'aphrodisiac' in particular, although he expressed a readiness to reconsider the other proposed cuts. In the event matters were not resolved until Otto Preminger himself visited London early in November to meet Watkins, when they agreed that the BBFC would after all allow (1) 'Steaks, liquor and love' in place of 'Steaks, liquor and sex', (2) 'The most powerful love potion in the world' instead of 'The most powerful aphrodisiac in the world', and (3) an alternative line to 'there is more joy in heaven over one sinner that repenteth'. Preminger accepted the rest of the BBFC cuts. The print submitted in July of 8,977 feet was reduced to 8,550 feet, the cuts amounting to about four minutes and 45 seconds of running time, on which basis the film was at length passed on 27 November 1953.

Its British release followed early in 1954, when almost all the critics expressed mystification as to why there had been any American opposition. Roy Nash in *The Star* of 8 January described the film as 'an innocent a piece of "obscenity" as he had ever come across', while Beverley Baxter in the previous day's *Evening Standard* thought that it showed how ridiculous Leagues of Decency could be when they invaded the entertainment world. Most critics commended the film and the acting of the principals, although one or two found it tedious or claustrophobic.[30] Nevertheless, on the strength of the overall favourable critical reception, United Artists lost no time in asking Watkins on 12 January, before the film went out on general release, to reconsider the 'X' certificate, which one or two critics had questioned. Watkins would not give way, affirming,

We do not consider that a film whose theme is whether or not a young girl will submit to seduction and in which the dialogue refers frequently and explicitly to this theme is suitable for young persons under 16 . . . The views expressed by one or two critics on the classification reflect, we think, a misunderstanding of the true scope and purpose of the 'X' category. They appear to believe that the 'X' category must denote something rather 'shocking' or distasteful and that consequently any film which does not deserve these epithets ought not to be graded 'X'. This fails to take account of the obvious fact that a film could be free of all objection and still unquestionably adult and suitable only for adult audiences.

Afterwards only one local authority, Warwickshire County Council, enquired of the BBFC on 14 January about the reasons behind the 'X' certificate, but when the council received these, it took no further action. More widely, the BBFC did not receive a single complaint from the general public, which suggests that its decision was correct, but all the same Trevelyan went to see the film on 5 February 1954 at the Regal cinema at Sidcup in Kent. He reported that the cinema was packed with various age groups, and that audience reaction was enthusiastic, which he regarded as a refutation of film industry contentions that 'X' films automatically lost money. Watkins initialled Trevelyan's report without comment on 12 February. In the aftermath of the film the play was revived at the Vaudeville Theatre with a different cast from March to July 1954.

Nowadays television showings of *The Moon is Blue* contain the BBFC dialogue cuts, while on 3 August 1988 the BBFC restored them when it passed the video version in full.

Irma La Douce

As the 1950s progressed and the cinema was declining in the face of television competition, screen and stage challenges to publicly accepted sexual manners, of which *The Moon is Blue* provided an early symptom, gathered momentum in various forms in Britain until in 1959 the Obscene Publications Act passed through Parliament. The Act defined obscenity as material having a tendency to deprave and corrupt when taken as a whole, which applied to stage plays but not to films. However, important as this change was, it scarcely influenced the censorship treatment meted out to *Irma La Douce*, a French play by Alexandre Brefford.

This was concerned with the love of golden-hearted prostitute Irma La Douce for hoodlum Nestor le Fripe, whose jealous nature compels her to promise to have only one 'steady' client in place of her customary large number of customers. Nestor decides to check up on Irma by disguising himself in a beard, naming himself Oscar and picking her up on the street as a casual client. In this way he becomes her 'steady', and during his daily visits he pays her a great deal of money. Soon the 'real' Nestor grows jealous of Oscar and *vice versa*, and Nestor decides that Oscar must disappear from Irma's life. But when he does so, Nestor is arrested and charged with Oscar's murder, even though of course no body has been discovered. Nonetheless tried and found guilty, Nestor is sentenced to penal servitude on Devil's Island, but, tormented there by the fact that he has impregnated Irma, he escapes, along with other convicts, and eventually makes his way back to Paris. There he finds a price is on his head as Oscar's escaped murderer, which makes it impossible for him to lead a normal life with Irma and their unborn child. Consequently he reverts to his beard and attempts to convince everyone that Oscar is alive after all. However, the resurrected Oscar is liable for heavy back taxes, which Nestor cannot pay, so that he bids Irma a fond farewell, telling her that he must rejoin his family in the United States. He then reappears as Nestor just in time for the birth of what turns out to be their son, celebrated on stage in a Christmas tableau before his Devil's Island fellow escapees emerge with gifts as the Magi at the Nativity.

In April 1957 the Globe Theatre in the West End submitted a French-language scenario to the LCO, where it was allowed in only that particular version, conditional upon minor amendments and an altered ending in whatever language was to be employed.[31] It had opened in Paris as a musical comedy during 1956 and was still running there in February 1958, when an English translation was forwarded to the LCO. In this version the birth again takes place at Christmas but without the appearance of the escaped convicts, while this time Irma gives birth to twins, so that the resemblance to the Nativity in Brefford's finale is eliminated. The Lord Chamberlain passed this version after two petty dialogue cuts, but no performance followed, and some four months later Donmar Productions sent another English-language script to the LCO for a scheduled tour in Bournemouth and Brighton before a transfer to the West End. However, this version restored the original French ending. Lord Scarbrough, the Lord Chamberlain from 1952 to 1963, was prepared to allow the play only if the first English-language ending was retained, and it was on this basis that the play came to enjoy a long London run, from July 1958 to March 1962, after ecstatic reviews. The 1959 Obscene Publications Act did not cause Scarbrough to recall the play on account of its prostitution theme, and only three letters of complaint from the general public reached him during the London performances.

In 1960 the play came to the attention of irreverent Hollywood director Billy Wilder, who was keen to adapt it into a film without the songs, while he and co-scriptwriter Isadore (I.A.L.) Diamond also decided to carry out significant changes to the plot. Nestor now became an innocent young cop who, unaware that the Paris police force habitually turns a blind eye to Irma's whoring, arrests her and, in a one-man raid on the brothel from which she operates, picks up his own inspector. Sacked from the force for this transgression, he becomes Irma's protector, falls in love with her and suffers from acute jealousy because of her numerous customers. He disguises himself as a wealthy British peer and pays her sufficiently well to keep her off the streets. She returns this money to him as her protector, but when his cash dries up, Nestor takes a back-breaking job in a meat market and grows too tired to make love to Irma as the British peer. As a result, Irma reverts to prostitution, Nestor promptly 'murders' his disguised self, and they marry in church just before she rushes off to give birth to their baby in the vestry. As a supposed murderer he has been sentenced to fifteen years in prison, but when the truth emerges, he is able to return to the police, while Irma becomes a reformed wife and mother.

On the surface there appeared little in these alterations to concern the BBFC unduly, but with two excellent comedy co-stars in Shirley Maclaine as Irma and Jack Lemmon as Nestor, Wilder's approach was at times provocative. When *Irma La Douce* was presented to the BBFC on 8 July 1963, it was viewed by Trevelyan, now the Secretary, senior examiner Frank Crofts and examiner Newton Branch, who all agreed that several scenes were censorable. This led four days later to a meeting between Trevelyan and representatives from distributors United Artists, where it was decided that Trevelyan would give the detailed BBFC objections in writing. This was done, Trevelyan simultaneously pointing out that the film would necessarily be 'X' owing to the prostitution background. He was anxious mainly about the peer's feigned impotence, which he thought was not in good taste and which he wanted removed altogether. In addition the double-entendre dialogue went rather too far, while the climactic scenes in the church would probably offend people to whom the church and the sacraments were sacred.

The required cuts were: (1) the peer referring to himself as 'only half a man . . . a hollow shell', the first part of which the BBFC interpreted as castration or impotence, (2) dialogue by Irma of entertaining men for prostitution purposes and her phrase of '. . . pick up their marbles', marbles allegedly well known in Britain as a slang word for testicles, (3) in a short scene between Irma and other prostitutes there was innuendo dialogue about her activities with the peer running, 'We played a game.' 'That's more like it.' 'He beat me nine times in a row. His wife used to do it, but she won't any more. She's got something going with the gardener', (4) the peer receives an offer of other prostitutes, accompanied by a reference to 'something interesting and unusual', (5) Irma and the peer are seen entering a hotel together with his lines, 'I've been practising. Let's get on with it', (6) an entire scene in which Irma stimulates the peer's imagination in order to make him sexually potent, (7) the wedding scenes were to be considerably reduced to eliminate shots of prostitutes dressed as bridesmaids, of the priest being urged to hasten the sacrament and, as far as possible, of labour-pain sounds during the marriage service, and (8) shots of Irma naked, although these might be acceptable when the BBFC had seen the re-edited version.[32]

This letter produced on 29 July a meeting between Trevelyan and one of the film's Hollywood producers, Walter Mirisch, who offered some counter-proposals for the re-editing but wanted Wilder to be involved in whatever cuts were decided upon. In a follow-up letter Trevelyan emphasised that the sexual impotence problem might be hard to resolve, although he hoped that Wilder would come up with a solution, but in any case the wedding scenes would have to be cut along the lines of his previous letter before the BBFC would view the re-edited film.

The revised version arrived at the BBFC a month later, when Lord Morrison, the BBFC President from 1960 to 1965, together with Trevelyan, Crofts and experienced examiner Audrey Field, viewed it before upholding most of the objections already notified to United Artists. All of this was forwarded to United Artists on 30 August, but it was not until mid-October, when matters were discussed with Hollywood executives and with Wilder, who appeared to be co-operative but maintained he was encountering technical difficulties with some of the required cuts, that action was taken. The eventual upshot was the removal of 'only half a man . . . a hollow shell', the retention of 'marbles', the removal of the dialogue about games, the retention of 'I have been practising. Let's get on with it', the removal of most of the dialogue in the bedroom scene between Irma and the peer, which Trevelyan had taken exception to, and of the reference to 'something interesting and unusual', the reduction in the wedding sequence of the priest's words but not of the shots featuring the prostitutes as bridesmaids, and the retention of Irma's nudity. In this form, and with some reluctance over the bedroom scene, the BBFC finally allowed the film as 'X' on 4 November 1963.

The censorship of Wilder's film at the BBFC occupied all but four months. In the process the footage was reduced from 12,850 to 12,690, cuts amounting to almost two minutes' running time, and the British release was delayed until early 1964, when the reviews were overwhelmingly unfavourable purely on cinematic grounds. It is doubtful whether all the trouble the BBFC took to arrive at an acceptable version was justified, for only one individual complaint materialised, and even this pointed out that the film does not show the seamy side of prostitution and tends to glamorise it. In his reply Trevelyan conceded the point but stated that 'the portrayal of prostitution was in many respects an unusual one, and that there was a gaiety and light-heartedness about the film which would probably lead most people not to take it too seriously'. After its release *Irma La Douce* drifted into obscurity in Britain, but the BBFC cuts to the film were fully restored in the video version passed on 24 May 1990. Nevertheless the early 1960s treatment of the film demonstrated how far the BBFC had moved since *The Moon is Blue* ten years previously.

Notes

1. Lord Chamberlain's Plays Correspondence Files, *Damaged Goods* 1917/837. Play reader's report, 17 April 1914. All references hereafter come from this file.
2. Home Office papers, HO45/10955/312971/55 and 69.
3. Lord Chamberlain's Plays Correspondence Files, *Desire Under the Elms* LR 1925/2. Play reader's report, 19 March 1925. All references hereafter come from this file.
4. Lord Chamberlain's Plays Correspondence Files, *Mourning Becomes Electra* 1937/659. Play reader's report, 27 September 1937.
5. Lord Chamberlain's Plays Correspondence Files, *Desire Under the Elms* 1938/1958. Play reader's report, 5 November 1938.
6. Lord Chamberlain's Plays Correspondence Files, *The Shanghai Gesture* 1956/9617. Play reader's report, 27 January 1926.
7. Lord Chamberlain's Plays Correspondence Files, *The Shanghai Gesture* LR 1926/2. Note by Cromer, 4 May 1929 on Assistant Comptroller's memorandum, 2 May 1929. All references hereafter come from this file.
8. John Baxter, *The Cinema of Josef von Sternberg* (London and New York: Zwemmer and Barnes, 1971), p. 154.
9. See James C. Robertson, *The British Board of Film Censors: Film Censorship in Britain, 1896–1950* (London: Croom Helm, 1985), pp. 140–1.
10. Lord Chamberlain's Plays Correspondence Files, *The Shanghai Gesture* 1956/9617. Play reader's report, 16 November 1956.
11. Lord Chamberlain's Plays Correspondence Files, *Tobacco Road* 1947/8737. Play reader's report, 27 January 1946. All references hereafter come from this file.
12. Leonard Mosley, *Daily Express*, 20 August 1947, and W. A. Darlington, *Daily Telegraph*, 20 August 1947.
13. For a more detailed discussion, see Brian McFarlane, 'Outrage: *No Orchids for Miss Blandish*' in Steve Chibnall and Robert Murphy (eds), *British Crime Cinema* (London: Routledge, 1999), pp. 37–8.
14. Lord Chamberlain's Plays Correspondence Files, *No Orchids for Miss Blandish* 1942/4286. Play reader's report, 16 March 1942. All references hereafter come from this file.
15. *The Times*, 19 and 20 May 1942.
16. Further details appear in James C. Robertson, *The Hidden Cinema: British Film Censorship in Action, 1913–1972* (London and New York: Routledge, 1989), pp. 92–3.

17. Chibnall and Murphy (eds) (1999), *British Crime Cinema*, pp. 17–21.
18. McFarlane, 'Outrage', in ibid., pp. 37–50.
19. British Board of Film Censors (BBFC) pre-production scenarios, 113a and 113b, 30 December 1947.
20. *Sunday Dispatch*, 31 October 1948.
21. Lord Chamberlain's Plays Correspondence File, *Pick-Up Girl* 1946/7147. Minute by Clarendon, undated but probably 17 May 1946. All references hereafter come from this file.
22. BBFC pre-production scenarios. 36 and 36a, 7 and 10 October 1946.
23. *The People*, 6 January 1947.
24. Lord Chamberlain's Plays Correspondence File, *The Moon is Blue* 1953/5663. Play reader's report, 6 June 1951.
25. *The Star*, 26 June 1953.
26. *Variety*, 1 July 1953.
27. *Daily Express* and *News Chronicle*, 1 January 1954; *Variety*, 3 March 1954.
28. *Variety*, 15 July 1953.
29. BBFC file on *The Moon is Blue*. Watkins to United Artists, 29 July 1953. All references hereafter come from this file.
30. In particular Fred Majdalany, *Daily Mail*, 8 January 1954 and Peter Wilsher, *Sunday Chronicle*, 10 January 1954.
31. Lord Chamberlain's Plays Correspondence File, *Irma La Douce* 1958/763. Gwatkin to Globe Theatre, 24 April 1957. All references hereafter come from this file.
32. BBFC file on *Irma La Douce*. Examiner's report, 8 July 1963 and Trevelyan to United Artists, 15 July 1963. All references hereafter come from this file.

CHAPTER 3

Foreign Affairs

The Lord Chamberlain after 1909 was obliged to ban any play that might impair Britain's diplomatic relations with any other country. The assumption behind this, that internal artistic expression should always take second place to foreign-policy considerations because these were based upon the royal prerogative, was scarcely an issue before 1914, since in the immediate pre-war period only some 60 per cent of adult males aged 21 and over and no women at all had the right to vote in general elections. In consequence public opinion was at most a minor influence upon the making of foreign policy, but in 1918 all adult males and all females of thirty years of age and above were given the franchise. The emergence of a new mass electorate coincided with the Labour Party's development into a major force in domestic politics, one superficially devoted to the international creed of socialism. As a result, giving automatic priority to foreign policy over public opinion carried more censorship hazards between the two world wars than before 1914, as the cases in this chapter demonstrate. After 1945 political censorship in plays and films gradually died away.

Auction of Souls

This began life as a 1919 film which focuses upon Aurora Mardigan, a young Armenian girl who in real life had allegedly escaped death at the hands of her Turkish oppressors and later been sold to a Turk as a slave. The film shows, sometimes in graphic detail, the 1915 Turkish massacres of the Armenians, the accompanying barbarities and the slave auctions of naked Armenian women. The film's purpose was the mobilisation of public support for the newly formed League of Nations and its protection of persecuted minorities. To this end, the film was shown privately in October 1919 at the Queen's Hall in London to a large invited audience of public figures, including T. P. O'Connor, the BBFC President from 1916 to 1929.

The Foreign Secretary of the day was Lord Curzon of Kedleston, a former Viceroy of India who had no knowledge of the cinema but feared that a wide release for *Auction of Souls* might exacerbate anti-Turkish feeling in Britain, Turkey having been a German ally in the First World

War, and complicate the Anglo-Turkish peace talks then taking place. Curzon was also concerned that the film's anti-Christian subtitles might provoke Moslem uprisings against British rule in Egypt and India as an indirect result of the notorious Amritsar incident of April 1919. Then a British force had fired upon a demonstrating Indian crowd, causing 379 deaths, many more casualties and an upsurge of fierce anti-British resentment throughout the Moslem world. As a result, the Foreign Office placed pressure on both the Home Office and the BBFC for the suppression of the film, on the pretext of harm to public morals if no other reason could be found.

The BBFC was seemingly ready to fall in with Curzon's wishes, but his desire to suppress the film clashed with the recently established League of Nations Union, which had already arranged a twice-daily, three-week run for the film at the Albert Hall for January 1920. Just before this run was due to start, Scotland Yard personnel visited the film's distributors and apparently threatened them with prosecution if the Albert Hall showings went ahead. Such action was legally questionable, the League of Nations Union promptly protesting to the Home Office over what it regarded as a violation of civil liberty. Since the Union was supported by many people prominent in British public life, the Home Office beat a retreat, and on 17 January one of its civil servants, together with two Scotland Yard officers and C. Hubert Husey as the BBFC's chief examiner, viewed the film and did so again two days later. The upshot was that the Albert Hall run was allowed to proceed as planned, but two crucifixion sequences in the film were reduced and the word 'Christian' was removed from all the subtitles. *Auction of Souls* was never officially submitted to the BBFC and does not appear in its surviving records. After the Albert Hall run only one British cinema, at Twickenham in Middlesex, went on to screen the film. This action resulted in Middlesex County Council taking the cinema owners to court on the ground that the BBFC had not awarded the film a certificate. The council won the case, while the film itself, probably lost, passed into film history.[1]

With BBFC connivance, the Foreign Office succeeded in a near total suppression of the film in Britain. Nevertheless the brief Albert Hall season had made an impact upon the theatre world, although this did not become evident until after Turkey had signed the peace treaty in August 1920. However, even after this Anglo-Turkish relations remained uneasy, and when towards the end of 1920 Betty Fairfax, a leading repertory actress, forwarded her play based upon the film to the LCO, Lord Sandhurst, the Lord Chamberlain, decided to ban it. Undeterred, Betty Fairfax tried again in February 1922, when Anglo-Turkish relations had to some extent settled down. In her play, due to open at the Palace Pier in Brighton during the following month, Aurora is loved by an Englishman but is pursued by Casim Bey, a Turk who attacks Armenians and badly maltreats a Christian priest before carrying off both Aurora and her sister. The two women are brutally handled but refuse to submit themselves to him, whereupon Casim decides to sell them at a slave auction. The English lover's attempt to rescue them fails, Aurora's sister is killed, while Aurora herself and a third sister are sold to another Turk, Kiamil Pasha, and taken to his castle. Under torture, Aurora agrees to convert to Islam, but her lover manages to rescue her and in the process tortures Kiamil. The fugitives seek refuge in a monastery, but Casim and his soldiers slay a Christian priest before once again making off with Aurora. She yields to Casim after he has threatened to kill her mother, now also his captive, but during a storm he is killed by a falling tree, while she and her lover finally make their escape.

This play represented barely concealed exploitation theatre, and George Street, the Reader of Plays at the LCO, thought there was too much torture, and that at least some of these particular scenes should be removed. From a wider perspective, he observed,

> The Turks are of course abused all through. It is regretted that England and France no longer protect the Armenians. The period, however, is during the war, as at the end 'Allenby has swept Palestine'. I do not know if Mohammedans would be offended. The opposition of Christians and Mohammedans is insisted on throughout. I think it probable if the Lord Chamberlain refused a licence there would be an outcry: the Turkish atrocities may be exaggerated but are based on facts real enough. The Lord Chamberlain might like other advice on these points . . . I do not know if representing Kiamil Pasha (who may be a real person) as a disgusting brute matters or not.[2]

Lord Sandhurst's successor as Lord Chamberlain in 1921 was Lord Atholl. Probably due to continuing tension between Greece and Turkey after serious armed clashes between them in Asia Minor during August 1921, Atholl chose to consult his Advisory Board, which came out unanimously in favour of a ban. However, this time Betty Fairfax did not acquiesce as tamely as she had done in 1920, and on 16 March 1922 she asked for the precise objections to her script and offered to amend it in whatever way Atholl required. The outcome was that in July she reapplied for a licence on the basis of a scenario that omitted all the torture material and all religious references in the dialogue. With these amendments and because the Turks were now described merely as brigands, she was successful, Street commenting, 'I should think it doubtful that the play would have vogue enough to attract any political attention.' On 14 August, when the play

opened at the Ambassadors Theatre in Southend-on-Sea, Street's prediction seemed likely to be correct, but two weeks later Turkey launched a
major attack upon the Greeks in order to recover land in Asia Minor lost to
Greece in the 1920 peace treaty. Within a matter of days the Greeks were
routed, and Turkish forces were marching towards the British position in
the neutral zone at Chanak on the Asian side of the Dardenelles. During
much of September 1922 an Anglo-Turkish war looked imminent, but
although by early October the crisis had largely abated with a halt to the
Turkish advance, these events had once more aroused Moslem sensitivities.

This became clear when in October 1922 the Fairfax play was staged at
the Grand Theatre in Brighton, where it was seen by Khwaja Kamaluddin,
the imam of the mosque at Woking in Surrey, who wrote to Lord Atholl to
ask that the play's licence be revoked on the grounds that it libelled both
Turkish troops and the nation's new leader, Mustapha Kemal Pasha. The
imam complained that *Auction of Souls* represented a shameless attack
upon the principles and faith of Islam, which was likely to create a disastrous impression upon Moslems everywhere, especially India. Atholl
was sufficiently concerned to order that a report on the play should be
carried out to ensure that the licence conditions had been and were
being respected. This revealed that although the Turks in the play were
described as merely brigands, the setting, place names and use of words
such as 'effendi' were entirely Turkish. In addition the name of Kiamil
Pasha had been changed only to Kiamil Basta, while Christians were
depicted as regarding some of the brigands' prayers as blasphemous. At
this news Betty Fairfax was summoned to the LCO on 17 November and
instructed to make the necessary script changes. She agreed to do so, but
by 12 December, with the play due to be performed in Sheffield shortly,
Atholl had not received a new script. The planned Sheffield run did not
take place, a revised script was eventually sanctioned on 27 March 1923,
and again no performances seem to have followed.

In November 1925, by which time Anglo-Turkish relations had
improved, a very similar play by May Dana for performances at His
Majesty's Theatre in Barrow-in-Furness was allowed by Lord Cromer,
Atholl's successor, on condition that a whipping scene was not made too
realistic and that the name of a minor character was altered from Kemal
Effendie to Abdul, doubtless to avoid any inferred similarity to Mustapha
Kemal, by then the Turkish president. Cromer received no public com-
plaints about this version, *Auction of Souls* finally vanishing from the
British entertainment scene.[3]

Both the film and the plays were seen by only a small minority of the
British public, and there was no detrimental effect upon Anglo-Turkish

relations. This might be seen either as effective censorship or as wide-spread British apathy to post-war Middle Eastern affairs.

Dawn

At daybreak on 12 October 1915 a German firing squad in Belgium executed Edith Cavell, a fifty-year-old British nurse working in Brussels, for aiding allied servicemen to escape from German clutches. According to international law, she was guilty of espionage and the German action was technically legal, but by pre-1914 standards this capital sentence was unduly severe, which handed Britain the opportunity for a propaganda coup. Immediately after her death novelist Edgar Wallace wrote a script for a film entitled *The Martyrdom of Nurse Edith Cavell*. The BBFC passed this uncut on 11 November 1915 but insisted that the title should be changed to *Nurse and Martyr*, and that Edith Cavell's name should not appear on the screen or in advertising material. These conditions were imposed out of deference to Cavell family feelings.

In 1920 the Edith Cavell statue was built near the junction of St Martin's Lane and Charing Cross Road opposite the National Portrait Gallery, where it still stands. With a memorial to her heroism in the very heart of London, it was all but inevitable that sooner or later a play would be written about the events leading to her execution, and the first such drama, by Eva Elwes, was submitted to the LCO early in 1925. This play opens in the house of Farmer Morgan, Edith's uncle, where his daughter Cecily flirts with Lieutenant Beckwith. Edith arrives, together with Captain von Corlessburg, whom she has nursed during his illness and who has proposed to her. She turns him down in order to devote herself to her nursing, after which he is recalled to Germany. After the war has broken out in 1914, Beckwith arrives at her hospital in Brussels as a wounded prisoner of the occupying German forces, and she helps him to escape. She is discovered, put on trial and condemned to death by a German court martial, despite von Corlessburg's testimony on her behalf during the trial and the protests of the American consul afterwards. At the end two tableaux portray her execution and the unveiling of her statue.

As the Reader of Plays, George Street, commented, this script was a crude attempt to exploit the continuing British public interest in her case, but nevertheless he recommended that the play should be given a licence. This recommendation is worth quoting at length, for it pinpointed the difficulties relating to theatrical reconstructions of comparatively recent events and portrayals of the dead when Parliament in 1909 had laid down neither a definition of 'recent' nor how the Lord Chamberlain's censorship should function if the dead person concerned was also a historical figure at the centre of a national tragedy. Street observed,

> There are two obvious objections. 1. The general outrage on good taste is exploiting Nurse Cavell's heroism. It would be answered to this that the intention is good and that she is represented as a noble woman. Also that she cannot be regarded as a private person, but belongs to history. 2. The offence to her relations. But one cannot be sure of this without enquiry, in an age in which the nearest relations of distinguished people print their most intimate letters when they are dead.
>
> It is a difficult matter to advise on. On the whole I think that the celebrity of the subject and the insignificance of the play, which is never likely to be heard of again, put together make it inadvisable to ban it. Perhaps the first scene, since it deals with the alleged private life of Nurse Cavell, is even more objectionable than the others but in itself there is no particular harm in it. I think Tableau 1 should be cut out as too harrowing to anyone who remembers the event at all. It is with great reluctance that, even with this excision, that [sic] the play is recommended for licence.
>
> P.S. I assume that Farmer Morgan and his daughter and Beckwith are imaginary. If they happen to exist the play would be an outrage on private and living people.[4]

Lord Cromer, the Lord Chamberlain, decided to consult the Cavell family, which in 1925 consisted of Edith's two sisters, who felt that the play was historically inaccurate, and that a fairly fictional account of the event should not be allowed. Consequently Cromer banned the play on 2 March 1925. Its possible impact upon Anglo-German relations did not influence this decision, and the matter rested there until an announcement more than two years later, in the *Evening Standard* of 17 September 1927, of film producer/director Herbert Wilcox's intention to make the film *Dawn* with American star Pauline Frederick as Edith Cavell. One week later the Alexandra Theatre in South Shields applied to the LCO for a licence to stage a slightly revised version of the Eva Elwes play from 6 October. Lord Cromer gave this application exceedingly short shrift, despite his aware-ness of Wilcox's forthcoming film, noting that 'so far as any play is con-cerned I think the whole thing too recent and I am not prepared to pass it for the reasons given in 1925'.[5] The Alexandra Theatre's response was the alteration of the title to *The Price She Paid*, while the names of Edith and her mother were changed to Ada and Mrs Deane, on which basis Lord Cromer allowed it on 18 October 1927. *The Price She Paid* ran in South Shields for several months, but in February 1928, due to the events recounted below regarding Wilcox's film, the title of the play was altered once again, this time to *Dawn*.

The prospect of a film dealing with the Edith Cavell episode came at a delicate moment in Anglo-German relations. Since 1925 the 1919 European peace settlement had been supplemented by the Locarno treaty, in which Belgium, Britain and Italy guaranteed the Franco-German frontier, and by German membership of the League of Nations. Thereby Germany had moved from being a pariah state to a respected part of the international community, a position it was trying to exploit away from the public gaze by pressing for an early evacuation of all allied forces from German soil, due in 1935 at the earliest in the 1919 settlement. The German Foreign Office grew alarmed that Wilcox's film would arouse anti-German feeling in Britain, in this way damage Anglo-German relations and prevent the projected early troop withdrawals. Germany first approached Britain about the forthcoming film as early as 26 September 1927, when the Foreign Office refused to intervene directly and proposed instead a German overture to Wilcox.[6] Either this idea was not acted upon or Wilcox proved to be unco-operative, for Germany evidently brought pressure to bear on Belgium, where a part of *Dawn* was being filmed. According to Wilcox almost forty years later, his leading actress, Pauline Frederick, was in Brussels ready to start work on the film when on 19 October she abruptly withdrew from the project, citing as her reason pressure from the German embassy in Brussels.[7]

On 1 November in Berlin the matter of *Dawn* was elevated to a high diplomatic level when the German Foreign Minister himself, Gustav Stresemann, asked the British ambassador, Sir Ronald Lindsey, to ascertain whether the British government would take steps to 'discourage' the production. Stresemann made it clear that he took exception to the subject matter itself rather than to the way Wilcox intended to present it. In subsequent dealings with both Belgium and Germany, the Foreign Office clung to the principle of governmental non-intervention in film-censorship policy while in practice it acted to subvert this. Behind the scenes it was decided to approach Wilcox unofficially if all else failed.[8] However, by the end of November 1927 filming was well under way, and during December and halfway through January 1928 the Foreign Office, acting under direct instructions from Foreign Secretary Sir Austen Chamberlain, concentrated upon, first, gathering factual material on the Cavell execution with a view to discrediting Wilcox and his film and, second, contacting the Home and War Offices in the hope that they would bring pressure to bear upon the BBFC.[9] By mid-January these tactics had reached a dead end, Chamberlain then having either to remain inactive and put in jeopardy a full Anglo-German reconciliation or to place pressure on the BBFC and leave the government vulnerable to the charge of political film censorship with a general election less than two years ahead. In either case Anglo-German relations might deteriorate, so that Chamberlain brought the question to the Cabinet which on

18 January 1928 instructed him to discuss the matter personally with T. P. O'Connor, the BBFC President.[10]

Accordingly Chamberlain met O'Connor that same evening, after which the former, as he informed the German ambassador in London, Friedrich Sthamer, expected the BBFC to reject the film. Moreover, as acting Home Secretary at that time, Chamberlain arranged for the Home Office to draw the attention of the leading local authorities to *Dawn* in case Wilcox attempted to bypass the BBFC. All in all, while Chamberlain was unable to give Sthamer an absolute guarantee, he was optimistic that the now completed film would be suppressed.[11] On 26 January the Home Office tackled Rosamund Smith, the Conservative chairman of the London County Council theatre committee, with a view to a ban. Just to make sure, lest the London County Council banned the film and Wilcox then submitted it to other local authorities, the Home Office intended also to approach them and so informed the Foreign Office.[12]

Although Wilcox probably did not realise how far Chamberlain was prepared to go in his efforts to suppress the film, the former was not a man to be easily intimidated. Amid a mounting background of British press speculation in early February over German official efforts to bring about a ban on the film, Wilcox issued a public invitation to Chamberlain to view *Dawn*. The film covers the activities of Edith Cavell (Sybil Thorndike) in Brussels, her imprisonment by the Germans, the court martial and execution in mainly non-controversial fashion, although one member of the firing squad is shown refusing to fire, which was a fiction. Wilcox's purpose in making the film was solely commercial, a wish to cash in on the success of American mid-1920s anti-war features without simultaneously aggravating germanophobia among the general population in Britain. Mindful of German official reaction, Chamberlain declined Wilcox's invitation and in his published reply of 10 February went out of his way to express his personal aversion to such a film. He was shortly to face questions in the Commons, answers to which elicited his admission that he had contacted O'Connor over the film but otherwise were a combination of falsehood, half-truth and evasion to conceal the involvement of both the Cabinet and Stresemann as well as to gain time for the BBFC to view and reject the film.[13]

Meanwhile Wilcox had delayed his submission of *Dawn* to the BBFC, doubtless relying upon increasing press and parliamentary criticism of the Foreign Office to see the film through censorship. He arranged twelve showings for MPs and the press in addition to a private showing for the famous playwright George Bernard Shaw, moves which led Wilkinson, the BBFC Secretary, to ask Wilcox for a print of his film. Wilkinson viewed this at the BBFC on the morning of Saturday, 18 February, simultaneously

Figure 2 Sybil Thorndike as Edith Cavell in *Dawn* (GB, 1928). British and Dominion Film Corp./The Kobal Collection

with Wilcox's private showing for Shaw, according to Wilcox, which there is no reason to doubt in the light of events soon to follow.[14] Two days later the BBFC's decision to reject *Dawn* was conveyed to Wilcox by O'Connor in person after consultation with Wilkinson and chief examiner Husey, but, as with *Auction of Souls*, the BBFC's register of rejected films gives no indication that the film was ever viewed there. O'Connor announced the BBFC's decision to the press and defended it on the ground of possible harm to Anglo-German relations, even though there is no clear evidence that he himself ever saw the film.[15]

In this statement O'Connor omitted the fact that Wilcox had never officially submitted *Dawn* to the BBFC, which had acted on its own initiative purely to steal a march on Wilcox, possibly as the result of Foreign Office pressure. No doubt Chamberlain and O'Connor had hoped that the BBFC rejection would stifle the controversy, but by then it was public knowledge that the Foreign Office had been deeply embroiled in the censorship of *Dawn*. On 22 February 1928 this was deemed so constitutionally questionable that *The Times* even devoted a leading article to the subject, which was critical of both Chamberlain and O'Connor but nonetheless concluded that 'recent personal tragedy is not a fit subject for the screen'. On 27 February and again two days later Chamberlain fended off Commons questions by continuing the public cover-up he had initiated in mid-December 1927.[16] In the interim Wilcox had submitted the film to the London County Council. This screening occurred towards the end of March and was followed a few days afterwards by a debate of the full council. An all-night sitting developed before a vote was finally taken at 4 a.m. on 4 April. Despite the best efforts of Rosamund Smith to have the film banned in London, as Chamberlain wanted, the council decided otherwise by 56 votes to 52, provided that the scenes in which a German soldier was himself threatened with death if he did not fire at Edith when the firing squad did so and their two graves alongside each other in the final sequences were removed. In this version *Dawn* was screened in London from 5 April 1928 to mid-May, while over the remaining months of 1928 and during early 1929 most local authorities followed London County Council's lead. Wilcox had defeated the Foreign Office and the BBFC combined, but no harm was inflicted on Anglo-German relations, perhaps because Stresemann appreciated that Chamberlain had done his utmost to suppress the film. Furthermore, by the time it was ready to be released in many parts of Britain as a silent film, many cinemas were converting to sound. Thus the film was not shown as widely as had seemed likely when Germany had first exerted pressure on the Foreign Office for its suppression.

Although *Dawn* occasionally indulges in fiction for dramatic effect, it is fundamentally a serious examination of the Edith Cavell tragedy, which produced a stage equivalent by Erwin Pagan, due to be performed at the Garrick Theatre in Charing Cross Road, very close to the Cavell statue. Entitled *Edith Cavell: Her Passing in the Image of Christ*, the play was presented to the LCO on 23 February 1928, when the uproar over the BBFC rejection of the film was at its height. The play covers the period from Edith Cavell's arrest to her execution in heavy melodramatic style and remains faithful to the facts as then known. Reader of Plays George Street reacted,

Previous plays on the subject have been banned because their vulgarity offended Miss Cavell's relations. I should hardly think they would object to this unless on the natural ground of *any* play about her being repugnant. But the question can hardly be separated from that of the film *Dawn*. It will have been seen. . .that the play is perfectly fair – possibly more than fair – to the Germans. It does not deny their legal right to execute Miss Cavell and represents those on the spot as intensely anxious to prevent its ghastly blunder and save her for her own sake. They are the victims of 'the machine' working ignorantly at Berlin. Apart from *Dawn* there is the consideration that war plays have gone on up to now, but they were imaginary and this is actual.

In face of all the difficulties it is obvious that I cannot advise a licence without further consideration.[17]

Lord Cromer, the Lord Chamberlain, decided to seek the views of Edith Cavell's two sisters and was informed that both resented the fact that Wilcox had not seen fit to consult them before making his film, whereupon Cromer indicated that if they objected to this play, he would ban it. Since he had not consulted the Foreign Office in any way, his continuing ban would in theory not lie open to the accusation of political pressure. One of Edith's sisters then read Pagan's play, regarding it as unobjectionable but historically inaccurate because it whitewashed the Germans, but in any case both sisters felt it was still too early for any stage reconstruction of Edith's tragedy. Upon receipt of this news, Cromer was inclined to maintain the ban, but when he met Pagan and the Garrick Theatre manager a few days later, Pagan remonstrated with him and expressed the view that although he was willing to consult the Cavell family on points of detail, he felt free to select his own subject. Once again Cromer resolved to consult the two sisters in an effort to overcome their objections, but privately he realised that even if he was successful in this, he would also have to confer with the Foreign Office. This change of tactic was probably induced by Cromer's fear that, with the outcome of the film furore still in the balance, either Pagan or the Garrick Theatre management would reveal the fact of the ban to the national press. This would inevitably give rise to suspicions that Cromer himself was acting in accordance with Foreign Office wishes and to resulting unfavourable publicity. He wasted no time in contacting the two sisters again, but nevertheless when the London County Council allowed the film on 4 April, the question of family objections to Pagan's play remained unresolved. After the film had been shown in London, the two sisters asked Cromer to reach a decision without regard to family feelings in the knowledge that the film appeared likely to be widely seen. Accordingly Cromer decided to pass Pagan's play with the omission of the subtitle reference to Christ, subject to Foreign Office agreement, although the latter's involvement in the matter was to be withheld from all the interested parties concerned. On 13 April a member of the LCO met Sir William Tyrrell, the Foreign Office Permanent Under-Secretary and a future BBFC President from 1935 to 1947, who accepted that, in view of the London County Council's decision over the film, the play would also have to be given a licence. Even so, Cromer delayed doing this until a definite date for the planned Garrick opening was known. However, there had very recently been a change of management at the theatre, and the new management did not wish to present the Pagan play, which was neither awarded a licence nor ever produced.

Professor Mamlock

From the Bolshevik revolution in Russia in late 1917 to 22 June 1941, when Hitler unleashed his forces against the Soviet Union, Soviet feature films were extremely hard to see in Britain for commercial and political reasons. During the 1920s the BBFC rejected the pro-revolutionary classics Sergei Eisenstein's *Battleship Potemkin* (1925) and Vsevolod Pudovkin's *Mother* (1926), but the rejection of the former with the Home Secretary's knowledge and approval came to light during the *Dawn* affair in 1928, and to avoid future charges of political censorship, the BBFC relaxed to some extent its previous rigid hostility towards Soviet features. However, the Board was secure in the knowledge that such films, silent until 1934, were unlikely to receive a wide distribution in Britain, like foreign films in general. Even so, into the 1930s the BBFC continued to regard Soviet films very suspiciously and rejected those which implicitly advocated revolution and were set outside the Soviet Union, such as Ilya Trauberg's *The Blue Express* (1929), rejected on 20 April 1931, and Abram Room's *The Ghost That Never Returns* (1929), rejected on 9 February 1931. Between the two world wars no Soviet feature of any genre was shown in a British licensed public cinema outside London. Even in the capital the four public cinemas that screened Soviet films – the Academy in Oxford Street, the Berkeley in Berkeley Street near Piccadilly, the Everyman in Hampstead and the Forum in Villiers Street next to Charing Cross Road station – all catered for middle-class, well-educated audiences and charged high admission prices. The films also required the approval of the London County Council, which fell under Labour control in March 1934.

The small minority British interest in Soviet features was increased during the 1930s by the advent of Nazism in 1933-4 and Hitler's consequent threat to European security. Many British left-wing intellectuals during 1938-9, when German territorial expansion into Austria and Czechoslovakia was soon reinforced by strong pressure against Poland, saw an Anglo-French–Soviet alliance as the best method of containing Germany and preventing war. Against this international background Soviet anti-Nazi films were produced, one of which, *Professor Mamlock*, was unique as the solitary inter-war Soviet film based upon a play attacking the domestic policy of a nation with which Britain theoretically enjoyed friendly diplomatic relations until war broke out on 3 September 1939.

Professor Mamlock is a Friedrich Wolf play, written in 1934, dealing with the rise of anti-Semitism during the Nazi seizure of power in Germany in 1932–3. It centres upon the plight of one individual German Jew, Dr Mamlock, an eminent apolitical surgeon who had fought for Germany during the First World War. The play opens in May 1932 in Mamlock's clinic, where his staff are arguing among themselves about the imminent presidential election between Hitler and the incumbent non-party president, Field Marshal Paul von Hindenburg. From this discussion it becomes apparent that two of the doctors, Hellpach and Inge Ruoff, are Nazi supporters and anti-Semitic. When Mamlock arrives, he cuts short the discussion but makes it obvious that he favours a von Hindenburg victory. The scene then moves to the Mamlock household in February 1933, soon after the re-elected von Hindenburg has appointed Hitler as Chancellor and the Reichstag building has been set ablaze, a key event in the establishment of the Nazi dictatorship. Mamlock's loyal wife is a Gentile, his son, Rolf, is a Communist, much to Mamlock's displeasure, and his schoolgirl daughter, Ruth, is pro-Nazi. By April the Nazis have taken a firmer grip on power and stepped up their persecution of Jews, events which intensify the Mamlock family divisions. However, Ruth finds that her pro-Nazi sentiments do not prevent her from being forced to wear the yellow Star of David on her coat, while her brother, Rolf, sells Communist leaflets openly on the streets. In love with Rolf despite their political differences, Inge Ruoff saves him from arrest by Nazi storm troopers just as Hellpach is informing Mamlock that he has been dismissed from his own clinic. Incredulous at this news, Mamlock turns up at the clinic as usual, but Nazis assault him and he is compelled to wear the yellow star. In the last act Mamlock cheerfully returns to the clinic after the Nazi government has decreed that war veteran Jews can retain their positions. Anxious merely to resume his professional work, Mamlock finds Hellpach, himself keen to engineer Mamlock's removal so that he can take over the clinic, armed with a list of Jewish assistants whom, Hellpach claims, Mamlock must dismiss. The latter indignantly protests with remarks which Hellpach chooses to interpret as anti-Nazi. He demands that all those staff present sign a statement to that effect, but all refuse to do so, even Inge, by now thoroughly disillusioned with Nazi anti-Semitism in practice. Despite this show of loyalty by his colleagues, Mamlock nonetheless shoots himself.

The Westminster Theatre submitted Wolf's script to the LCO on 6 November 1935 for a run due to commence on 3 December. Reader of Plays George Street commented that the depicted events were now two years old and out of date because Nazi anti-Semitic persecution had recently intensified. The play was ineffective for British audiences, who did not need to be informed that anti-Semitism was irrational. The play also suffered from a translation into pronounced American, especially the use of the word 'bullshit', although this was not a sufficient reason for a ban.[18] In accordance with Street's recommendation, Lord Cromer allowed the play on condition that 'bullshit' was removed from the dialogue, but he also wrote, 'I suppose the Germans cannot object?' Although it was close to routine practice for the LCO to consult the Foreign Office about plays with possible implications for Britain's foreign relations, there is no direct evidence in the Lord Chamberlain's correspondence about *Professor Mamlock* that Cromer took such action in connection with Wolf's play. All the same there is circumstantial evidence that contact with the Foreign Office did in fact take place. Indeed it would have been surprising if it had not done so at a time when Britain was spearheading the League of Nations into an apparently head-on collision with Italy over the latter's recent invasion of Ethiopia. With a war against Italy in prospect, Britain was unlikely to risk extra, unnecessary problems with Hitler, at least while the Ethiopian crisis lasted, when only two months earlier Germany had enacted the sweeping anti-Semitic Nuremberg laws. Nevertheless on the surface there was no reason why *Professor Mamlock* should not have proceeded as scheduled after it had survived the Lord Chamberlain's censorship. But in reality the run did not take place. The previous play at the Westminster Theatre was suddenly extended by several days and the next one brought forward at short notice into the week after the *Professor Mamlock* performances had been due to start. This suggests official pressure from some quarter, possibly not recorded at the LCO for fear of press disclosure and a repetition of the *Dawn* events eight years previously. As it happened the press appears to have missed the *Professor Mamlock* cancellation entirely.

However, the LCO was not yet done with the play, for on 5 January 1939 it was resubmitted with the same plot and slightly amended dialogue for a performance at the Congregational Church Hall in Nottingham on 14 January. By then pre-war Nazi anti-Semitism had reached its zenith in the notorious Crystal Night pogrom of 9–10 November 1938, while Hitler had disclosed his aggressive intent in Europe through German armed intervention in the Spanish Civil War since 1936 and Germany had more recently annexed Austria and the Sudetenland in Czechoslovakia during 1938. In the light of these events and resulting international tension, the LCO attitude to the play was different from 1935, Reader of Plays Henry Game noting, 'If we are to adhere to the rule, that if authors want to write anti-Nazi plays, they must cast them in Ruritanian form, I cannot possibly recommend this play.'[19] However, he had joined the LCO only in 1936, while Lord Clarendon had become Lord Chamberlain in 1938, so that initially both were unaware that *Professor Mamlock* had already been allowed. When this came to light at a late stage before the arranged performance, there was little option but to allow it again on the ground that the play was based upon historical fact. Neither Lord Clarendon nor any of his staff appears to have known that the 1935 run did not take place, and in 1939 only a dialogue reference to the Nazi use of torture was removed.

The Nottingham performance went largely unnoticed, and the play might at that stage have passed into obscurity but for the fact that it had already been filmed in the Soviet Union during 1938. Wolf, a German Communist, was a refugee there from Nazism and he co-authored the film, along with fellow Communist exiles Adolf Minkin and Herbert Rappoport, who also directed. Filmed against the background of the Nazi *Anschluss* in Austria of March/April 1938, the ensuing overt anti-Semitic outrages in the streets of Vienna and the mounting German threats against Czechoslovakia, the feature intensified the play's anti-Nazi content. This was done, first, by having Mamlock (Sergei Mezhinski) paraded through the streets and labelled 'Jew' on his clothes rather than simply having his clothes torn and being made to wear the yellow star and, second, by making his suicide attempt at the end unsuccessful. While he is lying in bed in his clinic on the road to recovery, he briefly sees his son Rolf (Oleg Zhakov), who has escaped en route to a concentration camp. Rolf manages to flee before the Nazis arrive at the clinic, but Mamlock is roused by their presence to deliver an impassioned anti-Nazi tirade on the clinic balcony before the Nazi storm troopers mow him down with a machine gun.

The film was released in the Soviet Union early in September 1938. Shortly afterwards its strident anti-Nazism was given added topicality by the transfer to Germany of the mainly German-speaking Sudetenland area from Czechoslovakia in the international Munich agreement and, more directly, by the Crystal Night events in Germany six weeks later, which horrified European opinion. These bestowed upon the film a valid prophetic quality it had not possessed when made and consequently exacerbated anti-Nazi feeling in Britain. The Film Society, a private London club founded in 1925 to present to educated audiences films otherwise unlikely to be seen in Britain, screened *Professor Mamlock* in March 1939, and a few weeks later it was reportedly on its way to the BBFC. The Board announced in advance that the film would be rejected.[20] This unprecedented action was probably taken with the *Dawn* controversy in mind in an effort to discourage any submission, for the real reason behind the BBFC's concern was the film's uncompromising assault on a point of German domestic policy. With the growth of anti-Nazism and germanophobia in Britain after Germany violated the Munich agreement by occupying the whole of Czechoslovakia on 15 March 1939, the Academy cinema submitted the film to the BBFC on 12 May. Despite its advance declaration of intent, the Board took two weeks to reject it. Taking a leaf from Herbert Wilcox's book over *Dawn*, the Academy then turned to the London County Council, which allowed it uncut on 26 July. By that time rising German pressure on British- and French-guaranteed Poland was assuming menacing proportions and arousing the serious prospect of a general European war. In the event the Academy screened *Professor Mamlock* just days before the German invasion of Poland on 1 September and the Anglo-French declaration of war on Germany two days later. On 14 September the BBFC reversed its previous rejection of the film and passed it with meagre cuts. However, it was not a good commercial proposition even in wartime, and it received only a limited general release in January and February 1940. The Academy revived the film in September 1944, when knowledge of Hitler's genocide of European Jewry was becoming public and the Red Army was sweeping through Poland, but it has not since been seen in Britain due to unavailability. On the other hand, the play was given a public performance at a provincial theatre in 1947.

Notes

1. Further details of this episode can be found in the Home Office papers HO45/10955/312917/92, 94 and 98 and in James C. Robertson, *The Hidden Cinema: British Film Censorship in Action, 1913–1972* (London: Routledge, 1989), pp. 14–16.
2. Lord Chamberlain's Plays Correspondence Files, *Auction of Souls* 4357/22. Play reader's report, 24 February 1922. All references hereafter come from this file.
3. For the information in this paragraph, see Lord Chamberlain's Plays Correspondence Files, *Auction of Souls* 6448/25.
4. Lord Chamberlain's Plays Correspondence Files, *Edith Cavell* LR1925/1. Play reader's report, 20 February 1925. All references hereafter come from this file.
5. Lord Chamberlain's Plays Correspondence Files, *The Price She Paid* 1927/7894. Note by Cromer, 27 September 1927, on play reader's report, 26 September 1927.
6. Foreign Office papers (FO), FO395/418, P1008/7/150, 26 September 1927 and FO395/427, P104/18/150, 5 October 1927.
7. Herbert S. Wilcox, *25,000 Sunsets* (London: Bodley Head, 1967), p. 73.
8. FO 395/418, P1124/7/150, 1 November 1927, and P1053/7/150, P1124/7/150, 18 November 1927.
9. See FO 395/418, P1199/7/150, 16 and 20 December 1927; FO 395/427, P49/18/150, 12 January 1928.
10. Cabinet minutes 23/57, 1/3, 18 January 1928.
11. FO 395/427, P104/18/150, memorandum by Chamberlain, 24 January 1928.
12. FO 395/427, P129/18/150, 27 January 1928.

13. Fuller details appear in James C. Robertson, '*Dawn*: Edith Cavell and Anglo-German relations', *Historical Journal of Film, Radio and Television*, 4, 1 (1984), pp. 17–22.
14. Herbert S. Wilcox, *25,000 Sunsets* (London: Bodley Head, 1967), pp. 79–82.
15. *Daily Express*, 21 February 1928.
16. See House of Commons debates, vol. 213, cols 1056–7, 16 February 1928, and vol. 214, cols 14–18, 429–30, 27 and 29 February 1928; FO 395/427, P251/18/150, 15 February 1928.
17. Lord Chamberlain's Plays Correspondence Files, *Edith Cavell: Her Passing in the Image of Christ* WB 1928/1. Play reader's report, 23 February 1928. All references hereafter come from this file.
18. Lord Chamberlain's Play Correspondence Files, *Professor Mamlock* 1935/14401. Play reader's report, 7 November 1935. All references hereafter come from this file.
19. Lord Chamberlain's Plays Correspondence Files, *Professor Mamlock* 1939/2259. Play reader's report, 9 January 1939. All references hereafter come from this file.
20. *The Times*, 20 April 1939.

CHAPTER 4

The Quest for 'Quality'

Film and theatre censorship as exercised in Britain during the 1950s shared much in common. Both the British Board of Film Censors and the Lord Chamberlain's Office employed a system of censorship which depended as much on the application of pre-production scrutiny as it did on post-production review. In one key regard, however, there were vital differences. Cinemagoers constituted a mass audience and were therefore considered different in character and nature from theatregoers. Thus, the censorship criteria applied to cinema set standards of 'quality' differing from those in effect for the stage. With the advent of a new 'X' certificate from January 1951, moreover, the BBFC sought to initiate a category of film classification which not only limited cinemagoing audiences to people over sixteen years of age but was also meant to promote the production of films that were construed as 'good adult entertainment'.

The difficulties in defining 'good adult entertainment' became acutely apparent when, on 5 January 1955, director Ronald Neame informed the British Film Producers Association that he felt 'the "X" certificate was no longer serving the purpose for which it was intended'. 'The British Board of Film Censors had stated at the outset that it was intended to encourage the production of films for adult audiences,' he argued. 'In fact, however, the "X" certificate was being wrongly exploited and was assisting considerably wider distribution of Continental films in this country than might otherwise be possible whilst, at the same time, attempts by British producers to make films suitable for adult audiences had, more often than not, failed.'[1]

The problems posed for the film industry in setting 'quality' standards for mainstream cinema different from those which obtained in regard to theatre were made abundantly clear during the 1950s. Here, we shall be examining them from the point of view of the representation of women; next, we shall be scrutinising the depiction of youth; and, subsequently, we shall be looking at changes in the image of masculinity across both the 1950s and 1960s.

Women of Twilight

Helen Allistair runs a home for unmarried mothers. She pretends to be a philanthropist but is, in fact, a thoroughly bad lot who lives on the money she extorts, in one way or another, from her unfortunate boarders. A nice young woman, Christine, is sent from the maternity hospital to Helen's place, and there makes friends with a girl, Vivianne, who is pregnant with a child by a young gunman (who is presently hanged). Christine very soon tumbles to the situation, but Helen is a slippery character and extremely difficult to catch out. Her wits, and fortuitous circumstance which plays into her hands, enable Helen to escape exposure once or twice. But, in the end, Vivianne learns from a feeble-minded servant that Helen is something only a very little short of a murderer and that there is an infant corpse buried in the garden which needs explaining. When Vivianne tries to go to the police, Helen prevents her by force. Premature labour is brought on. Helen, hoping Vivianne will die, does not summon the doctor. But when Vivianne does not die and will presently face unwelcome publicity as the ex-mistress of an executed criminal, she decides to perform the social service of exposing Helen as the horrible hypocrite she is. Christine, who has lost her own child (another victim of Helen's duplicity) and is now happily married, will adopt Vivianne's little girl, which is Vivianne's dearest wish.

Written by Sylvia Rayman, a 28-year-old part-time assistant at a snack bar in Swiss Cottage, *Women of Twilight* was first staged by Jean Shepheard at her small repertory theatre, The Regent, in Hayes on 30 July 1951, where it was produced by Rona Laurie with an all-female cast (which included Ann Jellicoe). 'Although the play deals with a social evil of our time, urging greater humanity to the unmarried mother,' Laurie stated in her producer's note to the published script, 'this theme is woven into the texture of the drama and never becomes mere propaganda.' 'The situations are strong, the language sometimes crude,' Laurie continued, 'but this strength and crudeness heighten the moral effect of the play as it challenges the social conscience of the audience.'[2]

Interestingly, given its controversial subjects of 'unmarried mothers' and 'baby-farming', the Lord Chamberlain's Office found little to query in Rayman's play when presented for pre-production scrutiny, and their reader demanded just two revisions, albeit that they were considered crucial. A line of banter about 'the girl guides' motto' ('Be prepared – it's the finest motto in the world') had to be dropped in view of its clear sexual innuendo in context. And the dialogue relating to one woman's account of rape, followed by the retort 'There's nothing wrong in being raped', was required to be rewritten. Once these amendments were forthcoming, however, the play was licensed and proceeded to enjoy a successful first run, whereupon it was snapped up by Anthony Hawtrey for production on 15 October 1951, with a new cast including René Ray (as Vivianne), at his Embassy Theatre in Swiss Cottage. After a three-week presentation, the play was transferred by impresario Jack Hylton to the Vaudeville Theatre from 7 November 1951 (where it ran for 235 performances) and, then, to the Victoria Palace (where it ran from 18 June to 1 November 1952) with Freda Jackson now playing Helen.[3]

Perhaps predictably, the critics gave *Women of Twilight* mixed reviews. 'No one would put this among the Plays Pleasant,' commented J.C. Trewin in the *Observer*, 'but it does seize the mind.' 'For all its faults,' Harold Conway commented in the *Evening Standard*, 'it does project vivid characters, dramatic atmosphere, and sustained theatrical tension.' 'This all-women play, in which the housing shortage, unmarried mothers, sadism both sluttish and refined, child murder, baby-farming, high rents and street walkers, are mixed together in glorious and humourless confusion,' stated the *Sunday Times* critic, 'is as great an advance on the Embassy's recent offerings as Neanderthal man was on the anthropoid ape.' And the *Daily Telegraph* reviewer added, in similar vein: 'Unrelieved femininity is popularly supposed to breed neurosis, and certainly this is the most hysterical play I have met for many years.'[4]

The film producers, John and James Woolf of Romulus Films, discovered the play even before it was presented at the Embassy and immediately recommended it to Daniel M. Angel for co-production. They are 'very keen to make it into a film with me,' Angel told the British Board of Film Censors on 26 September 1951, and their proposed cast comprised no less a trio than Flora Robson, Ida Lupino and Sally Gray in the leading roles. His letter to Arthur Watkins, the BBFC secretary, also included a copy of the play and the crucial promise that 'as you know from the Woolf Bros' and my previous films, the script and direction will be in the best of taste, as we do not want to set out to make a "sensation" film.' Angel was seeking BBFC advice on the potential censorship problems they might encounter. But short of informing him that 'Any film based on this play would, without any doubt, have to be placed by the Board in the "X" category,' Watkins maintained that he could say little more until a film script was available and 'detailed observations' might be made. In the meantime, Watkins handed the play over to his script readers for comment on its worth, and went along to see the Embassy stage presentation for himself.

Thus, when a screenplay (written by Anatole de Grunwald) was forthcoming on 21 April 1952, Watkins was already well armed with his readers' thoughts on the play script, his own reactions to the stage production, and, moreover, the fruits of early discussions on the matter with the BBFC president, Sir Sidney Harris. His readers' responses to the *Women of Twilight* film script subsequently confirmed Watkins's opinion that 'It is a sordid story but there are many moving moments and human touches.' Given that 'At least two of the characters are sympathetic,' he continued, 'I do not think there are any grounds on which we can bar this film from the "X" category.' But what he required from the film-makers by way of modifications was more, certainly, than those proposed by his readers. Harris agreed that 'This is a better script than many and with discreet direction and good acting it would make a worthy "X".' Yet he, too, wished to see changes made.[5]

The extent of the considerable revisions recommended to Angel was forthcoming on 1 May 1952. In addition to emphasising 'the need for discretion and restraint' in production generally, Watkins highlighted several principal areas of concern. On the question of 'language,' for instance, the words 'bastard' and 'bitch' were especially singled out to be deleted, not least in view of the fact that they occurred numerous times. And various telling phrases used in the women's accounts of their unwanted pregnancies – such as 'Lots of women die in childbirth,' 'I was raped,' 'Only you wasn't sure which one it was,' 'They'd be blaming the curate,' and 'I would never have let it go so far' – were also to be dropped. 'I think we must do rather more in the direction of making it less obvious that Jess is a prostitute,' was the comment made on one character, while 'the whole episode of Helen throwing Vivianne downstairs and leaving her to have her baby without medical aid is very unpleasant' was the judgement forthcoming on an important scene at the film's climax. 'If the episode is to remain,' Watkins argued, 'the greatest restraint will have to be exercised in the handling and we hope that special attention will be paid to this point in order to avoid trouble when the film comes up for censorship.' In the event, anyway, Watkins was adamant: 'There must of course be no actual shot of Vivianne lying at the foot of the stairs.'

Watkins need not have worried unduly. Committed, as they were, to making a film 'in the best of taste,' the Woolf brothers and Angel dutifully obliged with the requisite changes on almost every front. 'Bastard' was altered to 'brat' whenever it was found, and 'bitch' to 'cat,' 'kid' or 'fool,' although Angel stuck by his guns over 'You old cow' and was allowed to keep it (just as, surprisingly, the censors never queried his use of 'You lying slut'). By the same token, Angel continued to retain a proposed shot of Jess striking Vivianne which was also permitted as, indeed, was a heavily ironic reference made by one mother of her child, when departing for Germany,

Figure 3 Press book advertising for Gordon Parry's film of Sylvia Rayman's play *Women of Twilight* (GB, 1952). Courtesy of Steve Chibnall, British Cinema Archive

as 'my little souvenir from England.' But frequent usage of offensive words like 'hell,' 'bloody' and 'God' was amended to innocuous remarks such as 'heck,' 'blinking' and 'garn'. And all the troublesome phrases employed in the women's personalised accounts of their plight were removed – 'I was raped' being eventually replaced by 'I was taken advantage of' and shorn of its explicit incidental aspects. In the final analysis, moreover, the climactic scene to the film was done entirely by means of a close-up upon the arch villain's face while the sounds of Vivianne, injured and on the verge of childbirth, were served up merely as background. There was, as required, no shot seen of her lying at the foot of the stairs.

In one vital regard, yet again, the producers had made changes of their own, thereby further compromising the force and import of Rayman's original play. Where, previously, she had an all-woman cast with not a man on stage, now interestingly, in the screenplay, room was found for a male character, and a key one at that. Although Angel and the Woolfs had seen fit finally to employ Freda Jackson, René Ray and Vida Hope in the roles they had made their own on stage (as well as offering choice parts to Lois Maxwell and Dora Bryan), clearly they felt it necessary to write in a new leading character for the up-and-coming Laurence Harvey. Given that Harvey was already contracted to the Woolfs, after all, it made sound business sense to promote his career in this fashion. And obviously it was the commercial imperative and then received industry notions about the film's marketability that accounted for the apparent need for a male figure at all (the journeyman director, Gordon Parry, probably had little say in either the script or the casting). But, in the process of adding and foregrounding a prominent role for Harvey – as Vivianne's imprisoned lover who is hanged for murder (previously only referred to in the play) – the producers did scant service to Rayman's former purpose or her project.

The BBFC, for their part, were happy enough to pass the completed film, which they did in July 1952 once the President, Secretary and three other censors (including John Trevelyan) had seen it and confirmed that it could only be given an 'X' certificate. In view of the fact that it was the first British film to be put in the 'X'-rated category of classification, they must have been especially interested to see the reactions it provoked. So, too, must Angel and the Woolfs, whose hopes were doubtless riding high on their venture together. In the event, the film critics were hardly impressed and, for the most part, *Women of Twilight* received a negative, even hostile, response.

There were occasional dutiful nods in the direction of recognising the film's socially conscious themes and issues. Thus, Paul Dehn praised its 'blazing, missionary sincerity' in the *Sunday Chronicle*, while Ray Nunn of the *Daily Sketch* maintained: 'In my opinion here is an adult, honest drama which focuses attention on a real-life problem, to which none of us should close our eyes.' 'You may find it distasteful. You may regard it as something of a social document,' Ewart Hodgson commented in the *News of the World*, but 'One thing is certain. It's a film that cannot be ignored.' Campbell Dixon echoed these sentiments in the *Daily Telegraph* when commenting: 'If it helps to awaken the public conscience and sharpen official vigilance it will be justified.' And if Dilys Powell of the *Sunday Times* considered it 'not at all badly done,' although little more, Virginia Graham of the *Spectator* found it to be 'a seemingly plausible record of man's inhumanity to woman and a woman's attempt to cash in on it'.

But most critics damned the film in no uncertain terms. It 'fails to live up to the pathos of its subject,' Fred Majdalany argued in the *Daily Mail*. It was 'Not my idea of an enjoyable evening out' according to Reg Whitley of the *Daily Mirror*, and 'Not a film to be proud of in Coronation year,' in the eyes of *The People*. 'If you enjoy watching women snarling, scratching or pulling each other's hair in sordid surroundings, this is your picture,' Roy Nash added in *The Star*, while Jympson Harman of the *Evening News* maintained: 'They order this matter better in France.' Clearly, in the eyes of some critics, *Women of Twilight* still remained too much of a woman's film. Where, moreover, Thomas Spencer of the *Daily Worker* felt it invited audiences to 'wallow in the sordid with a comfortable feeling of taking part in some high-minded sociological investigation,' even the *Monthly Film Bulletin* was prompted to comment in similar supercilious tones that 'The problem of finding accommodation and the danger of overcrowding are not confined only to the unmarried mothers in contemporary Britain.'[6]

I Am a Camera

I Am a Camera is a play derived from the Berlin stories of Christopher Isherwood. The action takes place in a Berlin pension where Isherwood is trying to write and being too easily deflected. Here, his friend Fritz introduces him to Sally Bowles, who afterwards comes to live in the same house. Sally is our old friend, the Innocent Tart. She is English, of good family, but with an inherent and unselfconscious libidinousness that drives her, not exactly on to the streets, but into the arms of not-very-carefully chosen men. Isherwood gives English lessons to Natalia, daughter of a wealthy Jewish shop-owner. Fritz tries in vain to get off with Natalia, until he confesses (just after the anti-Semitic troubles begin: the period is about 1930) that he is himself a Jew. Meanwhile Isherwood and Sally have been taken up by one of Sally's boyfriends, a rich American. They go around drinking together and the American buys them expensive and useless presents. He even suggests a trip round the world but in the end slips back, bored, to the United States. Sally, who has had an abortion, gets tight one evening and contacts her family – more or less by accident. Her mother flies to Berlin and assumes that Isherwood is her lover. This is not so, even though appearances would seem to indicate the opposite. Sally says that she will not return to England with her mother. Isherwood finds that he must return to England, as his money is running out. But Sally cannot change her way of life and she reappears in her usual night club while Isherwood, having written a book about her, fades out.

Successfully launched at the Empire Theatre in New York on 28 November 1951 – where it ran for 262 performances – John van Druten's play of *I Am a Camera* was immediately seen as an attractive proposition in the eyes of various British stage and screen producers. It was first tendered to the Lord Chamberlain's Office for pre-production scrutiny by Laurence Olivier Productions on 12 March 1952, where the script reader, Charles Heriot, instantly dubbed it 'a static play,' but maintained that 'If this play were set in Paris and written by Anouilh, it would receive louder praise than I expect it will get.' Despite the free-spirited nature of its principal character and the various instances of her libidinous lifestyle, Heriot's reservations about its viability for stage presentation centred upon just three key areas of concern. There were, to begin with, too many references to 'whores' throughout the play and it was felt that some should be omitted and the producers should 'only retain the word where dramatically necessary'. Second, the line 'Throw her on a couch and ravish her' should be cut. And, third, Sally's reasons for securing her abortion should either be altered or dropped altogether – 'I imagined how it would grow up and how after I'd put it to bed at nights I'd go out and make love to filthy old men to get money to pay for its clothes and food.' Though reference to abortion itself was allowed, clearly, this was considered to go too far.[7]

Once Brigadier Sir Norman Gwatkin, the Lord Chamberlain's Assistant Comptroller, had communicated the extent of the required alterations to Laurence Olivier Productions, they soon fell out of the reckoning as regards likely producers. In the autumn of 1953, however, the impresario Donald Albery revived the idea of mounting a production of John van Druten's work. A dynamic newcomer to the London theatrical scene, Albery wrote to the Lord Chamberlain on 23 December that he hoped to present it in early spring 1954, that the playwright had agreed to come over from the United States to direct the piece himself, and that Dorothy Tutin – fresh from her recent West End success in Albery's presentation of Graham Greene's *The Living Room* – would take the leading role of Sally Bowles.

It was proposed to open the play at the New Theatre, St Martin's Lane, on 12 March 1954 after a week's run at the Theatre Royal in Brighton. Already alert to the problems which had been singled out previously, however, Albery willingly consented to the deletion of 'an odd "whore" or two' on the basis that it 'would probably go unnoticed and might even be to the advantage of the play.' However, he then asked the Lord Chamberlain to reconsider the other two stipulations and, canny producer that he was,

Albery cited as reasons the fact that certain notable critics, such as Ken Tynan of the *Evening Standard*, had already seen the American production and most would probably have read it anyway. 'I do not want, with this play, to have any suggestion that it has been censored,' he argued, 'as this sort of thing is too often used for cheap publicity purposes.' To retain the offending lines 'would undoubtedly have a value in explaining the mental processes of these particular characters in the particular period in which the play is set,' Albery maintained, and besides, he concluded, action could still be taken to amend matters at the last, should need arise, since 'the Lord Chamberlain reserves the right, if he thinks fit, to require the cuts to be made.'

It was a cunning ploy, but the Lord Chamberlain's Office was not so easily deceived. On 4 January 1954, Gwatkin replied: 'The Lord Chamberlain feels that there would inevitably be more publicity if cuts were required after the play had been produced than if they were made before.' Reiterating their concern that the offending passages should be moderated, Gwatkin added, for good measure, that 'there is no need for anyone outside your office to know that such alterations were not made by yourselves'. His bluff called and trumped, Albery returned one day later, on 5 January, with the proposed alterations which he had 'just received' from John van Druten and with an assurance to the effect that 'We are, of course, perfectly prepared to accept your suggestion that we should ourselves appear to have altered these few lines by a managerial-cum-author decision.'

Though, occasionally, the word 'whore' was still deemed dramatically essential in van Druten's eyes and retained where necessary, in three instances he had simply substituted it with 'tart'. The other lines had been changed, respectively, to 'Knock her down. Throw her on a couch or something', and, 'I'd go out with filthy old men to get money to pay for its clothes and food.' Since, crucially, the words 'ravish' and 'make love' had been altered, the Lord Chamberlain was now content to let the play proceed into production, and a licence was issue for public performance on 5 January. When, furthermore, Albery returned on 16 February with a few additional alterations made during rehearsals and which appeared to him to be 'relatively harmless', these too were allowed to pass.

I Am a Camera opened as planned on Friday 12 March 1954. This was, in fact, its fifth 'first' night following four charity preview performances earlier in the week, thereby prompting the ever-idiosyncratic drama critic, Harold Hobson, to note that the play 'could be amongst the most distinguished productions in London' but that, for the moment, the cast 'seemed to me utterly exhausted, as well they might be'. Yet Hobson's modest diatribe against previews – admittedly made 'at the risk', as he put it, 'of being in a minority of one' – could not disguise the opinion that he still found it 'a fine though episodic play' (*Sunday Times*). His caveats were echoed or amplified by a small number of critics. But the majority were unstinting in their praise of both the play and production, not least for Dorothy Tutin's undoubted acting prowess, which was variously described as 'sparkling,' 'a triumph', 'a sensation' and 'vivid perfection'. 'No young actress in recent years has given a performance of such outstanding brilliance,' A. E.Wilson commented in *The Star*.

The role of Sally Bowles, everybody agreed, was especially demanding. 'Such a part can only be made plausible by an actress with certain particular gifts,' stated W. A. Darlington of the *Daily Telegraph*: 'She must be able at least to suggest depravity, yet she must have a quality of spiritual integrity which, underlying her deplorable behaviour, shows that in spite of all she is somehow good'. 'These qualities Dorothy Tutin has,' he concluded, and 'By a happy coincidence, the part and the actress have timed their arrival so as to meet at just the right moment.' If the critics, Hobson apart, were pretty unanimous and fulsome in praising Dorothy Tutin, there was less certainty about the morals of the piece, which some considered highly dubious and 'shocking.' Though the *Sketch* thought it 'a civilised night at the theatre,' the *Manchester Guardian* maintained 'The play has no moral, makes no point, or even a gesture of summing up.' A. E. Wilson was not alone in commenting upon 'the play's disregard of moral standards', and most noted that 'An inconvenient baby is not given the chance to be born.' There were repeated references in reviews, albeit brief and passing, to Sally getting 'rid of an unwanted, illegitimate baby before it is born'.

Ivor Brown also concentrated upon moral issues in his column for the *Observer*, where, through a muddled confection of mixed metaphors, he managed to outline what he perceived to be the dilemmas posed by the play's success. 'I remember thinking of a Restoration Comedy that it was perfectly written, perfectly acted, and perfectly filthy,' he stated, 'and I have in my dour, Platonic way, a strong conviction that this piece (or at least this production) might have been an honest gin-and-bitters, but has had a strawberry ice cream sloshed over the top of it.' 'We are now in a period as tolerant as that of the Restoration,' he continued, 'and, when the artist is skilful, to enjoy all is to pardon all.' 'Standards are slipping,' was Ivor Brown's considered opinion, but 'If the morals are bad, the "theatre" is unquestionably good.'[8]

Others were less sure of that, even, especially among the ranks of the Public Morality Council. And, on 6 May 1954, the General Secretary of the Council's Stage Plays, Radio and Television Sub-Committee wrote to the Lord Chamberlain conveying its 'surprise and regret' that *I Am a Camera* should have been licensed for public performance. The point and purpose of the Public Morality Council's letter was soon made clear and in no uncertain terms:

> In the view of my Sub-Committee, as the entire theme of the play is fornication, treated in such a way as to have a most damaging effect on all who see it and especially the younger element in every audience, it has no redeeming feature. I remind your Lordship that the girl in the play was not forced by any tragic compulsion or material need to live the life of a harlot, but only did it because she liked it, thus making Ivor Brown (*Observer*) say it was 'perfectly acted, perfectly produced, and perfectly filthy'. What seems to be particularly regrettable is that at a time when all are agreed that there is the greatest possible need for a tightening up of the moral fibre in the whole country, that a play such as this, which cannot but have the most deplorable effect on public morals, should have been licensed. Is it not possible, even at this stage, for the licence to be withdrawn?

Norman Gwatkin's reply of 12 May sought to defuse the issue by pointing out the production's credentials – it was the work of 'a well-known author', was being presented here 'under the aegis of Mr Donald Albery' and 'had played for some time in America' – as well as emphasising that the Lord Chamberlain had indeed given the matter 'considerable thought' and insisted upon 'certain cuts'. While recognising that the general theme of the play was 'promiscuous fornication', nevertheless, he felt that it 'is not put in at all an attractive light and should act more as a deterrent than as an encouragement to anyone whose thoughts run in that direction'.

Undeterred, however, the Public Morality Council responded on 29 June with another letter of complaint, contesting the Lord Chamberlain's judgement once again, and seeking yet further review of the performance licence awarded the play. This time, Lord Scarbrough felt compelled to go and see it for himself. Though his opinion remained the same, the arguments marshalled in its favour took on increasing statistical force, as his letter of 8 July revealed:

> From our experience here, we have usually found that we received a number of complaints from members of the public when there is a doubt as to whether or not a play should have been licensed. With regard to this particular play, it has now been on for some 4 months and has been seen, I have ascertained, by over 100,000 people and I am informed that except for your letter, we have not received a single complaint about it. I think this worth mentioning as it tends to confirm the view to which I have myself come after seeing the play.

Thus, when subsequent letters arrived at the Lord Chamberlain's Office from disaffected theatregoers who also complained about *I Am a Camera*, they were greeted by the simple expedient of citing the production's credentials, adding a note about the play serving 'more as a deterrent than as an encouragement', making slight amendment to the quantity of complaints received ('a single complaint' changed over time to 'very small number'), but contrasting them, finally, with the increased majority that had seen the play without demur.

The woman from St John's Wood who believed that 'Its filth and obscenity and general low character are a disgrace to the English stage' was sent such a reassuring reply. So, too, was the woman from Mapledurham, south Croydon, as well as the 31-year-old man from Fulham who had spent four years in the army and considered himself 'fairly blasé' until he took an Irish nurse, aged twenty-one, along with him to see the play. 'I was absolutely disgusted with this show and left early,' he stated. 'I felt ashamed to be English and a Londoner especially.' By the time he was sent a letter from the Lord Chamberlain's Office, however, the number of theatregoers contentedly seeing *I Am a Camera* had increased to 200,000 strong, while the number of complaints was still 'very few indeed'.

Only one correspondent appeared to cause even mild concern among the Lord Chamberlain's men. 'One is forced to conclude that the reason that all this is allowed to go out is that it is "good box office",' the woman from St John's Wood adamantly maintained on returning a second time to the fray. 'Can you truthfully state that this is not the case?' 'Oh dear', Brigadier Sir Norman Gwatkin wrote in confidential comment and blue pencil on the margin of her letter, 'What a leading question.'

Despite the occasional protest from disgruntled members of the public, however, *I Am a Camera* proved a considerable success with theatregoers. Its London run lasted for fully ten months, until 8 January 1955, and then, with Moira Shearer succeeding Dorothy Tutin in the lead part of Sally Bowles, it began a twelve-week provincial tour at the New Theatre, Oxford, from 7 February. Given the critical and commercial acclaim it had enjoyed, moreover, the play inevitably attracted the attention of film producers. West End theatrical successes traditionally turned out to be a source of steady supply for adaptation to the cinema and John van Druten's play was no exception.

I Am a Camera had, in fact, been spotted within a month of its London opening by director Henry Cornelius (whose previous credits included *Passport to Pimlico*, in 1949, and *Genevieve*, in 1953), and producers John and James Woolf of Romulus Films. On 13 April 1954, in time-honoured fashion, Cornelius proceeded to send a copy of the play script to Arthur Watkins, secretary at the British Board of Film Censors, with a view to obtaining the Board's opinion as to its likely viability for transposition to the cinema screen. He was adamant from the outset that what he intended was a 'quality' film, that he was 'not in any way interested to emphasise or stress the moral controversial points of the play', and that he was seeking to draw out 'the contrast between the growing Nazi movement and the individual lives of the characters in the play'.[9]

Watkins immediately set one of his readers the task of reading and evaluating the play's potential problems and pitfalls. To nobody's surprise, Audrey Field's detailed and summary report highlighted a number of possibly contentious areas. The question of 'language' and the characterisation of Sally Bowles were paramount among her concerns. 'This is not an immoral or even an amoral story,' she stated initially, 'just the picture, against the background of a crumbling world, of two young people adrift and at a loss.' 'It captures the flavour of the thirties very well,' she continued. 'But I can find very few pages of dialogue in the whole script which are not "X", and there are some lines which would not be in accordance even with our "X" standards.'

The prospect of an 'X' certificate was very worrying to film producers, of course, since it instantly curtailed a film's box-office potential by confining exhibition to 'adult' audiences alone, and cinemagoers over sixteen years of age. Hence, to help matters, Audrey Field suggested that the focus of the story could be shifted away from the character of Sally, with the result that her role would be 'groomed into relative respectability and much reduced'. The advantage here was obvious, she felt, since 'This would give Mr Cornelius the chance of developing a good story on the courage of persecuted Jews in pre-War Berlin.' The disadvantage of prompting Cornelius to proceed along these lines, so as to secure an 'A' certificate and possibly larger audience, was that the finished film would not bear 'very close relation to the play'. Not only did this seem an unlikely proposition in itself, but the chances of persuading him to follow such a course of action seemed further diminished when taking into account Field's distinctly jaundiced, if highly realistic, conclusion that 'it won't be like what we know of film producers if he cheerfully and willingly jettisons all promiscuity, drug addiction and abortion'.

Once armed with Field's comments, Arthur Watkins reported back to Henry Cornelius the first fruits of the BBFC's findings. 'Obviously the play could be modified in several ways in order to squeeze the film into the "A" category,' he stated, though with inevitable consequences of a sort that would doubtless prove unwelcome to both the author and director. As far as he was concerned, however, 'The answer is a simple one, namely, that a film based on this script would fall unquestionably into the "X" category.' Even then, of course, there would have to be changes. But to Watkins's mind, these were 'minor points' and 'would not cause any trouble'. 'The play, as I am sure you will agree, is adult from beginning to end,' he maintained, 'and one of the reasons for the existence of the "X" certificate is to enable the Board to pass stories of this kind.' The incentive for the film-makers seriously to contemplate taking an 'X' rating was immense, in short, as Watkins made abundantly clear in his parting remarks: 'This is a natural "X" subject and for that category we would place no serious obstacle in the way of a film adaptation.'

Lest he had missed anything by way of unforeseen hazards in his seeming enthusiasm for the project, however, Watkins also availed himself of the opportunity, in the time it would take for the film-makers to come up with a screenplay, to send no fewer than four of his examiners along to watch, on the Board's behalf, the stage production of *I Am a Camera* during the course of its London run. Clearly, pre-production scrutiny by the British Board of Film Censors entailed extensive theatrical 'vetting' as well, when it was deemed necessary. But the reactions of the four examiners only served, in this instance, to fuel further Board debate about the play's merits or viability as a film.

John Trevelyan (later to be BBFC secretary, in his own right, from July 1958) and Mary C Glasgow went to see it on 18 June 1954. Glasgow noted ironically in her report, written the next day, that 'The occasion was memorable for the harmony of the examiners' views – the first of the kind on record.' Then she proceeded to spell out their unanimous judgement of its worth:

> We have no hesitation in saying that we regard this material as unsuitable for a film. Apart from the dialogue, which is appallingly vulgar but could presumably be pruned at the script stage, we consider the whole subject unacceptable. It may be argued that this account of a decadent section of society, without standards of any kind, moral or sexual, is interesting historically – although we did not find it so in the play. As a film, we cannot see how it could be other than harmfully degrading to the cinemagoing public. We may add that the play contains references to religion and to politics which are at least tasteless and at worst offensive.

Such unanimity was soon shattered when, somewhat predictably, Audrey Field stated: 'I do still consider that there ought to be room for a film based on this play.' Furthermore, on 24 June, she elaborated at length her sincerely felt and strongly held feelings in favour of allowing it to go ahead and, preferably, under Cornelius's direction:

> I agree that there are a number of 'shock' lines and, for a film, a great many of them would have to go . . . As to the story, admittedly Sally does not get her just deserts by, e.g., being raped by her brother-in-law and going mad; nor, on the other hand, does

she reform and qualify for a good man's love. She goes off to Italy with a man who says he is going to put her in a film. But is not this sort of thing what more often happens to a promiscuous woman in real life? And, in an 'X' film, doesn't integrity count for something? Of course, opinions differ as to whether the play has integrity; but I myself believe that it has . . .

No one, I believe, would come away from this play believing that promiscuity led to happiness. On the contrary, I thought that the scene in which Sally tells Christopher that she is pregnant and how she feels about it, and the scene in which she describes her state of mind after she has had the operation, were of more moral worth than the whole boiling of so-called 'sex instruction films'. I was deeply moved. So were my neighbours, a pleasant elderly couple from Lincoln; and the house as a whole was attentive and completely quiet. Christopher also, though still at the time of this story, a drifter, is plainly sprouting a sense of moral values, and his advice to Sally emphasises this . . .

I believe that the cleavage of opinion between JT and MCG on the one hand and myself on the other respects a violent difference of opinion which exists among responsible members of the playgoing public about the play. I had no hint of this when I read the play; it has only gradually come to my notice since, from little things I have heard. Nevertheless, I firmly believe that a director of Mr Cornelius' calibre can, if he wishes, present to the cinema public something which will command *and* deserve success by shunning the cheap way of depending on shock lines to raise inane laughter; and by laying bare the integrity and moral power which I believe I have detected in the play, so enabling us to say to critics, 'We are confident that we were right in giving a hearing to this controversial film'. It is, indeed, partly confidence in Mr Cornelius which has emboldened me to stick my neck out. I only hope he will not let me down.

The fourth and final examiner, Gerald Sharpe, took his wife with him to see the play several months later, on 8 September 1954, and was clearly not averse to giving the BBFC secretary the benefits of their joint, if ultimately mixed, assessment:

My wife and I turned to one another at the first interval in this play and agreed that it would be quite impossible to put anything like this on the cinema screen. While quite understanding that the heroine was deliberately setting out to shock Christopher Isherwood at the outset, by painting herself even blacker than she was, and that this was a legitimate story point, we felt that even when toned down, it would be very strong meat indeed for the cinema. The whole business of the unwanted baby, while again dramatically powerful and providing a reason for drawing Isherwood and Sally closer together, was distressing and it is difficult to imagine how one could present it in an acceptable manner even to an 'adult' cinema audience. As the play progressed, its better features became apparent: concern at Nazism and persecution of the Jews; very realistic reconstruction of the German atmosphere. And the under-lying moral tone is undoubtedly good. Our final conclusion was that a film based on the play *could* be acceptable. I understand that the Board is in fact committed to passing the film in the 'X' category in one form or another. Naturally the more flagrant pieces of dialogue would be quite inadmissible in the cinema. (My wife and I are by no means prudes but she was deeply shocked in particular by the references (a) to Fraulein Schneider's bosom, (b) to Sally's preference for going into the man's bed, and (c) to syphilis. For myself, I would like to see the last of the unwanted baby and the abortion arrangements and aftermath.)

Given the sheer weight of his examiners' opinions on all sides of the debate, Arthur Watkins must have turned with some relief to the long-awaited draft screenplay for *I Am a Camera*, written by Henry Cornelius and John Collier, when it actually landed on his desk in late October 1954. Advance warning of its imminent arrival, sent in a letter from producer John Woolf on 22 October, promised that 'whereas of course the main characterisation remains the same as the play, we have asked the writers considerably to tone down some of the dialogue'. In addition, though, Woolf was already expressing misgivings about the box-office potential for their film if Watkins persisted in his promise of consigning it to the dreaded 'X' classification: 'If you think there are any slightest alterations which will ensure an "A" certificate, we should be only too happy to give them every consideration as we would naturally much prefer this to an "X".' Watkins, for his part, was exceptionally well prepared to mount a ready and robust reply which he sent on 25 October: 'From reports I have received on the stage play, I do not see any possibility of a film based on it getting into other than the "X" category, but we will of course keep an open mind when we read the script.'

Audrey Field and Gerald Sharpe were given the task of reading and commenting upon the film script. Both expressed themselves 'deeply disappointed' with the outcome and Field, in particular, found it unacceptable in large measure. Where, previously, she had been a firm advocate of the project proceeding into production, now she had considerable and profound reservations. Her report of 28 October 1954 outlined extensively what she saw as its new-found redeeming as well as damning features:

The play has undergone very extensive alterations and the 'shock' points have been toned down. A great deal of the prohibitive dialogue has disappeared (though not all). An abortion is mooted but does not happen; instead Sally first decides to have the baby and accepts Chris' offer of marriage, and then tells him she has made a mistake and is not going to have a baby after all. She decides to accept an offer from a friend of Clive, the American, to 'make a film in Paris'. The mother does not come into the film at all. The affair between Fritz and Natalia is more prominent and brought into sharper focus by glimpses of Natalia's family, and something is seen of Nazi disturbances in the streets of Berlin. Chris' own awakening to some sense of responsibility, and to the grief and menace of the world in which he lives, is made more clear. The fact that the story is a period piece (very important from our point of view) is emphasised by telling it in the form of flashback. These points are all to the good. On the other hand, the nature of the framework is disastrous. The story is told by way of flashback from a cocktail party to which Isherwood has come to meet a new literary 'lioness' – the Sally Bowles of today, who has just written her 'Confessions' and become a best-selling authoress. At the end of the film Isherwood meets her again, finds that she has just been asked by the manager to leave her hotel because of a rowdy party, so invites her to come and stay in his house – an offer which is accepted. This sort of framework won't do. Also the comedy scenes have been so multiplied and laid on so thick as to suggest to the undiscerning that Sally's way of life is a huge joke, instead of the tragedy which the play implied. Moreover, whereas the play was visually entirely free from suggestiveness, the film makes a great feature of drunkenness and rowdy parties and, in an early scene, of undressing and underclothes. A great deal, therefore, will need to be done.

Gerald Sharpe echoed many of Field's sentiments a day later. 'While most of the objectionable dialogue from the play has gone,' he noted, 'so has the good moral tone together with the strong feeling of sympathy for Sally who, in the play, is so obviously headed for an unhappy future.' In one regard, especially, he found himself totally in agreement with Field's contention that 'Sally must not be allowed to "get away with it" and appear as a present day success.' And, clearly sharing some of Audrey Field's tangible disillusion at what they had been presented with for consideration, moreover, Sharpe concluded with a wry comment made at both their expense: 'Cornelius' statement on his letter of 13 April that he is "not in any way interested to emphasise or stress the moral controversial points of the play", now seems to take on a new significance.'

After he had collated his readers' observations and decided upon the appropriate course of action, Watkins then embarked on fully a month of painstaking and protracted negotiations with the film-makers to ensure that the BBFC got what was wanted even before production began. He started off with a letter to John Woolf, on 1 November 1954, in which he detailed precisely and exhaustively a long list of reservations regarding the proposed screenplay. It was intended to express their twin points of concern: principally, that 'We could not have Sally coming back prosperous and successful – a living advertisement for a shiftless and promiscuous way of life'; but also that the new framework, which looked upon events in 'flashback' from the present day, served merely to undercut what was formerly 'a period piece', in effect, and lend greater contemporary significance or resonance to the characters and proceedings. But there were many other matters raised besides and enough, certainly, to compel an immediate meeting with the producer.

John Woolf arrived the next day, on 2 November, accompanied by one of his scriptwriters, John Collier, and two colleagues from Romulus Films. It was clearly a bargaining session in which some ground was conceded by both parties while vital matters remained firm and fast. If, on occasion, the BBFC 'Agreed to waive our objection' to one issue or 'Agreed to *consider* allowing' another, it was invariably done on the strict understanding that they were 'reserving the right to maintain our original objection' in the light of what was finally forthcoming by way of a completed script or the finished film. But Watkins appeared to be relatively pleased with the discussions, not least when Collier outlined his ideas for yet another 'new prologue and epilogue' that he hoped would settle the BBFC's mind on the 'flashback' framework front. 'This sounded satisfactory since it made clear that Sally had by no means prospered since she left Chris,' Watkins reported, and 'It was agreed that the new material should be sent to us as soon as it was ready.'

Meeting the BBFC's exacting demands was easier said than done, however, and by 24 November Woolf was in a quandary. 'Several attempts were made to write along the lines we discussed with you but none of them met with Cornelius' approval and, in fact, somehow they were not satisfactory,' he wrote. Furthermore, 'After a lot of discussion it was therefore decided that Collier should attempt to modify and alter the present framework in an attempt to meet and overcome the objections you had to it.' The new pages were also submitted for Watkins's perusal, as Woolf proceeded to spell out the changes. 'The principal difference of course is that it is now made perfectly clear that Sally is poor and completely unsuccessful – that the book has been ghost-written for her and that there is no prospect of her making any money out of it,' he said. 'In addition, there is no suggestion that any amorous exploits of her past are to be the selling angle of her book.' 'I earnestly hope that they will meet with your approval,' was Woolf's desperate plea at the end, 'because in the event that they do not, both Collier and Cornelius seem to be completely out of ideas of how to proceed'.

Audrey Field commented upon the new prologue and epilogue in her usual pithy and succinct vein on 25 November 1954, within twenty-four hours of receipt:

> It is now clear that Sally has not prospered and that the book will bring her in nothing (until it has sold 200,000 copies). She is living in a depressing little furnished room. I do not mind the introduction to the film (but is 'Don't lick your lubricious lips', on p. 3, really necessary?). The title of Sally's book, 'The lady goes on hoping', seems to me all right. But I am less happy about the concluding pages: I wish the makers of the film were not so set on Chris and Sally setting up house together again. Nothing is gained, I should have thought, from their point of view or ours, by starting off on the same tatty story all over again. I do not know if it is prohibitive for the 'X' category, but it is certainly no help. P. 99: '*lascivious* looking critics' might be better out.

Watkins wrote back to Woolf, the same day, stating that he did not like the proposed modifications to the screenplay and proposing yet another meeting in view of the impasse they had reached. The meeting which followed on the evening of 29 November resolved matters to everybody's satisfaction – though not of course without some final demands being laid at the scriptwriters' door. If nothing else, clearly, the film-makers were resigned to their lot in accepting the worrying prospect of an 'X' certificate. Still, at least they were allowed now to proceed confidently with production – something which had, in fact, already lately started.

Shooting commenced in mid-October 1954 and was based largely at Walton Studios. In addition to Cornelius and Collier, the team assembled by John and James Woolf included Jack Clayton as associate producer and Guy Green on cinematography, with Clive Donner as editor and Malcolm Arnold scoring the music. Laurence Harvey, contracted to the Woolf brothers, was given the part of Christopher Isherwood, Anton Diffring engaged to play Fritz, and Ron Randell to take Clive. The Viennese actress Lea Seidl was recruited for Fraulein Schneider and Shelley Winters brought over from America for Natalia. So, too, was Julie Harris for Sally Bowles. Though better known as a film actress in Britain (for Fred Zinnemann's 1952 *Member of the Wedding* and Elia Kazan's 1955 *East of Eden*), Harris secured the leading role as a direct result of her considerable stage success in the part during the original Broadway run of *I Am a Camera*. Given that she was 'a star of stage and screen', and American as well, it doubtless made good business sense to engage her services. The commercial imperative was significant. But to many critics and fans who had witnessed Dorothy Tutin's triumph as Sally Bowles on the London stage, it seemed unfortunate all the same.

In the event, however, the film censors were not finished with *I Am a Camera*. Once it was completed and handed over for post-production review before the award of an appropriate certificate, the BBFC examiners took issue with one of Sally's lines of dialogue – 'Surely he hasn't got a crush on shoes at his age?' – which she uttered when throwing her shoe out of a window, in a fit of pique, and seeing it immediately pocketed by a young lad. 'The line must be deleted,' Woolf was dutifully informed after the BBFC had viewed his film on 9 May 1955. So it was, indeed, and replaced by alternative dialogue from Sally, which was obviously intended for comic effect: 'Perhaps he's got a one-legged sister.' The fact that the substitute line was greeted with instant approval, and *I Am a Camera* awarded its long-promised 'X' certificate accordingly, was perhaps an inadvertent sign, if such were needed, of the kind of film that Watkins had sought to aid and abet all along. What better way to defuse controversial and contentious issues than by means of humour?

Figure 4 Julie Harris reprised her Broadway stage success as Sally Bowles in the Henry Cornelius film of *I Am a Camera* (GB, 1955). Romulus/The Kobal Collection

Audrey Field had noted of the first draft screenplay, for instance, that 'The comedy scenes have been so multiplied and laid on so thick.' Perhaps Watkins promoted this approach on the scriptwriters' part precisely because he saw it as an easy way out of dealing with an otherwise difficult property and so that the humour would usefully serve, to borrow Field's words yet again, 'instead of the tragedy which the play implied'. What to her mind was a setback and source of disappointment may just have turned out as a boon and benefit to Watkins's way of thinking.

And when, on 15 August 1955, the Public Control and Licensing Committee of Surrey County Council wrote to Arthur Watkins enquiring as to the nature of the film, because it had not yet been given a trade show but the producers wanted permission for a Sunday 'preview' performance, the BBFC secretary's summary response was nothing if not interesting. The story 'centres on the capricious and unpredictable behaviour of the heroine', he replied on 17 August, but 'The whole theme is treated in a spirit of light comedy.' Watkins reiterated, nevertheless, that 'the Board considered it necessary to restrict the exhibition of the film to adults'.

For the critics who reviewed the film when it opened at the London Pavilion on 14 October 1955, however, the humour appeared out of place and hardly appropriate. 'I expected a bitter-sweet tale of a fascinating little amoral child–woman in the sad decadence of Berlin just before Hitler took over,' Jympson Harman noted in the *Evening News*, but 'The film only suggests the tragedy of the times. What was gentle farce on the stage now becomes roaring farce.' 'The new treatment seems wrong,' he continued, and 'Despite its "X" certificate *I Am a Camera* is nothing like as naughty as it should have been. Perhaps that is why it seems to falls between two stools.' The film was 'thin, pretentious and silly' according to Campbell Dixon of the *Daily Telegraph*, 'something of a mess' in the eyes of Derek Granger on the *Financial Times*, and 'a travesty of the original', Julian Symons maintained in *Tribune*.

Of the actors, in particular, the critics agreed in their opinion that Laurence Harvey was 'hopelessly miscast' as Isherwood. By contrast, Julie Harris's performance as Sally Bowles was considered to be one of the film's few redeeming features and 'a creation of pure joy' (*Daily Mail*) – except to those, like Harold Conway of the *Daily Sketch*, who remained convinced about 'How more effective was Dorothy Tutin's untutored, unconscious humour in the trolloping department.' For the most part, though, the film fared badly as far as the critics' reactions were concerned. So poor was the response, in fact, that many preferred to indulge themselves with a punning game of the sort instigated by the New York critic who had declared of the Broadway stage production – 'No Leica'. Thus, Alan Brien said of the British film that '*I Am a Camera* has been a victim of double exposure' (*Evening Standard*), while Donald Zec claimed that it 'seems badly out of focus' (*Daily Mirror*), and Paul Dehn stated that 'it does point the futility of substituting a mere lens for the eye of genius' (*News Chronicle*).[10]

Debate about the merits or otherwise of *I Am a Camera* surfaced several years later, once again, thereby providing a wry postscript to earlier events as well as offering further evidence of Arthur Watkins's intentions in dealing with it throughout. In April 1961, Associated Rediffusion Limited wrote to the BBFC enquiring whether the film might possibly be reclassified and given an 'A' certificate in the light of the fact they wished to broadcast it on television. In discussion among themselves, on 17 April, the BBFC examiners agreed that it now 'seemed pretty small beer for an "X" – especially because the film seems to have lost much of its impact with the passage of time'. 'In effect, there is very little feeling of realism about it,' they concluded, 'as compared with the punch of subjects like *Room at the Top*, *Look Back in Anger*, and *Saturday Night and Sunday Morning*.'

In the event, predictably, the examiners decided 'all this abortion business' meant *I Am a Camera* must still remain firmly in the 'X'-rated category and could not possibly be reclassified without re-editing. But the fleeting reference to the 'new wave' of British social realist films that emerged in the late 1950s was significant. It was significant because it afforded recognition of the fact that things had changed in British cinema. And the BBFC secretary from 1958, John Trevelyan, had done much to cultivate the 'new wave' in order to help provide precisely the sort of films that had been noticeably lacking throughout the earlier part of the decade. Crucially, Trevelyan succeeded in promoting the 'quality' mainstream British cinema that Watkins had signally failed to foster.

If though, as the examiners now agreed, *I Am a Camera* seemed 'pretty small beer' and had an air of 'almost *Carry On* farce about it', as they concluded, then this can only be attributed in large measure to the process of film censorship which obtained during most of the 1950s, when cinemagoers were protected and sheltered from anything worse than what usually was allowed by the BBFC. And if, indeed, British cinema carried greater 'punch' from the outset of the 1960s, it did so in part because film censorship had opened up sufficiently to allow of such. Some things were still prohibited, of course. The 1960 film of *Saturday Night and Sunday Morning* was no more allowed a successful or controversial abortion scene than *I Am a Camera* had previously. But the 1966 film of *Alfie* was permitted it, as we shall see. The times were certainly changing, in short, and British film censorship was changing with them.

In the late 1960s, moreover, *I Am a Camera* reappeared in a new-found guise, as a two-act musical called *Cabaret*, with the American character now named Clifford Bradshaw. It opened on Broadway during 1967, and a script was submitted to the Lord Chamberlain's Office in November 1967 with a view to a run at the Palace Theatre in the West End beginning on 28 February 1968. This time, it was uncontroversially allowed in the light of the interim, more liberal developments on both stage and screen, although the theatre management was warned that in a stage direction marked in the script as 'He hits the gong between her legs', the gong should be placed between the lower legs of the actress concerned. With a few lyrics altered by the production team, in addition to the Lord Chamberlain's warning, the play proceeded as scheduled. Lord Cobbold, the Lord Chamberlain since 1963, received not one single letter of complaint about the musical play from the general public.

In 1971–2, the memorable film version of *Cabaret*, written and directed by Bob Fosse, reverted more closely to *I Am a Camera* rather than that of the musical play it claimed to be based upon, although most of the songs were retained. By now the 'X' certificate and even stronger cinematic fare were firmly established in the cinemagoer's mind, with the result that the BBFC allowed *Cabaret* uncut on 1 March 1972, while retaining the 'X' certification (albeit that, from 1970, this was raised to eighteen years of age and over). However, after the film's release a member of the public from Worsley in Lancashire wrote to the BBFC to enquire about the reasons for the 'X' certificate. The reply hints at possible divisions among the examiners, for it was explained that while there had been no question of cuts, the 'X' certificate had been a marginal decision. But its entire tone was still deemed adult, especially in its depiction of the 'degenerate' Berlin environment of 1931. The wheel had truly come full circle.[11]

Notes

1. Quoted in Anthony Aldgate, *Censorship and the Permissive Society: British Cinema and Theatre, 1955–1965* (Oxford: Clarendon Press, 1995), p. 18, which discusses the question of 'quality' cinema and the 'X' certificate at length, with particular regard to the British 'new wave' cinema.
2. Sylvia Rayman, *Women of Twilight* (London: Evans, 1952), p. 5. There is useful background on Rayman in Oscar Lewenstein, *Kicking Against the Pricks: A Theatre Producer Looks Back* (London: Nick Hern Books, 1994), p. 83, and astute analysis of her play in Maggie B. Gale, *West End Women* (London: Routledge, 1996), pp. 128–32.
3. Lord Chamberlain's Plays Correspondence Files, Department of Manuscripts, British Library, *Women of Twilight*, 1951/3145. Play reader's report, 2 July 1951, and other memoranda or correspondence related to same. All references hereafter come from this file.
4. See the *Observer*, 21 October 1951; *Evening Standard*, 16 October 1951; *Sunday Times*, 21 October 1951; *Daily Telegraph*, 16 October 1951; and other reviews held in the dossier for the play at the Theatre Museum, London.
5. British Board of Film Censors file, *Women of Twilight*: letters from Angel to Watkins, 26 September 1951, and Watkins to Angel, 2 October 1951; see also a memorandum from Watkins to Harris, 29 April 1952, as well as handwritten comments to same by Harris of 30 April 1952. Remaining BBFC references to *Women of Twilight* cited hereafter come from this file.
6. See *Sunday Chronicle*, 18 January 1953; *Daily Sketch*, 16 January 1953; *News of the World*, 18 January 1953; *Daily Telegraph*, 19 January 1953; *Sunday Times*, 18 January 1953; *Spectator*, 16 January 1953; *Daily Mail*, 16 January 1953; *Daily Mirror*, 16 January 1953; *The People*, 18 January 1953; *The Star*, 16 January 1953; *Evening News*, 16 January 1953; *Daily Worker*, 17 January 1953; *Monthly Film Bulletin*, no. 227, vol. 19, December 1952; and other reviews on the microfiche for the film held at the British Film Institute, London. For more recent analysis of the film see Janet Fink and Katherine

Holden, 'Pictures from the Margins of Marriage,' *Gender and History*, vol. 11, no. 2, (July 1999), pp. 233–55, and, Kerry Kidd, '*Women of Twilight*', in Ian MacKillop and Neil Sinyard (eds), *British Cinema of the 1950s: A Celebration* (Manchester and New York: Manchester University Press, 2003), pp. 127–9.

7. Lord Chamberlain's Plays Correspondence Files, *I Am a Camera*, 1952/6249. Play reader's report, 17 March 1952. All references hereafter to the Lord Chamberlain's Office come from this file.

8. See *Sunday Times*, 14 March 1954; *The Star,* 13 March 1954; *Daily Telegraph*, 13 March 1954; *Sketch*, 24 March 1954; *Manchester Guardian*, 13 March 1954; and *Observer*, 14 March 1954.

9. British Board of Film Censors file, *I Am a Camera*: letter from Cornelius to Watkins, 13 April 1954. The remaining BBFC references to *I Am a Camera* cited subsequently are taken from this same file.

10. See *Evening News*, 13 October 1955; *Daily Telegraph*, 15 October 1955; *Financial Times*, 17 October 1955; *Tribune*, 21 October 1955; *Daily Mail*, 14 October 1955; *Daily Sketch*, 13 October 1955; *Evening Standard*, 13 October 1955; *Daily Mirror*, 14 October 1955; *News Chronicle*, 14 October 1955; and all other newspaper reviews on the microfiche for *I Am a Camera* at the British Film Institute Library, London. The BFI Library also holds John Collier's final draft screenplay, with later revisions (25 October 1954: S10373), and the release script for the film (July 1955: S10334).

11. Lord Chamberlain's Plays Correspondence files, *Cabaret*, 1967/1931, play reader's report, 11 November 1967, *inter alia*. See also BBFC file, *Cabaret*: Stephen Murray to D. J. Smith, 26 April 1973, et al. There is a lot of substance and insight on the musical and film of *Cabaret* to be found in Linda Mizejewski, *Divine Decadence: Fascism, Female Spectacle and the Makings of Sally Bowle*s (Princeton, NJ and Oxford: Princeton University Press, 1992). Save for its weak grasp of the subtle censorship machinations at the Lord Chamberlain's Office and the BBFC during the 1950s, this is a wonderfully inspired and brilliant book with much to offer.

CHAPTER 5

'I'm not a juvenile delinquent'

'In the forties,' Arthur Marwick maintains, 'the grown-up generation provided the semi-outcast figure who shocked the respectable and outwitted
the sluggish government: the spiv.' 'With the early 1950s,' he continues,
'there came the first nationally recognised figure representative of youth's
detachment from the rest of society and representative also of the fact that
for the first time working-class youth could take the initiative: the Teddy
boy.' By September 1956, the initial British screenings of the American
film *Rock Around the Clock* were accompanied by violence, vandalism and
the first 'rock 'n' roll riots'. Increasing affluence, greater leisure time, the
proliferation of popular culture in the various forms of records and comics,
and 'the birth of the teenager' were inextricably bound up with 'the consequent creation of an adult-controlled "youth culture industry"', to
borrow John Davis's words, that sought 'to exploit the emergent consumer
market amongst the younger generation.' As Davis goes on astutely to
argue, however, 'the coming of rock 'n' roll to Britain was in fact anticipated as a media event well before the first screenings of *Rock Around
the Clock* and the subsequent disturbances and moral panic of [that]
September'. So too, it should be noted, was 'the moral panic' associated
with the teenager and the Teddy boy in society at large, not least in the eyes
of the censors overseeing the British theatre and cinema that sought to
survey the changing representation of youth.[1]

Cosh Boy

Roy Walsh is a little brat, utterly spoiled by his widowed mother and his
grandmother. Both women have a sentimental idea of the innocence of
youth, and are wholly unaware that Roy is the brains behind a gang of
hooligans who operate in the district. Roy is caught, but gets off and is put
on probation. The probation officer is a well-meaning but ineffectual
person who irritates Roy by his 'soft' attitude. Roy goes from strength to
strength, from bag-snatching to the seduction of the fifteen-year-old sister
of his slightly mentally disturbed henchman, Alfie. The police get seriously on his track. Meanwhile, his mother meets and falls in love with a

decent Scottish widower and, in due course, marries him. She does not tell Roy because she is afraid of what he may say. Roy enters during the wedding celebration and insults his mother – whereupon his new step-father clouts him. This does not improve relations nor does the hysterical entry of Alfie's mother with her daughter, who is pregnant. The mother is a common woman and we are certain that she will not let her daughter give birth, and so there is the making of an ugly scandal. Moreover, the police are now well on the way to arrest Roy. His stepfather dismisses the wom-enfolk, announcing that he will deal with Roy on his own. Roy, who has been listening to all this, emerges from his bedroom with a razor. The step-father disarms him and is about to give him a sound thrashing, under duress, when he stops and tells Roy that the only way he can indicate that he has a spark of decent feeling left in him is by submitting voluntarily to his punishment. Roy's response is to snatch up the razor and dive for the window, where he is caught by the waiting policemen.

The play script of Bruce Walker's *Cosh Boy* was presented for pre-production scrutiny to the Lord Chamberlain's Office on 10 March 1951, where it was immediately greeted by one reader as 'a sound tract for the times'. 'The language is pretty strong in places,' Charles Heriot felt, 'but I believe this to be a serious attempt to present a solution to the problem of the juvenile delinquent.' Although recognising that 'The moral seems to be that if boys are beaten by their parents they won't become menaces to society,' Brigadier Sir Norman Gwatkin, the Lord Chamberlain's Comptroller, certainly had reservations about the language used – not least words such as 'sod', 'bloody', 'Charlies' and 'by Christ'. But Gwatkin also complained that 'it seems a pity to make the Probation Officer out to be a fool – they have a difficult enough job anyhow,' and, in view of the play's con-tentious themes generally, he asked to see the author when Walker was next in London.

The meeting which followed two weeks later between Gwatkin, Walker and the play's director, Terence de Marney, soon ironed out all the difficulties. Once Walker had undertaken to make the necessary revisions to the offensive language, as well as to the characterisation of the proba-tion officer – 'any suggestion, as we assured you the other day, of this char-acter being at all "odd" will be completely deleted both in the script and during production' – *Cosh Boy* was licensed for stage presentation and opened at the Embassy Theatre, Swiss Cottage, on 17 April 1951. After a successful provincial tour, which incidentally revealed that 'the title is considered very horrific', the play moved into London's West End and the Comedy Theatre on 18 December 1951, under the new title of *Master Crook*.[2]

Although opening in the week before Christmas and hardly traditional festive fare, as all the critics noted, *Master Crook* was well received and garnered considerable plaudits for James Kenney's performance in the lead role of Roy Walsh. He was instantly acclaimed as 'a brilliant young actor' by W. A. Darlington of the *Daily Telegraph*, who went on to praise the play as 'a relentless study of a juvenile delinquent which is not only theatrically effective but psychologically right'. Opinions differed, predictably, as to the cause of juvenile delinquency and the author's intent in that regard. 'Society is the real villain of this piece,' argued Cecil Wilson in the *Daily Mail*. 'It indicts a world which takes war for granted and lets children loose in an age of lawless bloodshed.' 'The author is not perhaps quite certain how to account for this little brute,' *The Times* countered. 'Should he blame the state of the world or rest on the present spare the rod and spoil the child? He is theatrically shrewd and follows both courses.' There was greater unanimity, however, about the play's effectiveness. 'Those who believe that cosh-and-razor boys can be cured by some happy hours of psychotherapy will not like it,' commented the *Observer*, 'But many playgoers will.' 'I have no doubt that this play will have a salacious appeal,' the *Evening Standard* theatre critic noted before stating, ominously if presciently, 'and be made into a triumphantly sadistic and sordid film'.[3]

Just before that happened, however, the Lord Chamberlain received a worried letter from the Chief Constable of Oldham, quoting from a report made by two of his policemen after a visit to the Theatre Royal in Oldham, where they had watched a local performance of Bruce Walker's play. They expressed their fears accordingly:

I respectfully report for your information that on Monday, the 21st instant, I visited the above theatre in company with PC 82 Thompson and witnessed the first performance of the play *The Master Crook*, by Bruce Walker . . . The action of the play is presumably set in the East End of London. It is, where the situation warrants, stark and raw, the language being unrestrained, the following expressions being used: 'I'm the bloody boss around here'; 'You know my daughter too bloody well, don't you?'; 'You seduced her – you dirty little bastard'; 'I'll get that dirty little bastard if it's the last thing I do'; 'The little bastard'; 'If you think I would give a lousy bastard like you a chance . . .'; 'You dirty bitch'; 'The old bag said she would fix it that there would be no kid, didn't she?'; 'I beat the whole bloody lot of you, didn't I?'

At the end of the performance, in company with PC Thompson, I interviewed Mr L. Mather, the Licensee, and asked if he was in possession of the licensed script. Mr Mather produced a script which he termed the licensed script but which, in fact, was a script version of the play supplied by Messrs Samuel French Ltd, Publishers. Mr Mather said that the company was working to that version and, as far as they understood, it was the licensed version of the play. I told him that a report would be made to the Chief Constable for his information.

The Chief Constable's letter of 22 April 1952 asked, in short, whether the Lord Chamberlain had indeed licensed the play with the script as presented in Oldham. 'The play is a tract for the times,' was the reply forthcoming, 'and although the Lord Chamberlain felt the language was pretty strong in places, he cut only the absolutely impermissible, feeling the remainder was necessary for the authenticity of a play which has some claims to be a serious study of what is rather euphemistically called "juvenile delinquency" '. Suitably mollified, the Chief Constable of Oldham let the matter drop and, thankfully for prospective film-makers of the stage property, the way was clear for them to proceed further.[4]

In fact, a screenplay of Walker's stage play, written by Vernon Harris and film director Lewis Gilbert, was ready within a short while and presented by producer Daniel Angel for the BBFC's consideration on 21 May 1952. The script was noticeable for including several innovative features. A brand-new character was added, for one thing, in the comic figure of Queenie, a London prostitute clearly intended to be a ready source of light relief and numerous jokes, but also the subject of a vicious attack by Roy's gang of cosh boys. For another, the stepfather was changed from a Scotsman to a Canadian, and a whole new scene was added, in which Roy robs the local Palladrome at gunpoint and shoots its manager in the process. In addition to highlighting the use of coshes and razors by street gangs, in short, the film-makers now proposed to feature armed robbery as well.[5]

Inevitably, the screenplay posed problems for the BBFC. 'Although the author could justly argue that a subject like this necessarily entails brutality, raw sex, and crime,' commented one script reader, Frank Crofts, 'I think there is too much.' The cosh was singled out, in particular, as 'a weapon we have always tried to keep out of films'. But the difficulties there were likely to be compounded by the fact that 'Roy also has a razor before taking to a pistol.' The scenes in which 'The profession of the prostitute, Queenie, is dragged in' as the butt of numerous jokes were hardly to be recommended. And the climactic incident in which Roy's new stepfather threatens to thrash the boy with his belt was only marginally better: 'Although a belt is not welcome as an instrument of punishment in films, it is the usual one with this class of people and Roy is more or less grown-up.' If Crofts was prompted at the last to concede that the screenplay 'has a strong moral thread running through it,' nevertheless it was felt that the film would have to be an 'X' and that 'A good deal will depend on how this film is directed: it might be impressive but it might also do more harm than good.'

The second BBFC reader, Mary Glasgow, was less equivocal on all fronts, and found little to condone in the prospect of Bruce Walker's play being adapted for the cinema:

A film on this subject is going to give offence to three main groups: the Magistrates' Association, the Probation Officers, and Youth Clubs. The story underlines the failure of the probation system in the case of Roy Walsh and his gang, and the well-intentioned stupidity and (from the sound of it) Sunday school atmosphere of a youth club. It also clearly advocates corporal punishment and shows the police turning a blind eye to its administration, although it is no longer allowed by courts. All this seems particularly unfortunate after the humane approach of films like *I Believe In You* [1952]. I find it a nasty and altogether unhelpful script. Graham Greene can handle the subject of razor gangs and get something mystical, as well as unspeakably horrible, out of the result: but this author has nothing to say except 'beat the wretches, and enjoy yourself doing it'. The ending of *Master Crook*, with Bob Stevens 'swinging his belt', walking slowly towards Roy, followed by Roy's screams dying away with the fade-out, would be revolting and surely most unfortunate. This may be meant to be a cautionary tale, but I cannot think its effect would be anything but unhealthy.

In the final analysis, therefore, as far as Mary Glasgow was concerned, the objections to the film going ahead in the manner intended were twofold: first, 'offence will surely be given to various public bodies', and, second, there was 'the more debatable point, which I think needs careful consideration, that the film might easily do more harm than good to the young gangsters who it may be supposed to frighten'. In that regard, moreover, an 'X' certificate might serve simply to whet their appetites. 'Apart from the actual attractions they may find in the activities of Roy and his friends,' she concluded, 'an "X" certificate would only stir their curiosity.'

The long letter which Arthur Watkins sent to Daniel Angel on 6 June 1952 highlighted all these matters for urgent attention, and more besides. 'Much will depend on the handling and treatment,' he stated emphatically at the outset, before outlining the precise areas of concern. Probation officers and youth clubs, in particular, should not be presented in 'an unsatisfactory light', there should be no 'belittlement of their efforts', and care should be taken to ensure that they are not personified as 'a target for fun' or 'ineffectual characters'. 'Even for an "X" film on this subject, there is too much emphasis on the use of the cosh, both visually and in the dialogue,' Watkins continued, and 'There is similarly far too much emphasis on the use of razors.' Numerous instances and examples were singled out to be deleted on both fronts.

'The scene in which Roy seduces Rene should be handled carefully and be as brief as possible,' Watkins informed Angel. 'There should be no shot of

Figure 5 James Kenney and Joan Collins star in Lewis Gilbert's film version of *Cosh Boy* (GB, 1953). Daniel Angel–Romulus/The Kobal Collection

him ripping her blouse . . . no shot of Rene scratching Roy's face or of a slow trickle of blood down his cheek. It should be quite sufficient here for her to slap his face.' By contrast, although some of Queenie's more obvious lines were cut, a lot was allowed to pass by way of innuendo and *double entendre* about her activities. And, interestingly, the most that Watkins felt compelled to say in regard to the final 'belting' scene was that 'Roy's screams as the picture ends should not be overdone. There should only be as much as is necessary to indicate what is happening.' On the matter of the shooting incident, moreover, Watkins had nothing to say whatsoever. In this respect, clearly, he was trusting in Angel's integrity. As he put it succinctly in a parting comment: 'If the producers' concern is to present this important theme in an effective manner without sensational exploitation, there should be no difficulty from our point of view and we shall be prepared to co-operate in any way we can.'

The producers lived up to expectation, once again, although not before a team of four BBFC censors had viewed a rough cut of the film on 15 September 1952, and declared that 'the screams were overdone and unduly prolonged' in the final scene of Roy being beaten by his stepfather.

A further viewing on 23 September, this time with the president and secretary in attendance, confirmed that following new-found revisions all was now well but that the completed film, which had reverted to using the play's original if contentious title of *Cosh Boy*, should definitely be put into the 'X' category of classification.

Thereafter, the film fell foul of circumstances which could hardly have been expected or anticipated. On 2 November 1952, Police Constable Sidney Miles was shot dead by Christopher Craig during an attempted robbery at a confectionery warehouse in Croydon, Surrey. On 11 December 1952, Craig and his friend, Derek Bentley, were convicted of murder. Craig had fired the fatal shot but, at sixteen, was too young to hang. Bentley was nineteen and, despite the fact that he was under arrest at the actual time of shooting, was sentenced to death on the grounds that he had taken part in a joint enterprise. Derek Bentley was hanged at Wandsworth Prison on 28 January 1953.[6]

Cosh Boy, unsurprisingly, soon became inextricably linked with this chain of events. Even before it was given a premiere or release, the *Daily Mail* ran a story by Cecil Wilson on 18 Deceember 1952 – exactly one week after a verdict was handed down in the recent court trial – about the film's 'unexpected topicality', which recounted that the BBFC intended to stick by the award of an 'X' certificate in view of the fact that it served 'as a social document and a warning to parents of what can happen when they lose control of their children'. Cuts had been made by the BBFC 'to tone down the brutality', Wilson stated, but Daniel Angel had been reassured that 'the certificate they granted it two months ago, before the public heard of Craig, still holds good'. 'We welcome the film as a sincere attempt to awaken parents to their responsibilities,' Arthur Watkins was reported as saying. 'It paints anything but a glamorous picture of crime and the boy cannot be said to come very heroically out of it.' 'If I had made *Cosh Boy* today people would accuse me of trying to cash in on the Craig case,' Angel maintained. 'As it is I finished the film last summer, but it is quite uncanny how closely the boy resembles Craig in his whole behaviour – even in the things he says.'[7]

It is little wonder, therefore, that by the time the film was released in January 1953, newspaper columnists and reviewers alike were drawing even closer ties with the Craig and Bentley case. 'It is a dangerous film,' John Prebble argued in the *Sunday Dispatch*, while also pointing out that it was symptomatic of 'those gangster films which Christopher Craig went to see thrice weekly'. He urged that 'There's only one thing the film industry can do with *Cosh Boy*. BAN IT.' Such opinions were quickly echoed far and wide. Even when they were not, the film continued to receive scathing censure as *The Times* showed in a column headed 'Violence on the screen. Crime that Pays', which ran: 'The fact that *Cosh Boy* has an unhappily –

happily for the producers – topical interest, is beside the point; if the film is vicious it is vicious through its inherent content and not through any fortuitous circumstance.' Those critics who praised it, or had a longer memory or a sense of irony, such as the one on the *Sunday Graphic*, were few and far between: 'I don't say this is a first class film . . . But it is a gripping, up-to-the minute story – and I don't remember much of an outcry when it was played on the London stage. I suppose they assume that theatregoers are far steadier fellows than the film public.'

When, however, various local authorities started banning the film from exhibition in their vicinity soon afterwards – Birmingham, Coventry, East Suffolk, Hove, Hull, Nottingham and Surrey among them – Angel decided that matters were getting out of hand. On consulting the BBFC and 'as a result of discussions with several licensing authorities', he sought to alleviate the situation by making 'a very short cut early in the film', as well as adding 'both a foreword and an end word by way of roller title'. It condemned the cosh as 'the cowardly implement of a contemporary evil', decried juvenile delinquency as 'a post-war tragedy', yet stressed that 'This film is presented in the hope that it will contribute towards stamping out this evil,' and concluded: 'Our judges and magistrates and the police, whose stern duty it is to resolve the problem of the juvenile delinquent, are agreed that its origins lie mainly in the lack of parental control and early discipline.'

Serious Charge

The genesis of Terence Young's 1959 film, *Serious Charge*, lay in Philip King's play of the same name which was first presented for consideration to the Lord Chamberlain's Office in March 1953 with an anticipated presentation date of November that year. In time-honoured fashion, one of the Lord Chamberlain's readers, Charles Heriot, began his report of 16 March with a synopsis of the play's essential plot and story line.[8]

Howard Phillips is a thirty-year-old vicar in a village. He is unmarried, lives with his mother, has a flair for interior decoration and rather too obviously repulses the advances of a spinster, Hester Byfield, who is thereafter too liable to believe anything bad about the parson. A village girl, pregnant by the local bad lad, comes to the vicar for advice and on her way out sees his maid in the arms of her seducer. She flings herself under a car and is killed. The vicar has discovered that Larry Thompson is the man and sends for him to tell him he is morally guilty of the girl's death and to warn him to mend his ways. Larry is thoroughly rotten – the vicar has also discovered him to be a thief and has thrown him out of the choir for 'talking smut' – and, when he hears a ring at the front door, shouts for help and smashes ornaments and furniture. When the visitor enters – it is Hester – Larry accuses the vicar of trying to make a pass at him. Hester is horrified and disgusted; she is also a gossip. The mischief is done. The village hounds its vicar and matters are reaching a point at which he must leave when Larry visits Hester to brief her about what she may have to say. Unfortunately he cannot keep his fingers out of her cash box. She sees him and in the ensuing row realises that he has lied. He tries to silence her and she defends herself with a pair of scissors. She tries to summon the vicar by telephone but only manages to stammer out a broken phrase before Larry closes with her. The scissors pierce her breast and she staggers out of the room. Larry thinks he has murdered her and collapses. Then the vicar arrives and everything is duly disentangled. Hester is not dead and is able to testify against the unspeakable Larry and save the vicar's reputation.

Heriot, for his part, thought the play 'strong and sensible'. 'We are in no doubt at any time that the vicar is innocent of the "serious charge",' he commented, and 'therefore, though the forbidden topic of homosexuality shadows this play, it does so in an inoffensive manner.' 'In my opinion,' Heriot concluded, 'the play is recommended for licence.' To be sure of his ground, however, he marked the controversial passages in the play and sent it on to the Lord Chamberlain and his comptrollers for further scrutiny. By no means all the theatre examiners agreed with Heriot's judgement.

'How can you pass this if we are to be at all consistent?', asked Brigadier Sir Norman Gwatkin, the Lord Chamberlain's Assistant Comptroller. 'But I am being consistent,' Heriot responded. 'Here there is no suggestion of real homosexuality – it is all lies.' Gwatkin, adamant in his own conviction that the play transgressed the bounds of propriety, replied: 'This is where we want the Solomon touch.' And he duly passed all comments on to the Lord Chamberlain himself, Lord Scarbrough, for final consideration. Scarbrough sensibly played both ends towards the middle. 'I am not convinced by the retort that because the accusation was untrue no question of propriety can arise,' he argued, 'but neither am I convinced that the relevant part of the play should be cut or altered.' 'Though it is conceivable that some embarrassment might be caused,' Scarbrough concluded, 'I think on the whole no great harm will be done and that the play should be licensed.' 'There you are. The judgment of Solomon has been given,' Gwatkin noted tartly, 'and May God have mercy on your soul.' He, for one, remained convinced it should not be allowed.

Serious Charge was licensed for all that, however, and proceeded into production. It opened at the Adelphi Theatre on 8 November 1953, where it was presented by the Repertory Players, with Nigel Stock in the role of Howard Phillips and Alec McCowan as Larry Thompson, and produced by Joan Kemp-Welch. 'The piece was splendidly served by the company of eight,' *The Times* commented, and 'It is a pleasure to find in Mr Nigel Stock a stage clergyman who can see beyond the end of his nose.' Alec McCowan, too, was especially commended with the only slight note of reservation among the critics being that he 'seemed an urban rather than a rustic type of delinquent'. W. A. Darlington of the *Daily Telegraph*, in particular, felt the play 'tells a good story plausibly and with a sufficient degree of skill.'[9]

One member of the public who saw this production was distinctly unhappy, however, and wrote to the Lord Chamberlain expressing her distaste at the whole proceedings. Signing herself anonymously and simply as 'a mother', she produced a scathing denunciation of the decision to award the play a licence:

> The argument would appear to plead the innocence of men charged with such offences and postulates the corruption of youths making such complaints. In view of the number of grave cases of this nature which have recently engaged public attention, does the Lord Chamberlain consider this is the moment for public performance of a play on this theme? The writer respectfully suggests that plays on the subject of inversion are attended in the main by those who are themselves perverts or near perverts. The author of this play is himself a well known homosexual whose life is spent amongst men of the same type and the sincerity of the play's argument is open to the gravest suspicion. The attention of the nation has recently been drawn to this evil and the authorities are engaged on investigating the matter and I would suggest that a play of this kind is an attempt to commercialise the subject. A work which seriously examines the problem of the corruption of the very young by men of this class, if written by a serious minded man who was himself above suspicion, might conceivably have a not altogether pernicious effect (though even this is open to doubt). The theme should be left to the Royal Commission, to the psychiatrists, to the police and to social workers; while those who are themselves corrupters of youth should not be permitted to explore the subject for their own enrichment.

The Lord Chamberlain, perhaps sensibly in this instance, declined to reply. The Adelphi booking was a trial run, in effect, but in view of the favourable critical and popular response the play received, generally, *Serious Charge* was later given a full-scale professional production at the Garrick Theatre from 17 February 1955, where it was directed by Martin Landau and starred Patrick McGoohan.

Even as the play was enjoying the first fruits of its 1955 London run, a film producer expressed interest in transposing it from stage to screen. The West End theatre was a rich and regular source of supply for British films throughout the 1950s, as ever with British cinema, and none was quicker off the mark than the eagle-eyed John Woolf, who proved keenest to adapt

Philip King's *Serious Charge* for the screen and Romulus Films. Within a month of the play's opening, Woolf sent a copy of the script to the BBFC secretary, Arthur Watkins, with a view to ascertaining whether it would pass pre-production scrutiny or stand much chance of progressing easily into production into a film. 'It would be our intention to use the services of a distinguished director,' he assured Watkins on 17 March 1955, 'and not in any way to sensationalize it.' 'I naturally realize it would fall into the "X" category,' Woolf maintained, 'but think it such a powerful play that it would be worth taking the risk.'[10]

The BBFC moved into action immediately. Two examiners, Frank Crofts and Audrey Field, were dispatched by Arthur Watkins to watch the Garrick Theatre production. They were not pleased with what they saw of *Serious Charge* on stage – nor, especially, the likelihood of a film arising from it. They had 'strong misgivings' about the whole project and 'were agreed in thinking the central incident (which is essential to the story) intolerable for "A" and very undesirable for "X"'. 'It will make it very nearly impossible to reject other films of a melodramatic kind which flirt with the topic of homosexuality,' they stated, 'and we think this unsavoury flirting is just as bad as depicting a real homosexual on the screen.' Though the examiners recognised the play had already been licensed for the stage, in short, they drew a significant line of divide between what might be tolerated for a small band of theatregoers and what should be allowed for the mass of cinemagoers. 'We think that the imitative aspect should not be lost sight of,' they added, and 'We do not believe the Lord Chamberlain himself would think the story fit for the mixed and immature provincial cinema audience which would see even an "X" film' was their considered, if jaundiced and distinctly elitist, reaction. It was a revealing remark.

Not that all the BBFC scrutineers were of the same opinion. Another examiner, Newton Branch, went along to see the play as well and produced an extensive report of his own on 29 March 1955. He offered something of a dissenting judgement in that he considered *Serious Charge* to be 'a well constructed play' and thought it had much more to offer besides by way of a potentially salutary film vehicle. 'Directed by an Anthony Asquith, the play should make a very powerful film, and one which would very properly have an "X" certificate,' he stated, and 'My conclusions are based on the supposition that any film of *Serious Charge* would be made with artistry and great integrity.' He continued:

In my opinion, we should ignore the harm which this film *might* cause to or for a vicious minority of adolescents. It seems to me that the people to be educated (and so protected) in this case are adults – especially those particularly vulnerable to blackmail: clergymen and teachers. Moreover, the film would come as a sharp warning to the small minority of those professions who *have* homosexual tendencies and whose tragic follies make headlines in the *News of the World* and limericks about vicars and choirboys. And I think that the great majority of young people over 16 would be profoundly impressed by the rights and the wrongs of this affair. They know that they will soon be adults with all sorts of fearsome responsibilities and challenges. And they are in the best position to deal with the young villain of *Serious Charge* – if they choose to do so.

Unsurprisingly, Arthur Watkins at the BBFC proceeded to tell producer John Woolf that 'under no circumstances could any film based on this play be placed in any other than the "X" category' and that 'we are not prepared to commit ourselves even to an "X" category without further consideration [of a screenplay].' Given, however, that *Serious Charge* had plainly caused much controversy within his examiners' ranks, no less a person than the president of the British Board of Film Censors, Sir Sidney Harris, went along to see the play for himself. His judgements on reading the play script alone then watching the stage production make an illuminating contrast. On 21 March 1955, for example, he stated:

> I am rather surprised that this squalid melodrama was thought worthy of presentation on the stage, and it might be worth while to find out from the Lord Chamberlain whether he received any complaints. It would make a very unpleasant film and one liable to sensational exploitation. For the reasons given by the examiners I think we should have nothing to do with it. The 'X' certificate would only exclude persons under sixteen and the greatest risk of damage would be to persons of sixteen and seventeen who form a large part of the average cinema audience. Incidentally, I dislike the picture of the country vicarage with the worldly mother and the ineffective vicar whose method of dealing with Larry is so unwise. We see many films in which Roman Catholic priests appear as dignified and spiritually-minded persons. Why should the British film depict Anglican clergymen either as figures of fun or of incompetence? This is not entirely irrelevant to censorship.

But on 24 March 1955, by comparison, after viewing the stage presentation of *Serious Charge*, Harris felt compelled to revise his initially hostile opinion:

> I saw this play yesterday and I must allow that I was pleasantly surprised. I found little to complain about. It is admittedly a rather squalid story, but this aspect of it is largely forgotten in the tautness of the play and the good acting. It remains, in my view, melodrama rather than a serious social problem play, though towards the end it does become rather more serious. It might have been a better play if the author had not overdrawn (in particular) the character of Hester Byfield. The whole moral of the play is good and if we are to have a film on such a subject, we might do very much worse. The main trouble is that once we allow this topic we may find it rather

a slippery slope, but I do not see how we can possibly refuse this story for the 'X' category.

Having been prompted by Harris to find out what the Lord Chamberlain's Office had thought of the stage play, moreover, Watkins reported back the fruits of a discussion he had held with Sir Norman Gwatkin on 28 March 1955:

> He told me that they had received one or two individual letters of complaint about the play since its opening at the Garrick Theatre. They were on the lines of the individual playgoer having been 'embarrassed' at the introduction of the subject of homosexuality into the theatre. Sir Norman added that, in his own personal view, his department had made a mistake in licensing the play and he was opposed to the decision. He remained of the view that it would be better to keep this subject out of plays altogether. He confirmed that the decision to pass the play was based on the fact that no character in the play was actually a pervert and no more than an unfounded charge was involved. At the end of our talk, he confirmed that although some letters had been received, there had been no serious volume of complaints.

None of this was communicated to John Woolf, needless to say, who returned on 28 March 1955 to tell Watkins that he was now set upon purchasing the rights of the play and would submit a film script in due course while reiterating, for good measure, that 'it is not our intention in any way to sensationalise the subject any more than it is in the play'. The screenplay that was tendered finally for BBFC consideration almost four months later, on 23 August 1955, did as much as the producer promised and more besides. It had dispensed entirely with the original 'serious charge' at the heart of Philip King's controversial play and even Woolf was inclined to describe it in correspondence with Watkins as an 'emasculated' version 'which I am sure will please you'. Plainly, despite Woolf's protestations throughout that he would be only too happy to see the film in the 'X' category, given its adult themes and nature, at the last he was making a desperate attempt with the changes to see whether it might not yet be allowed for an 'A' certificate rating.

'The curse has been removed', commented the first BBFC reader of the screenplay, Audrey Field: 'It is now a girl (Dora), not a boy, who accuses the vicar of trying to interfere with her.' 'I really think the story has lost nothing of value in losing the homosexual element,' she continued, 'The "emasculated version" does in fact "please me" (see Mr Woolf's covering letter) and I really don't care how silly he thinks us to want the change as long as he sticks to the present version and makes the change.' Not that everything was acceptable in the new script as it stood. Profound misgivings were expressed about the fact that the girl was just seventeen years of

age and only two years out of school. And fears were evident about the proposed ending to the film, which all readers felt should be changed yet
again: 'We are told that Dora is to "get her deserts", so presumably the
lorry driver episode will go (our point would not be satisfactorily met by
Dora being raped and killed, in case that should be what they have in
mind).' 'But we are so well out of the homosexual element,' it was noted,
'that it would be a mistake to be too captious.'

'This is certainly an improvement from our point of view,' Watkins
concurred in his summary report to the BBFC president, though noting
that 'The present ending, of course, will not do at all.' 'It is, in any event,
a very bad ending,' he added, 'and I think that, from the artistic point of
view, the last ten pages of the script are weak and should be strengthened
so as to leave in no doubt the rehabiliation of the vicar in the minds of his
parishioners.' Sir Sidney Harris, for his part, certainly felt that something had been lost in the adaptation and was equally as intent upon
further fostering the projected image of the vicar as a salutary and
commendable figure in the eyes of the community, as he pointed out on
7 September 1955:

> I agree generally but we seem to have got rid of our main preoccupation by exchan-
> ging it for a grubby story which can only be saved by good acting. In particular, it
> would be wise to stress the importance of presenting the vicar as a fine character
> facing a squalid situation in a dignified and manly way. I agree as to the complete revi-
> sions of the last ten pages. If we are to contemplate an 'A' certificate we should meet
> *all* the points made by the two examiners and yourself.

In the event, as it turned out, no more work was needed for John Woolf's
purposes since he proceeded, thereafter, to withdraw from the project. The
reasons why he did so are difficult to fathom with any degree of certainty.
Perhaps he tired of the BBFC's continuing vacillations; perhaps he felt the
'emasculated' version had gone too far down the path, anyway, of selling
out on an otherwise laudable idea for a screenplay; or, maybe, he encountered problems in negotiating the rights on King's play. It was, to be sure,
an unusual occurrence for an eminent film producer like John Woolf to
drop out of the running.

Whatever the deciding factor as far as Woolf was concerned, the film
censors had not heard the last of *Serious Charge*. It resurfaced again
exactly three years later in the hands of Mickey Delamar of Alva Films.
Much had changed during the intervening period in the fabric of British
society, of course, not least with regard to its burgeoning youth culture.
Delamar consciously sought to appeal to that quarter, moreover, and,
much to the film censors' consternation, he reverted to Philip King's story

line for the inspiration of the screenplay he tendered to the BBFC early in September 1958. 'The story point is the same as in the original play,' Audrey Field commented on 8 September 1958, 'i.e. it depends on a charge of indecent assault by the vicar upon a youth.' But other matters were noted besides:

> The only important divergence from the stage play is that in the film script the vicar's mother persuaded the frustrated Hester to trap Larry into damaging admissions by vamping him and then staging a struggle which is interrupted by the vicar, Larry's father and other witnesses arriving just as Larry is protesting that the scene is parallel to the trumped up business at the vicarage. The picture of small-town life is filled out by rather unedifying sidelights on the life and loves of Larry and other potential Teddy-boys and girls; and the script has been, on the whole, somewhat vulgarised; but the vulgarisation of motion pictures intended for older teenagers has proceeded so fast in the past three years that it does not seem anything out of the way now.

John Trevelyan, who had taken on the position of BBFC secretary in July 1958, did not like the script at all and made that very clear. 'I do not consider the play as a serious exploration of a serious problem,' he stated. 'It is pure melodrama and should be treated as such. I think a good many adolescents will snigger at it, and it may, I suppose, give some of them an idea of how easy it is for them to do a bit of easy blackmail.' But he felt wedded in principle, at least, to extend to Delamar the same commitment to consider the project for the 'X' certificate that had been forthcoming to Woolf previously.

Ironically, any homosexual connotations to the assault were now deemed less troublesome in prospect, always provided the film-makers for their part were willing to contemplate an 'X' as well. 'We have not yet accepted the theme of homosexuality for anything other than the "X" category,' Trevelyan told Delamar on 15 September 1958, 'and I see no likelihood of our changing our policy.' But fears were expressed about the youth culture likely to be depicted in the film: 'I would suggest the Teddy Boy hooliganism, erotic dancing and necking in the empty house should be treated with care and not in such a way as to encourage adolescent imitation.' And Trevelyan's parting words were reserved for repeated admonition that 'from the angle of censorship it would be helpful if the vicar were shown as a thoroughly admirable person, effective at his job but landed through no fault of his own in a position of great difficulty'. Whereupon, in conclusion, he added 'one small point which is not a matter of censorship. On various occasions, the parsons are referred to as "the Reverend Phillips" and "the Reverend Peters". I think the term "Mr" would probably be used. Certainly no parson would address a colleague as "Reverend" as Howard

Figure 6 Cliff Richard made his screen debut in Terence Young's film of Philip King's play *Serious Charge* (GB, 1959). Alva/The Kobal Collection

does on p. 65'. Ever helpful to the last, in his way, Trevelyan left matters in Delamar's hands.

The problem for Delamar was that from the outset he was set upon securing an 'A' rating for his film and an 'X' would not do. Given, especially, that his intention was to cast the young British pop star, Cliff Richard, in the newly written part of Larry Thompson's brother, Curley, Delamar felt certain an 'X' certificate could only serve to deny him the guarantee of the idol's many teenage fans among audiences for the film. At the face-to-face meeting with Trevelyan which followed on 22 September 1958, producer Mickey Delamar and director Terence Young clearly did as much as they could to convince the BBFC of their willingness to compromise where necessary in order to achieve the desired result. As Trevelyan reported:

> We discussed the present script in some detail and I was told that this was only a pre-liminary script which Mr Young intends to revise personally. He has in mind mod-elling the parson on the David Sheppard type and wants either Anthony Quayle or Peter Finch for the part. He is quite prepared to tone down the Teddy-boy hooli-ganism and erotic behaviour with girls, and he wants also to alter the part of Hester considerably since he feels that at present it is overdrawn. Furthermore he proposes to have a completely different ending in which the parson realises that he must stay in the place because he is able to intervene successfully when one of the boys from his club is threatened with Borstal; indeed he wants to use this film to show what a live and forceful young parson can do with a boys' club.
>
> Both Mr Young and Mr Delamar realise that the nature of the 'serious charge' is a major difficulty, but they will consider whether it would not be possible to make the nature of the charge intelligible to the thinking adult and unintelligible to the child who knows nothing of such things. For instance, there might be the implication that the parson has physically attacked the boy rather than assaulted him sexually. All unnecessary emphasis on the nature of the charge . . . will be removed and the whole thing will be treated carefully and discreetly. I said that, in view of their proposed alterations, the only thing that really stood in the way of an 'A' certificate was the nature of the charge and that if this could be treated in a way that made it acceptable for the 'A' category so much the better, but I could not give any guarantee about it at this stage.

In the ensuing correspondence with Trevelyan, Delamar repeated that he was determined upon making 'an intelligent adult film of quality' and that he was 'hoping to get your "blessing" for the "A" (as against the "horror and sex" we want to steer clear of)'. Yet in the final analysis, neither party was able fully to deliver on its promises, as became instantly apparent when a rough-cut version was delivered to the BBFC for viewing, on completion of production, in January 1959. Delamar had secured the services of both Cliff Richard and Anthony Quayle, and

Andrew Ray for the part of Larry, as well as Sarah Churchill for Hester. But he had failed to resolve the screen depiction of the 'serious charge' to satisfaction and, moreover, his finished film now posed profound new problems for the censors besides.

Both the BBFC president and secretary, along with two more examiners, Frank Crofts and Audrey Field, watched the rough cut of *Serious Charge* on 13 January 1959. They were convinced the film could only be considered for the 'X' category, after all, and even then cuts should have to be made. Lines of dialogue like 'A bunch of creeps and fairies' and 'Who are you calling fairies?' would have to be excised for a start. The scene in which Larry tried to rape Hester when she was seeking to frame him would require to be shortened 'and the cut to Larry's father should therefore come earlier than at present'. So, too, would an opening scene where Larry and the village girl he seduced were shown dressing after making love: 'We are inclined to think that this scene is in fact unnecessary since their relationship is well enough established later, and that it starts the film off on the wrong note.' 'However, this is a matter of artistic consideration rather than of censorship,' Trevelyan recounted to Delamar on 15 January, 'although the visuals do present something of a censorship problem.' Other factors also loomed large:

> The scene in which the vicar confronts Larry and his gang in the Youth Club and is threatened by a flick-knife and bicycle-chain should be reduced with a view to removing as much as possible of the shots of these weapons. We appreciate that the scene provides a salutary lesson to the young hooligan, but, as I explained to you, we want to keep flick-knives and bicycle-chains (and all such weapons) out of films as far as possible since we do not wish to encourage any extended use of things of this kind. We are even more concerned about the bicycle-chain than about the flick-knife and I hope that you will be able to get rid of it either completely or almost completely.

In particular, Trevelyan stated, the censors were now distinctly worried about the introduction into the proceedings of a nude-bathing scene in which teenage girls, especially, were seen 'naked to the waist'. These, certainly, had to be removed. 'Since we have seen the film only in a rough cut version,' he said finally, 'it will be desirable that we should see the whole film again when it is completed. I do not anticipate that we shall ask for any further cuts but we must reserve to right to do so if we feel it essential.'

Some things were easily dealt with at Alva Films. The word 'fairy' was replaced by 'cissy' (sissy) on the two occasions in question, though Delamar regretted this could only be achieved at the expense of lip-synchronisation – 'I am afraid it is noticeable but that's our bad luck.' He also managed to shorten or eliminate the 'bicycle chain' shots. Three cuts were made to the nude-bathing sequence and he promised to further darken the grading of the final release print being processed in the laboratories in order to lessen its impact: 'I would point out that having run the film privately at the studios to several people who were viewing it for the first time, no one has, as yet, noticed anything unusual – and in point of fact, I often miss seeing anything myself when I run the film. In any case, at a grading session last Saturday morning the cameraman and I decided to bring the whole sequence down by one more point darker to give it more the required mysterious atmosphere I want.' Most of all, however, Delamar was distraught that his film might still end up with an 'X' rating, as he told Trevelyan on 9 March 1959:

> Finally, I would like to mention that so far people in the Trade who have viewed the picture privately have been kind enough to congratulate me on making a sincere and intelligent film of quality – and were most amazed when I told them you could only give it an 'X' certificate. In this day and age when we have to compete in Foreign markets to survive, and in view of the fact that *Serious Charge* is a meticulously 'clean' film with a moral lesson, it should most certainly not be classed with Sex and Horror pictures but receive an 'A' certificate – so I sincerely hope that you can reconsider your last decision in this respect, and in view of your kind help and encouragement to date I am sure that your sense of fair play will help me in this matter, particularly in view of the fact that otherwise respectable families and teenagers under sixteen will not be able to see a film meant for them.

Ironically, it was a judicious leak to the press about the censorship done to the nude-bathing sequence that captured some attention when the film was given its premiere on 14 May 1959, before being put on general release in ABC cinemas from 29 June 1959 – not least when it was revealed that the version made for overseas distribution had, in fact, retained the original and offending scenes intact. One particular report of the matter, in the *Birmingham Evening Dispatch*, so irritated Trevelyan at the BBFC that he felt prompted to write to Delamar, pointing out that 'As you know, we have a gentleman's agreement with the industry that details of negotiations between companies and ourselves are regarded as confidential by both parties.' 'Of course the press do get hold of things sometimes,' he added curtly, 'but I would be grateful if in future you would take some opportunity of reminding your staff of our agreement.' 'I can only assure you that no-one connected with my company, either directly or indirectly, has discussed or made statements to the Press in connection with any censorship negotiations that have taken place between you and me,' Delamar pleaded in response. Thereafter, in mitigation, he claimed that at the premiere gala party, 'where somebody mentioned that sequence as being in the French version,' he recalled 'Ann Todd said something like "it would always be worthwhile making the trip to Paris to see it"'.

That seemed to do the trick as far as Trevelyan was concerned. But in Delamar's eyes the major damage had been done at the point when the BBFC determined upon an 'X' certificate for his film. Moreover, press reviews appeared to bear out his ongoing concern when several critics noted that many of Cliff Richard's teenage fans were being denied the opportunity of watching their pop idol at the cinema in addition to listening to his various hit records. 'TV singer Cliff Richard makes his screen debut,' commented the *Sunday Dispatch*. 'His appearance will please those of his fans old enough to see the film.' In the words of Paul Dehn of the *News Chronicle*, there again, 'Cliff Richard has the voice of a young Presley and the soul of a young Wesley.' Most of the praise was reserved, however, for Anthony Quayle's performance as 'a muscular Christian', as *The Times* critic and William Whitebait of the *New Statesman* put it. If Andrew Ray also won considerable plaudits for his role as the young thug – 'horribly well played', in the eyes of the *Sunday Express* – Sarah Churchill's role as Hester was less well received with mixed reviews emanating from various quarters. 'The translation to the screen is creditable,' claimed Dilys Powell in the *Sunday Times* of the film overall, 'though I wish the cinema would give up equating rock "n" roll with juvenile delinquency.' And while many reviewers thought it 'an earnest and stagey film,' to borrow Peter Burning's words in the *News of the World*, most were in agreement with Derek Monsey in thinking that '*Serious Charge* makes a bid for intelligent contemporary film-making.'[11]

But Mickey Delamar, for his part, was intent still upon reversing the BBFC's decision to give his film an 'X' certificate and he returned to the fray in an attempt to overturn it on several occasions thereafter – not least when the prospect of a potentially lucrative reissue appeared on the horizon. His next try was forthcoming in December 1959 when he was firmly told that 'In the circumstances the film must remain in the 'X' category.' In his reply to Trevelyan of 7 January 1960, Delamar claimed he would doubtless return seeking an 'A' certificate given that 'at some time in the near future this may become a question which, quite bluntly, may affect my financial survival'. Thus, on 19 July 1961, he stated yet again:

> I know I don't have to remind you that as the film stands at present there is nothing in it that could be offensive or in bad taste, and when originally shown to officials of the Church and Youth Movements we were congratulated on the moral lessons it depicted. We have always felt the original certificate you granted us was a little unfair and more due to existing circumstances at the time rather than to the actual contents

of the film, and therefore think you might now see your way to treating us a little more leniently at this now later date.

Once more, the BBFC examiners dutifully trooped in to watch the film, and reread the final release script, as well. But to no avail. Frank Crofts, in particular, had little time for the argument in favour of letting more cinemagoers catch a sight of Cliff on the big screen, claiming wryly that the 'many teenagers who want to *hear* Cliff Richards [sic] sing will be able to do so whatever the category'. Thus, Trevelyan responded on 24 July 1961:

> We considered whether it would be possible so to cut the film as to make it appear that the charge was one of physical assault rather than of what is technically called 'indecent assault', but we find that there are a good many reactions from other people when the news gets out which would become nonsense if the nature of the charged was changed. Apart from this, Larry Thompson is not an 'A' category character. There is a certain degree of juvenile anti-social behaviour, there is the seduction of the French maid, and finally his attempt to make a sexual assault on Hester. There is in fact too much 'X' category material to get rid of without completely spoiling the story.

Finally, by 22 March 1962, Delamar settled upon an altogether different change of tack and a complete reverse of what he had argued previously. Seeking consciously to capitalise on what he saw as the principal setback, he now asked for complete restoration of the nude scenes in view of the fact his film was being considered for reissue and because it had, afer all, already been given an 'X' certificate:

> When first submitted, the film contained a 'night swimming pool' sequence with some nudity, which was, at your request, replaced by alternate footage. Briefly, I want the reissue version of this film to contain the original 'swimming pool' footage. I must emphasise that this sequence is photographed most tastefully and with complete discretion. It is neither salacious, nor dirty, and has not been included for any sensational value. It is entirely natural that this group of teenagers, deciding on an impromptu midnight bathe, should behave in this way and the sequence, which only runs for some 2 to 3 minutes, could not possibly give offence to anyone. I am aware that the Board's attitude to screen nudity has changed considerably since this film was first passed and, under today's standards, scenes such as this are, of course, commonplace in the many full length nudist features presently under distribution. In addition to this, it should be remembered that *Serious Charge* already carries an 'X' certificate (as opposed to the 'A' and 'U' on many nudist offerings) and we have no intention of seeking a change of category for this film.

Trevelyan was not to be persuaded by even this latest clever move, however, and it made scant difference to the BBFC's opinion. 'I can tell you quite definitely that we would not accept the original "swimming pool" footage under an "X" certificate today,' was his reply of 26 March 1962. 'Such changes as we have made in our policy on nudity do not relate to a scene of this kind in a feature film.' For all the conscious attempts at compromise on the part of the film-makers, *Serious Charge* was arguably an unfortunate victim during a period of cautious transition in British film censorship between the 'doldrums era' of the 1950s and the height of the 'swinging sixties'.

Notes

1. See Arthur Marwick, *British Society Since 1945* (Harmondsworth: Penguin, 1990), pp. 71–2, and John Davis, *Youth and the Condition of Britain* (London: The Athlone Press, 1990), pp. 160–1. For a fascinating survey of 'the spiv' during the 1940s see, also, Donald Thomas, *An Underworld at War* (London: John Murray, 2003).
2. LCP Correspondence, *Cosh Boy*, 1951/2740. Play reader's report, 15 March 1951, and all further correspondence related to same.
3. See *Daily Telegraph*, 19 December 1951; *Daily Mail*, 19 December 1951; *The Times*, 19 December 1951; *Observer*, 23 December 1951; and *Evening Standard*, 21 December 1951.
4. The Chief Constable of Oldham became something of a regular correspondent with the Lord Chamberlain, it appears, on matters of theatre censorship in his borough. For which, see the further examples of his attempted interventions cited by Kathryn Johnson in her excellent essay, 'Apart from *Look Back in Anger*, what else was worrying the Lord Chamberlain's Office in 1956?', in Dominic Shellard (ed.), *British Theatre in the 1950s* (Sheffield: Sheffield Academic Press, 2000), pp. 116–35.
5. The BFI Library holds a post-shooting dialogue script for the film (S9703). But the censors' comments and correspondence that follow come from the BBFC file on *Cosh Boy*, 25 May 1952 to 1 May 1953.
6. Derek Bentley's hanging had a profound impact upon British public opinion, with tens of thousands of people petitioning the Home Secretary for a reprieve, albeit to no avail. The conviction was finally quashed over forty-five years later, at a Court of Appeal held on 30 July 1998.
7. 'He filmed the Craig story before it happened', *Daily Mail*, 18 December 1952. The critics' reviews which follow are drawn from: *Sunday Despatch*, 11 January 1953; *The Times*, 9 February 1953; *Sunday Graphic*, 9 February 1952.
8. LCP Correspondence, *Serious Charge*, 1951/5355. Play reader's report, 16 March 1953, and other memoranda related to same.
9 See *The Times*, 9 November 1953; *Daily Telegraph*, 9 November 1953; and all newspaper reviews in the dossier for the play at the Theatre Museum, London. For more recent analysis of the play see John Johnston, *The Lord Chamberlain's Blue Pencil* (London: Hodder and Stoughton, 1990), p. 176;

Nicholas de Jongh, *Not in Front of the Audience* (London: Routledge, 1992), pp. 64–4; Alan Sinfield, *Out on Stage* (New Haven, CT and London: Yale University Press, 1999), pp. 241–2; and Dan Rebellato, *1956 And All That* (London: Routledge, 1999), pp. 170–2.

10. BBFC file, *Serious Charge*: letter from Woolf to Watkins, 17 March 1955. Remaining BBFC references thereafter come from this file. The BFI Library, London, also holds Guy Elmes's screenplay for the 1959 production (12 October 1958: S10429) and a breakdown for the film comprising set lists, dope sheets, location and studio shots, with inserts (S10428), as well as a microfiche of all newspaper reviews.

11. See the *Sunday Dispatch*, 17 May 1959; *News Chronicle*, 15 May 1959; *The Times*, 15 May 1959; *New Statesman*, 23 May 1959; *Sunday Express*, 17 May 1959; *Sunday Times*, 17 May 1959; *News of the World*, 17 May 1959; *Daily Telegraph*, 16 May 1959; *Daily Worker*, 16 May 1959; *Financial Times*, 20 May 1959; and *Observer*, 17 May 1959.

CHAPTER 6

Homosexuality and Lesbianism

In 1909 the Joint Parliamentary Select Committee recommended that the Lord Chamberlain should ban any play that encouraged vice, but the committee did not define vice, so that the Lord Chamberlain received absolute discretion in this area. Homosexuality remained a criminal offence until 1967, whereas lesbianism was legal, but the upper-class social conventions of late Victorian and Edwardian Britain considered both to be beyond the pale. In this vein successive Lord Chamberlains adopted an inflexible stance against single-sex liaisons until by degrees after the Second World War this particular taboo was lifted. BBFC policy followed much the same course.

Now Barabbas . . .

While serving in the Royal Armoured Corps during the 1944 allied land offensive against Germany, Captain William Douglas-Home refused to comply with an order on humanitarian grounds. He was court-martialled in October 1944 and sentenced to a short term of civil imprisonment, which he served in Wormwood Scrubs and Wakefield. He was a minor 1930s dramatist and also the son of a peer, and a week after his release in 1946 he started work on his play *Now Barabbas . . .*, a serious if over-dramatic study, possibly the first of its kind seen in the British theatre, of routine prison life, based upon his own experiences during his sentence. Perhaps conscious that the very theme might encounter the Lord Chamberlain's displeasure, Douglas-Home sets his play in a model prison, gives the convicts sympathetic characters and presents the prison staff, with one exception, as average human beings with strengths and weaknesses. The characters of the prison governor and the chaplain are written in much the same vein. The plot, such as it is, represents a combination of comedy and tragedy, and the various scenes occur in the men's dining room, the governor's office and the condemned cell, where a convict named Tufnell, an ex-paratrooper, is awaiting a possible reprieve from his death sentence for murdering a policeman. This is eventually refused, the execution taking place off-stage.

Now Barabbas . . . was first performed at a private club, The Boltons in Kensington, in February 1947, when the quality press reviewed it favourably.[1] Within days Douglas-Home forwarded the script to the LCO, where the chief concerns were hints of homosexuality and the implicit attack upon capital punishment through Tufnell's breakdown when he receives the news that he will not be reprieved. Of the latter, Reader of Plays Geoffrey Dearmer observed, 'People who go to see this play . . . expect this sort of thing and will no doubt share the author's anti-capital punishment opinions.'[2] His seniors agreed, but the question of homosexuality aroused a more detailed discussion. Dearmer continued,

> The only questionable side of the play is that of Richards. He is a not unpleasant 100% pansy. The only suggestion of perversion, and the subject is treated with complete reserve and delicacy, indeed barely hinted at, exists in Metcalfe's mind. Metcalfe is a gentle, educated prisoner with a *possible* tendency towards abnormality himself. He complains to the Governor that Richards's influence in the prison is unhealthy and he is sent to another prison. One gathers that Metcalfe is 'inside' for a similar offence himself. There is no suggestion that any improper behaviour has been practised at any time and the subject is so remote and briefly treated that I do not think any offence could reasonably be sustained. It could not be removed from the play without doing it irreparable damage, and no doubt this is a problem in prison life.

Dearmer went on to recommend dialogue cuts to the death-cell scene where Tufnell breaks down and abuses the chaplain upon learning that he will be hanged, and to prisoners' references to the warders as 'screws'. However, Henry Game, his immediate superior, commented,

> I have no doubt that homosexuality is a problem in prison, as it is outside – and more so. Yet if we allow it in this way, however 'remotely and briefly treated', I cannot see that we have any justification for disavowing the subject in the serious plays – and more particularly in those which deal primarily with this complex . . .

Clarendon, the Lord Chamberlain, resolved this disagreement in Dearmer's favour because of 'the fuss that might arise if all hints of homosexuality were deleted'.

The play was presented at the Vaudeville Theatre in the West End during early March 1947 and ran for almost four months with a cast that was largely unknown except for Tristan Rawson as the governor and Percy Walsh as the death-cell warder. The reviews were reasonably favourable, although that in the *Evening Standard* of 21 March complained about the background homosexuality running through the play. However, well over a year elapsed before it was converted into a film by producer/scenarist Anatole de Grunwald for Warner Bros. This time lag might have been due to the interim success of supposedly 'realistic' British films during the latter half of 1947 and throughout 1948, for *Now Barabbas* . . . was filmed in early 1949 at Teddington studios, then recently rebuilt after their destruction by a German rocket in 1945.

This time the cast was very well known – Richard Greene as Tufnell, Sir Cedric Hardwicke as the governor, Stephen Murray as the chaplain, and Richard Burton, Glyn Lawson, William Hartnell and Ronald Howard as other convicts. In addition there were small roles for Alec Clunes, Harry Fowler, Kenneth More, Dora Bryan, Kathleen Harrison and Dandy Nichols, while only Percy Walsh survived from the theatre cast. The script underwent extensive changes, most notably in the expanded characterisation of the female characters to accommodate the new flashback sequences. Before 1939 the BBFC had frowned upon serious depictions of British prison life, and *Now Barabbas* . . . was possibly the first time the Board was confronted with a serious treatment of the theme. An outright ban was impolitic owing to the fact of a West End production, but the BBFC cut the film before it opened at the end of May 1949. Without the relevant documentation, it is no longer possible to know what and how wide the cuts were, but the mostly favourable reviews suggest that the anti-capital punishment material was not only retained but was easily identifiable as such. This in itself was surprising in that the BBFC disliked films as social propaganda, and capital punishment fitted into that category since the Commons had voted for abolition on 14 April 1948 and the later Lords overthrow of that decision. However, not one single review as much as mentioned hints of homosexuality in the film, which tentatively indicates that this was the content the BBFC objected to, for BBFC policy towards the depiction of homosexuality followed that of the Lord Chamberlain.

Tea and Sympathy

This Robert Anderson American play is concerned with an eighteen-year-old at an American college who is accused by his fellow male students of being homosexual. His housemaster's wife feels sorry for him and by so doing alienates her husband, who himself harbours subconscious homosexual desires. To demonstrate his manhood, the young student tries to sleep with the local prostitute but finds himself unable to perform. When the college authorities find out about this escapade, he finds himself faced with expulsion, but before he leaves, the housemaster's wife, by now estranged from her husband, gives herself physically to him in order that he can express his heterosexuality.

During 1953 the play, directed by Elia Kazan with John Kerr as the young man, Deborah Kerr as the housemaster's wife and Leif Erickson as her husband, opened on Broadway, where it was such a runaway success that it soon attracted the attention of British theatre managements. As early as November 1953 the Globe Theatre unofficially submitted a script to the LCO, where both Sir Terence Nugent, Comptroller, and Sir Norman Gwatkin, Assistant Comptroller, read it and concluded that its official submission would be futile.[3] John Woolf of Romulus Films was also interested, and in April 1954 he invited Arthur Watkins to see the play in New York and asked him to read the script with a view to a film with the 'X' certificate. Watkins declined the New York invitation but read the script, which emphasised the supposed homosexual element more strongly than the play. Watkins then assigned this script to BBFC examiner Audrey Field, who reported,

Sincere, moving and entirely credible. It could happen just like this in the United States . . . It could not happen just like this in England . . . but, in essence, it could happen. Nevertheless, I hope that our present standards in regard to the discussion of homosexuality in the cinemas of this country will not be relaxed. It is a subject which ought now to be debated and further ventilated, but *not* in the cinema. The atmosphere is all wrong: who can doubt that a theatre provides the safer and cooler climate for the analysis of this sort of inflammable stuff? The audience, also, is largely wrong, except in a few 'specialised houses' in the West End of London. Millions of boys and girls of the 'working' classes, educated side by side, married in their late teens and early twenties, do not need to consider this problem at all, and if they need not it is a pity to thrust it upon them in the guise of entertainment. In fact, even if they see the film, they will not consider it at all seriously: imagine the guffaws of the local yokels when Laura [the wife] 'saves' Tom [the young man] . . . there is no need to make out to the rest of the world, and particularly to what is left of the Empire, that 'le vice anglais' is our sole preoccupation.[4]

The last sentence reflected her fear that if *Tea and Sympathy* was ever made, British film-makers would follow its theatre example. Watkins agreed and doubted whether the Lord Chamberlain would allow the play, seemingly unaware that its submission had been discouraged at the LCO five months ago, while Sir Sidney Harris, BBFC president from 1947 to 1960, stated tersely, 'We clearly could not pass a film based on this play.' Later in May 1954 Watkins informed both Woolf and a representative of Woolf's American associate, David O. Selznick, that the BBFC would reject the projected film.

By then the LCO had received an official submission from Donald Albery without any date or theatre in prospect. Reader of Plays Charles Heriot remarked that the theme was uppermost in the minds of most

American intellectuals. He supposed that an adolescent sexual atmosphere was common at all boarding schools, but 'the American kind, with its unusually adult swearwords and its furtive slavering after desire is too different from the English brand to be acceptable, even if there were no homosexual element'. Accordingly the play was banned, and several months later, following press reports in Britain that Metro-Goldwyn-Mayer (MGM) was contemplating a film, Watkins took the precaution of notifying MGM formally of the BBFC's likely policy. Nonetheless, as shall be seen, MGM pressed on with its plans, which possibly supplied the spur for impresario Hugh Beaumont in December 1954 to repeat his approach to the LCO on behalf of the Globe Theatre. Again the play was banned, but in the process Beaumont was surprised to learn that another theatre management had already submitted the play, as the American owner of the rights, Mrs Mary K. Frank, had no knowledge of this. Early in February 1955 Beaumont and Mary Frank met Nugent, who simply reiterated the fact that the Lord Chamberlain's censorship banned all references on the stage to homosexuality. Three months later Robert Anderson himself visited Britain while the play was on tour in the United Sates, but he accepted this policy without argument.

There matters rested for the moment, but MGM went ahead with the film, draining it of the play's overt homosexual references. This duly arrived at the BBFC on 12 September 1956, when it was viewed by Harris, Watkins, chief examiner Frank Crofts and Audrey Field. Two days later Watkins commented,

> The homosexual motif has been entirely removed from the story. There is no question of the boy being suspected of having immoral relations with the master [not Laura's husband but another master with whom the boy had been seen nude] or of his having homosexual tendencies. He is represented only as a sensitive, rather effeminate boy. There is no suggestion, either, that the housemaster has homosexual tendencies. The story otherwise follows the main lines of the stage play and it was agreed, in view of the episode in which the boy visits the local prostitute and the wife's final gesture in giving herself physically to the boy, to pass it in the 'X' category.
>
> I informed Sir Terence Nugent . . . of our decision and made it clear that we had only been able to pass the film because the homosexual motif had been wholly removed.

Shortly afterwards the film, with Deborah Kerr, John Kerr and Leif Erickson repeating their stage parts, was released in the United States but not yet in Britain, a delay which enabled Albery and Beaumont to join forces in submitting the play once again during October 1956. They even went so far as to arrange a private showing for Lord Scarbrough, the Lord

Chamberlain, Nugent and Gwatkin on 31 October, but Scarbrough was adamant that the play would be allowed only if the script was similar to that of the film. Evidently negotiations became acrimonious, for Albery was warned that if he went ahead with a planned private performance, then the present legal position of private theatre clubs might have to be reviewed. However, Albery decided to defy Scarbrough, for on 25 April 1957, with the film still unreleased in Britain, the play was staged by the New Watergate theatre club, with a reported membership of 50,000, at the Comedy Theatre with Elizabeth Sellars as Laura and Tom Sealy as the young student. The reviews were not unduly adverse, if a trifle mixed, and the Lord Chamberlain's censorship itself came under fire in the press over the ban at a time when the play was running in Paris with Ingrid Bergman as Laura and it was known that the film's British release would occur during August. This opening was expected to coincide approximately with the long-awaited report on homosexuality by Sir John Wolfenden and his committee, which had been set up in 1954. Cecil Wilson had already attacked the ban in the *Daily Mail* of 26 April 1957, while the *Daily Telegraph* not only did likewise but also published a leading article headed 'Sense and Censorship' suggesting that the Lord Chamberlain's censorship should either become more enlightened or be abolished. This so concerned the Home Office that it telephoned the BBFC on 3 May to enquire why the film had been allowed. When informed about the removal of homosexual references, the rejection of the 1954 script and the 'X' certificate, the Home Office was satisfied.

When at length *Tea and Sympathy* arrived in British cinemas, the BBFC in turn found itself under attack for the 'X' certificate, which one critic regarded as 'inexplicable'.[5] One local authority, Bedfordshire County Council, the licensing committee of which viewed every 'X' film as a matter of routine, awarded it an 'A' and the August issue of influential journal *Films and Filming* described the 'X' as 'quite unwarranted'.[6] This brought a fierce BBFC rejoinder, published in the October issue, defending its decision and explaining the general operation of the 'X' certificate. In this instance the critics were perhaps more forward looking than the general public, for the BBFC received only one letter of complaint about the 'X' for the film and the 'X' policy in general. By the time the film went on general release the Wolfenden report had been published to recommend the legalisation of homosexuality provided this applied only to men aged twenty-one and over as consenting adults and was carried out in private. This finding opened the way for a more open public debate on the question than hitherto and led to a policy change on homosexuality by the Lord Chamberlain, who accordingly allowed *Tea and Sympathy* in November

1958 for another theatre management. When the play was performed in Edinburgh in early 1960, Scarbrough received only one complaint and even this concerned the theme rather than the play itself.

The BBFC had not quite heard the last of *Tea and Sympathy*, for in April 1959 MGM requested an 'A' certificate, as a result of which the film was re-viewed by Harris, Trevelyan, and Crofts. Trevelyan believed that the 'X' should remain, but the others were inclined to grant MGM's request. However, Harris eventually decided upon the retention of the 'X' on the ground that an 'A' might be seen as a precedent for future films dealing with homosexuality. In any case, Harris thought, it was unwise to change decisions after such a short time. On this basis the film faded into censorship history.

Oscar Wilde/The Trials of Oscar Wilde

During the early 1890s the famous Irish poet and playwright Oscar Wilde's association with Lord Alfred Douglas led the former to sue the Marquess of Queensbury, Lord Alfred's father, for criminal libel on account of an alleged written accusation of homosexuality. Wilde's suit failed, for during the trial of April 1895 his sodomy with various young men of London's homosexual underworld came to light. As a result, in the following month a criminal trial against Wilde ensued, at which he was found guilty of pederasty and sentenced to two years' hard labour in Reading prison. After his release he wrote only two works of note and died in November 1900 at the age of forty-six in self-imposed exile in Paris. After his death Wilde's outstanding literary achievements were long overshadowed by the memory of the two trials and his criminal activities, and because of the latter any stage treatment of Wilde's life was considered to be out of the question by successive Lord Chamberlains. This formed a part of the general ban on homosexual references on the stage, which, as has already been seen, was not reversed until late in 1958, but even after that, although Lord Alfred had died in 1943, Wilde and Queensbury family sensitivities were taken into account.

The first play on the subject, by French playwright Maurice Rostand, was announced for a run at the private Gate Theatre in Villiers Street under the title of *The Trials of Oscar Wilde* in May 1935 with Frank Pettingell as Wilde.[7] However, these planned performances were abandoned following Lord Alfred's protests, even though the play was simultaneously running in Paris with Henri Baur. Nevertheless the Gate Theatre was determined to present the Wilde tragedy, and in September 1936 it performed *Oscar Wilde* by Leslie and Sewell Stokes, with Robert Morley in the title role,

Reginald Beckwith as Wilde's friend, Frank Harris, Harry Hutchinson as Sir Edward Carson, Queensberry's barrister at the first trial, and Andrew Cruikshank as Sir Edward Clarke, Wilde's own barrister. In this version neither Lord Alfred nor Wilde's wife appeared, and, after extensive but mixed notices, tentative unofficial enquiries were made to the LCO as to the possibility of a licence, but producer Norman Marshall was informed that the play would not be allowed.[8]

The subject of Oscar Wilde on a public stage was not broached again until June 1946, when the Playhouse Theatre submitted the Stokes script with a view to its production in September. Henry Game responded,

> This play is about perverts and perversion, and that its central character has been erected into a sort of literary martyr does not alter the fact. We do not licence [sic] plays about pederasts, and in my opinion rightly so . . . the Censorship is undoubtedly right in making perversion taboo as a dramatic theme. The theatre is an emotional place in which ugly things take on a false glamour. Wilde's story is tragic enough, but it is an ugly story. Wilde was the martyr of his own pride, not of British justice – and there is that to be said in this play's favour it makes that plain. But there it is . . . this is a play about perverts and perversion and for that reason I cannot recommend the play for licence.

Game's advice was accepted, and for the first time the ban on Oscar Wilde on stage became official. However, two years later the full details of Wilde's relations with young men, which had hitherto been omitted from his biographies, were published. These revelations led to a further private run for *Oscar Wilde* at the Boltons Theatre during August and September 1948, with Frank Pettingell finally playing the part of Wilde first allocated to him thirteen years previously.

This time the Lord Chamberlain's ban was criticised, for an anonymous *Daily Telegraph* reviewer on 31 August and Beverley Baxter in the *Evening Standard* of 3 September advocated that it should be lifted. Furthermore, Margery Vosper, the agent for the Stokes, had pointed out to the LCO that although the subject was unpleasant, it was questionable whether it was more unpleasant than *Pick-Up Girl*, while a homosexual incident had been allowed in *Now Barabbas* . . . In his defensive reply Nugent explained that the *Now Barabbas* . . . scene had been subsidiary rather than central to the plot, but even so, it had been toned down. This pressure proved sufficient to prompt Clarendon to send Heriot to see *Oscar Wilde* on 23 September, while Nugent himself, who had seen the play in 1936, also attended to refresh his memory. Heriot's long resulting minute deserves to be quoted in full for the light it sheds on the LCO attitude at that time towards both homosexuality as a stage theme and the theatre-going public.

It may be taken as axiomatic, I think, that it is nearly impossible to write a play around a single personality without that personality infecting, as it were, the whole atmosphere of the piece. This is exemplified in *Oscar Wilde*. The authors claim that they present a study of a man ruined by his own pride. I do not agree with them. To me, this play seemed a study of a convicted homosexual ennobled to the point of sainthood, so that one's instinctive reaction at the end of the play was, 'Oh, what a noble mind is here overthrown.' There was little or no indication of the psychological disintegration which is symptomatic of the last stages of most homosexuals. Now this implicit condonation of the vice is precisely what I presume the Lord Chamberlain tries to prevent in stage presentations. Further, the ignorance of the general public about what may be called the technical aspects of the crime has bred fear and its counterpart levity about the crime, so that there is on the one hand an unwholesome curiosity that would undoubtedly be stimulated by public performances of the play, and, on the other, a brutal kind of humour – either of which are [sic] opposed to the clinically detached attitude which I believe is the only one to be adopted when considering the subject. This is born [sic] out by comments overheard by me during the intervals last night. Many of the audience were puzzled by the two trial scenes. They did not appear to know the difference between criminal libel and sodomy, or that there had been two separate trials with different judges and prosecutions. (One young woman did not realise that the judges in the play were different until it was pointed out to her after the second act.) The other aspect was the general sympathy for Oscar shown by gushing young people of both sexes who had seen *The Importance of Being Earnest* and read the more lush poems included in a recently published edition of Wilde's works.

The authors claim that their treatment is not offensive. And this is so; but the text, when well acted as it was last night, seemed to skate on the thinnest of ice, so that what was *not* mentioned loomed with a reality larger than if it had been dragged into the open. What would happen to this play in the hands of bad actors or those themselves perverse, makes one shudder.

Clarendon simply minuted, 'I agree that the ban on plays about perversion and perverts must be maintained.'

For the moment the ban on *Oscar Wilde* thus remained in force, but over the next few years pressures gradually built up. The first of the relevant events took place in Paris in November 1950, when Wilde's son, who had taken the name of Vyvyan Holland, was invited to attend a ceremony at his father's tomb on the occasion of the fiftieth anniversary of Wilde's death to place the ashes of Wilde's friend and literary executor, Robert Ross, within the sepulchre. This would have been the first time that Holland had publicly acknowledged Wilde as his father, but he declined the invitation and his wife, Thelma, attended in his place. The second, related event was the anticipated publication of Wilde's letters by Rupert Hart-Davis in 1952, although in the event publication was delayed until 1962. All this exposed Holland to unsought press coverage, destroying his anonymity, and concentrated public attention once more upon his father.[9] One result was an approach to the BBFC in January 1952 by a British agent acting for movie mogul David O. Selznick, with an accompanying script based upon the Stokes play. To judge from the BBFC reports on this, the script followed the play with reasonable fidelity. It was perused by three examiners and then finally by Harris, a clear sign of how seriously the BBFC treated the theme. Audrey Field commented,

> It is clear that a number of good-looking but otherwise ill-endowed young men turned to homosexual practices for financial gain [which] is particularly contrary to public policy. The atmosphere of the cinema is particularly unsuitable, in any case, for considering this subject: one can well imagine the numbers of elderly degenerates whose interest would be rather in the audience than in the film.
>
> That the present approach is made by an American production company seems to me an added reason for caution: the alien outlook is apt to come through, even when the script is English, and put a delicate subject in even greater danger of offending British taste . . . the fact that the story is an English one will give it a very evil propaganda value in some parts of the world.[10]

She concluded that there was no chance the film would be allowed, even as 'X', and everyone else at the BBFC who read the script agreed, including John Trevelyan, the future Secretary. Harris noted, 'Oscar Wilde was a very clever dramatist, and it is better that he should be remembered by his own plays than by one which exploits the miserable tragedy of his life.' The BBFC notified Selznick's agent of this decision later on 25 January 1952, and Selznick apparently abandoned the idea.

However, theatre interest did not abate, for in April 1954 the Q Theatre near Kew Bridge submitted the 1935 Rostand play to the LCO for production in the following June. Heriot cryptically noted that apart from the fact that Wilde's son remained alive, the court evidence of the boys and the general atmosphere of sodomy justified by art was sufficient for the Lord Chamberlain to refuse to grant a licence.[11] The ban duly remained, and Wilde's appearance on either stage or screen in Britain looked to be blocked permanently until the situation was transformed early in September 1957 by the appearance of the Wolfenden report. As already noted, its recommendation that homosexuality between consenting adults in private should become legal provoked great public discussion of the subject, and within days of the report's publication an enquiry concerning *Oscar Wilde* was made to the LCO by producer Arnold Taylor, who was informed that the previous ban remained in operation. When Scarbrough discontinued the general ban on stage homosexuality in November 1958, this was announced publicly, in the light of which Taylor renewed his enquiry and was told that the play might be submitted, preferably with a letter from

Holland stating that he held no objection to a performance. However, Holland informed Scarbrough that he did indeed object very strongly because public performances would distress both his wife and son. At this news Scarbrough upheld his previous ban.

The Wolfenden report had also revived film interest in Oscar Wilde. In April 1959 Vantage Films unofficially approached Trevelyan with a screenplay for *Oscar Wilde*, which produced a discussion with a Vantage executive. Trevelyan recorded on the same day,

> In the first place we felt that the qualities of Oscar Wilde were less in evidence than they should be and thus did not bring out the real sense of tragedy. We also felt it was undesirable to have scenes in which Wilde flaunted young stable boys around in restaurants and elsewhere with his friends. We felt that full justice should be done not only to those who had compassion for Wilde but also for those who thoroughly disapproved of his conduct.

This assessment was indicative of the controversy stimulated by the Wolfenden report, of the government's unwillingness to commit itself and of the BBFC's desire to steer a neutral course. The Vantage executive agreed to provide a shooting script for the BBFC if the film went ahead, but on 5 June he telephoned Trevelyan to say he had learned that the Lord Chamberlain would have allowed the Stokes play but for Holland's pressure not to do so. He accordingly wished for clarification of BBFC policy, whereupon Trevelyan replied that he would probably adopt the same attitude. Matters were then left in abeyance until 17 November, when the *Daily Mail* reported that another film about Oscar Wilde was to be made by another studio with Ken Hughes as director. In the same report Holland was quoted as stating that he had not yet been consulted about this film and, until he saw the script, he would not know whether or not he approved.

This news probably expedited Vantage's plans, for on 19 January 1960 Twentieth Century-Fox, Vantage's parent company, presented to the BBFC a script entitled *The Oscar Wilde Story*, based upon the Stokes play. Trevelyan was now aware that, in the light of public knowledge that Holland was not opposed in principle to the presentation of his father's life on screen, it would be difficult for the BBFC to reject the script entirely. He was simultaneously well aware of the potential pitfalls of allowing such a film, as his lengthy reply to Fox makes plain.

> I think it would be true to say that people in general are about evenly divided on this issue. The Wolfenden report represented an advance in understanding but the government obviously feels unprepared to accept its recommendations since the pressure from those who condemn is still very strong . . . I just wonder whether the balance is not a little over-weighted in his [Wilde's] favour. This is probably due to

Queensberry's obsessional hatred of Wilde and his characterisation being perhaps a bit exaggerated. Carson, in the court scenes, is vindictive in condemnation but it might be thought that this was to some extent an act on his part in order to win the case for the defence. I think it really comes down to the presentation of Queensberry, which leads me to my second point.

I cannot help feeling that Queensberry's descendants might object to this presentation of their ancestor since he is made almost grotesque. We must admit that he was not unreasonable in wanting to get his son out of this crowd of homosexuals. I do not know enough of the history to know whether he did in fact turn his family out of his house to receive guests from Ascot including his mistress. If this presentation is fictional rather than factual it should, I think, be toned down, but there may be full justification for this.

How Wilde will come out of the film will depend very much on casting. The script makes me think that he might come out a bit too much of a martyr. After all he did like taking unsavoury stable boys to dine at Kettners, and there is little doubt about what happened there and elsewhere. It was all very tragic but it was also rather revolting.

The question of casting also arises very much in the case of Lord Alfred. Again I do not know what he was like, but I get the impression from the script that he is to be markedly a 'queer' and I think it would be a mistake to exaggerate this. Again his hatred of his father appears to have been obsessional and he was quite ready to sacrifice Wilde because of this.

I would hesitate to make any alteration to this script as written since I think it is admirable. I just wonder, however, whether there could be a little more discretion in the court scenes when Wilde is on trial. The questions to Parker are very direct about the 'acts of impropriety' . . . But I am not prepared at this stage to say that we definitely would not accept dialogue of this kind. I just think you might be wise to shoot these two scenes in an alternative version with somewhat less direct dialogue as well as in the version as scripted. This might help if you want the picture to be shown in the United States . . .

I think that we would want to be assured that you had safeguarded yourselves against any possible trouble with either of the families . . . I would like to know exactly what the position is. After all this story is to be told very frankly and we would not want to be associated with anything which gave rise to a court action.

Less than a week later Trevelyan held a discussion with Harold Huth, the producer of Warwick Films, an offshoot of MGM/United Artists, after which draft screenplays for Hughes's *The Trials of Oscar Wilde* were forwarded to the BBFC in early February and again in late March 1960, the latter two days after filming had commenced at Elstree. Audrey Field reported on the latter that the BBFC should have no trouble with this film and concluded, 'I only wish we could hope that other films about homosexuals will be half as seemly or dramatically gripping.'[12] For some weeks after this the BBFC does not appear to have been consulted again about the Vantage film, still entitled *The Oscar Wilde Story*, then being filmed at Walton-on-Thames in Surrey with Robert Morley repeating his 1936 London and New York stage role, this time under the direction of Gregory Ratoff. The final script was based upon the 1936 play but in reality was an extension of it, in that Lord Alfred and Mrs Wilde were now added to the list of characters.

In mid-April a letter to the BBFC from Holland's wife complicated matters, for it mentioned both films and while she did not appeal for them to be rejected in as many words, she requested that family feelings be taken into account. Her son was a 14-year-old English public schoolboy, and although her husband, along with the present Marquess of Queensberry and Lord Cecil Douglas, had acted as advisers on the Warwick film, her husband's advice had not always been heeded. She feared the worst because both film companies were American and would do anything for sensationalism and box-office returns. As a result of this letter Trevelyan contacted the Warwick company, but not Vantage, to ask whether it was completely satisfied that Holland and the Queensberry family approved of the production. In reply Warwick Films pointed out that over the past four months or so Holland had received the script at various stages. He had objected to some scenes towards the end of the first draft, but these had since been removed, after which he had expressed reservations only about minor dialogue and procedural points, raising no general objection. The Queensberry family was in much the same position over receipt of the scripts and had raised no objection. Moreover, both Holland and the Queensberry family had seen some of the film as already shot and offered no criticisms. Warwick did not know of Mrs Holland's concerns and suggested these might have been caused by press publicity surrounding the Vantage film rather than its own. All this was relayed to Mrs Holland, who indeed retained reservations about the Vantage film because, she wrote, it might contain some of the material in the 1936 play, particularly the erroneous implication that Wilde had died as an alcoholic in the Paris gutter.

In the event, without first submitting its completed film to the BBFC, Vantage arranged a showing for critics on 19 May prior to a public opening at the Carlton cinema in the West End three days later. It soon became clear that the two companies were engaged in a race to release their own film before the other, for the Vantage move produced a Warwick legal action for an injunction to delay the Carlton opening on alleged copyright infringement grounds, but the court decided in Vantage's favour on 16 May, so that the showing for critics, as well as the Carlton premiere, went ahead as scheduled amidst publicity misleadingly describing what was finally called *Oscar Wilde* as 'the frankest discussion of homosexuality ever seen in a cinema'. Against this background of cut-throat commercial competition, Vantage submitted its film to the BBFC only a day before the critics' preview, an action which gave rise to a stiff protest from Trevelyan.

The film was not awarded its 'X' certificate until the day after the critics had seen it, and indeed, according to one review, editing was still in progress only two hours before this performance began.[13] This suggests that the critics might have seen a fuller version than the public at the Carlton opening, for the final sequences of Wilde's drinking himself to death in Paris while reciting parodies of religious poems were removed at the BBFC, these cuts amounting to 149 feet of film or one minute, 40 seconds' running time. Mrs Holland was informed of this before the first Carlton performance, but some Paris sequences remained and, as Harris conceded in his letter to her, the grounds for her objections were not entirely removed.

The reviews for *Oscar Wilde* were good and the court scenes were highly praised, with the acting of Morley and Ralph Richardson as Carson receiving strong commendation, while the occasional critic complained that the film did not do full justice to the positive parts of Wilde's life.[14] Nevertheless the critics' reception was on the whole highly favourable, which apparently caused Warwick to submit *The Trials of Oscar Wilde* to the BBFC on 20 May, before the Vantage production opened at the Carlton, when it was allowed uncut, and to cancel a planned premiere at the Rialto on 26 May. Instead a West End opening was shunned altogether, apart from a charity midnight showing at Studio One in Oxford Street on 28 May, and two days later the film went on general release in an effort to steal a march on the Vantage feature. *The Trials of Oscar Wilde* was a much more lavish coloured offering than the monochrome Vantage film, with Peter Finch as Wilde, John Fraser as Lord Alfred, Lionel Jeffries as Queensberry and James Mason as Carson. Longer by almost thirty minutes than the Vantage film, its reviews were also favourable.

Both films are meritorious, and since they aroused no public controversy, Margery Vosper in the following December enquired whether the Lord Chamberlain would now allow the 1936 play. In the light of Holland's advisory role on *The Trials of Oscar Wilde* Lord Scarbrough agreed that the previous ban might now be reversed. Accordingly the play was submitted to the LCO in January 1961 without a planned date or venue for a run, although the script was embellished from its 1936 version, Heriot observing,

> There is nothing in the piece that has not already been dealt with in the films, and the subject of Wilde's perversion is handled tactfully (though truthfully) with stress laid on his overweening pride and the impossibility of ever changing his character.[15]

As a result of these comments, Scarbrough passed the play, but a licence was never issued, as the scheduled production was abandoned.

The Servant

The Servant began life as a little noticed 1948 novella by Robin Maugham, the homosexual nephew of W. Somerset Maugham and the son of a peer. Robin aspired to emulate the literary achievements of his illustrious uncle, and to this end he adapted his novella into a play almost eight years later. This is set in 1946, when Tony returns from Egypt for his demobilisation and finds waiting for him his close friend Richard, now a publisher, and Sally, with whom he had fallen in love while serving in Cairo. Richard has found Tony a Chelsea flat, while Tony, who has a private income, intends to resume his law studies. At the same time he enjoys luxury and advertises for a manservant. The apparently dull and obsequious Hugo Barrett applies, and although both Richard and Sally strongly disapprove, Tony engages him. Six months later Barrett virtually controls the entire household. Very well fed and freed of all domestic worries, Tony grows fat and drinks to excess.

Barrett then claims that he needs help with his work and introduces Vera, supposedly his niece but in fact his mistress and also a nymphomaniac, to Tony. She too enters the household, Barrett encouraging her to seduce Tony, which she is only too happy to do, while Barrett sets about excluding Richard and Sally from Tony's life. However, Richard possesses a key to Tony's flat, and when six months later Richard returns from the United States while Tony is away, he finds Barrett and Vera in bed together in Tony's bedroom. Richard and Sally believe that Barrett and Vera have committed incest and endeavour to exploit the illegality of this to break Barrett's stranglehold over Tony. On his return the latter plucks up courage to dismiss Barrett, but afterwards Tony misses Vera's physical charms, which shows Sally that she has lost him. Three months on Barrett, but not Vera, is reinstated, from which point Barrett acts as a pimp, providing young girls to satisfy Tony's libido, while Tony drinks more heavily than ever. By 1948 Tony is alcoholic, his kitchen has become a joint living room, and Barrett treats him as a social equal. In desperation Richard offers Tony a share of his own flat, but it is too late, for Tony has lost all his will power and is completely in Barrett's clutches.

The Connaught Theatre in Worthing, Sussex, submitted the play to the Lord Chamberlain on 10 March 1956 for a scheduled run commencing a month later. Troubridge, the Reader of Plays, unhesitatingly recommended a licence on the basis that the play's message was that 'a desire for comfort if pushed to excess may lead to the downfall of a character'.[16] Presumably because both Tony and Barrett were demonstrably heterosexual, Troubridge in pre-Wolfenden report days failed to recognise a possible implicit homosexuality in their relationship or in that between Tony and Richard, although there is nothing in the action or dialogue to suggest homosexuality, possibly Maugham's device to circumvent potential censorship obstacles. However, the play was not transferred to the West End, as Maugham had hoped, but earlier in the 1950s he had met Joseph Losey, the American film director in exile in Britain as a refugee from the anti-Communist McCarthyism then sweeping through the United States. Losey was interested in filming *The Servant* and might even have had a hand in the writing of the play, but for a variety of reasons the project had to be deferred until the first half of 1961 and the pre-filming preparations lasted until the very end of 1962.

Among these was an excellent Harold Pinter script. From the outset Pinter had appreciated that Maugham's 1948 story had been overtaken by events, for by the early 1960s post-war austerity had given way to increasing prosperity. In consequence domestic servants had become a rarity for the officer-type bachelor gentleman, overt class snobbery being much less in evidence after the mid-1950s. In updating the social milieu, Pinter eliminated the character of Richard, converted Tony into a social parasite and changed Vera into a carefree figure personifying early 1960s sexual permissiveness. Most crucially, he made Barrett less a stereotyped proletarian, from whom the upper classes would instinctively recoil, and more a symbol of emerging lower-class self-confidence. Pinter also included new material, with an orgy as the climax of Tony's degradation, as well as consistent verbal and visual suggestive references. These showed Tony having his breakfast served in bed by both Barrett and Vera, an early scene showing Barrett sleeping with his landlady and Barrett's lodgings with pages from cheap sex magazines, pornographic calendars and nudes stuck on to oil paintings, all sellotaped to the wall of his room.

Although there was nothing in Pinter's script that was directly homosexual, Losey kept in constant contact with Trevelyan before filming began and while it was in progress. Shooting opened on 28 January 1963 at Shepperton, but earlier Losey had met and written to Trevelyan, inviting him to see the rough cuts and to visit the set.[17] One week later the BBFC received the latest script amendments. On 1 March, Losey invited Trevelyan to see further rough cuts in about a week's time and then to discuss the way the film was proceeding, especially the orgy sequence, which, Losey hoped, Trevelyan would find 'less dangerous than as written'. Trevelyan evidently took advantage of this offer, for in the BBFC's documentation on the film there are undated notes in his handwriting listing his points of concern. Among these were (1) a dialogue exchange as follows: *Sue* (changed from Sally) 'Shall I bottle you?', *Tony*

'Yes,' *Sue* 'Shall I bottle you after dinner? Mmmm?', (2) a scene in which
Sue (Wendy Craig) and Tony (James Fox) roll around together on the
floor in a room of Tony's flat before Barrett (Dirk Bogarde) inadvertently
interrupts them, after which her dialogue opens with 'For Christ's sake'.
Trevelyan also expressed reservations about too much sexiness from Vera
(Sarah Miles) in her various sexual scenes with both Barrett and Tony and
objected to any nudity in scenes where a bed was visible and to obscene
photographs in the visuals of Tony's flat after Barrett has returned there
following his dismissal. Finally, Trevelyan was apprehensive of dialogue
with homosexual implications, particularly a line from Barrett at the end
of the orgy when he tells one of the women just as she is leaving, 'Make it
tomorrow . . . and bring John.'

Much of this was omitted from the final version of the film, but all the
same it is doubtful whether Trevelyan's undated notes tell the whole story.
For example, the orgy scene as originally written included crawling and
whipping, but this appears in neither Trevelyan's notes nor the released
print. Nor does an early scene with Barrett in bed with his landlady or a scene
showing Barrett serving Tony with breakfast in bed, although a brief one
with Vera doing so, when Tony is stripped to the waist beneath the sheets,
was retained. Trevelyan's reservations about the obscene photographs in
Tony's flat after the two men had become social equals, together with his
doubts about the dialogue line at the end of the orgy, reveal that he was well
aware of the homosexual implications of the Tony–Barrett relationship and
wanted these made less flagrant. Despite the Lord Chamberlain's and the
BBFC's recent relaxations on the subject of homosexuality, this remained
illegal and Trevelyan had to tread warily. The running time Losey filmed
amounted to approximately 140 minutes, but the released version was only
115 minutes long. Since these cuts have seemingly not survived, it is impossible to be sure of either what was filmed and then edited out or what was not
filmed at all from Pinter's script, which underwent constant revision while
filming was under way. Either Losey acceded to Trevelyan's objections as
shooting went along or made his own amendments to pre-empt Trevelyan's
likely reservations or for other reasons, probably a combination of the two.
In any case it remains impossible to trace to what extent Trevelyan influenced
the final version, although there is no doubt that he did influence it, if only
in a minor way.

Losey and Trevelyan viewed the film together on 19 March, when shooting was approaching completion, after which the latter voiced four chief
concerns. These were, first, the dialogue line from Sue after Barrett had
interrupted her love-making with Tony on the floor, 'Well, for God's sake,
restrict him to quarters', second, a scene with Barrett in the bathroom,

where Vera drops the bath towel wrapped around her nude body, third, Vera's 'soundless sexual laugh' while she is sitting on a table in a scene where she begins Tony's seduction and, lastly, Vera's off-screen banter with Barrett after Tony and Sue discover them in bed together in Tony's bedroom. For the moment there was no agreement, and all four points were left until later. By the end of March 1963 filming was over, although the editing occupied until early May, Losey meeting Trevelyan again on 25 May. In the event all four of the latter's final doubts are retained in the film, as is Barrett's line, 'Make it tomorrow . . . and bring John', which indicates that Trevelyan finally accepted the homosexual implications provided these were not direct and not accompanied by obscene photographs in Tony's flat while the two men are the only occupants.

At this point *The Servant* ran into distribution problems in Britain and was not officially submitted to the BBFC because it appeared unlikely to be shown at all until Losey succeeded in having it screened at the New York and Venice Film Festivals during September 1963. It was well received, and only then, on 30 September, was it presented to the BBFC, where it was at once allowed with the 'X' certificate. Even so, its British release did not take place until mid-November 1963, when the critics were rapturous, although the social-class aspect of the tale diverted their attention from the possible homosexual element in the Barrett–Tony relationship. The film was not a commercial success, but the favourable critical reception persuaded Robin Maugham to rewrite his play along the lines of Losey's film. This caused no problems at the LCO, the play opening at the Yvonne Arnaud Theatre in Guildford in 1966, but, like its 1956 predecessor, it has never been transferred to the West End.

Entertaining Mr Sloane

Joe Orton's 1964 *Entertaining Mr Sloane* opens with Kath, a nymphomaniac in her early forties, living with her nearly blind father, Kemp. Her homosexual brother, Ed, takes a guarded interest in them both and is well aware of his sister's sexual personality. After she picks up Sloane, a young man in his early twenties, in the local library and brings him home as a lodger, she makes sexual advances to him and he responds. Kemp believes that Sloane murdered his employer two years earlier, but Sloane brushes aside this accusation. Ed finds Sloane during one of his periodic visits to Kath and discovers that he himself is attracted to the young man. As a result, he offers Sloane a job as his chauffeur, which is accepted, but Sloane rejects Ed's homosexual overtures, while meantime Kath becomes pregnant by Sloane. Kemp grows increasingly hostile towards the latter, whereupon Sloane admits that he killed Kemp's employer, but when Kemp threatens to inform the police, Sloane murders him. Both Kath and Ed decide to conceal the murder, but Ed's price for his silence is that Sloane will live with him as his homosexual partner, while Kath is permitted trysts with Sloane from time to time.

Owing much to Pinter's earlier *The Caretaker*, with Sloane modelled on the homosexual Orton himself, *Entertaining Mr Sloane* relies heavily for its comedy effect upon the shock value of its cynicism as well as the widespread use of low-life language embodying the glib, irreverent spirit of the early 1960s. It commenced its run on 6 May 1964 at the private Arts Theatre Club, where it remained until the twenty-third of the same month. There it proved sufficiently popular for Orton to have the script presented to the LCO on 27 May with a view to a run at the Wyndham's Theatre commencing on 29 June. Reader of Plays Maurice Coles observed, 'Even if you are prepared to accept the thread of homosexuality which runs strongly through the play, there are nonetheless many cuts which will have to be made.'[18] Coles went on to list approximately twenty of these. This leads one to suspect that Orton was intent upon provoking the Lord Chamberlain in the hope that at least some of his dubious material would be allowed, for words such as prat, shit, bum, arse, bugger, pissed and vaginaltrous (apparently an Orton invention) as well as expressions like 'monkey's fart', 'sagging tits' and 'an old tart grinding to her climax' abounded.

Everyone at the LCO found the play unattractive, but the theme was not prohibitive and Orton's agent was informed that 'shit', 'arse', 'Oh, Christ', 'titties', 'vaginaltrous', 'a monkey's fart', 'bugger', 'sagging tits' and 'an old tart grinding to her climax' would all have to be deleted. Moreover, in a scene in which Sloane touches Kath's chest where he judges her nipple to be and she responds with, 'You wanted to see if my titties were all my own,' Sloane was forbidden actually to touch Kath's breast. Orton did not put up too much of a struggle over his provocations, suggesting the substitutions of 'twit' for 'prat', 'harris' for 'arse', 'rubbish' for 'shit' and 'actress grinding to her climax' for 'an old tart grinding to her climax'. However, he wished to retain 'tits' and 'titties', to which Lord Cobbold refused to agree, although he accepted all of Orton's other suggestions. In this form the play was passed, registering a dramatic impact on the theatre world as a black comedy. Madge Ryan played Kath, Dudley Sutton was Sloane, Charles Lamb was Kemp and Peter Vaughan was Ed.

The BBFC was fully conversant with the plot and general atmosphere of *Entertaining Mr Sloane* well before a film scenario arrived there from Canterbury Films on 30 May 1969, for Trevelyan had seen the play and disliked it.[19] Whether at this time he was aware of the cuts the Lord

Chamberlain had insisted upon is unclear, but some of these deletions reappeared in Clive Exton's script, while Canterbury Films had cast Beryl Reid as Kath in the aftermath of Robert Aldrich's *The Killing of Sister George* (see next section), Harry Andrews as Ed, Alan Webb as Kemp and Peter McEnery as Sloane. At this stage it was intended that Kemp would be a cemetery keeper living next to a Gothic lodge, where much of the action takes place, rather than the father of Kath and Ed. Recently recruited examiner Ken Penry at once pinpointed the crude language, either questioning its inclusion or suggesting amendments. In his view Sloane's line, 'Why don't you shut your mouth and give your arse a chance?' was unnecessary. In addition Ed's line, 'Why don't you speak to your only begotten son, you old twank?', 'This stuff smells like a knocking shop', 'I just don't give a monkey's fart' and 'Support the scout movement' (in a homosexual context) might give offence and required alternative wording, while a shot of Kemp breaking wind noisily would have to be cut. When these points were conveyed to Canterbury Films, the company accepted them all without protest, except the reference to the knocking shop, but by then a new script was being written, to consider which Trevelyan met director Douglas Hickox and Canterbury executive Doug Kentish on 8 August 1969. Trevelyan emerged from this encounter and from subsequent script rewrites with only minor reservations. The chief changes were the reinstatement of Kemp as Kath and Ed's father and the addition at the end of Ed presiding over a form of 'marriage' between Kath and Sloane, and Kath doing likewise for Ed and Sloane.

Canterbury Films could take liberties of this sort with the script, for in 1967 Orton had been murdered by his homosexual lover, Kenneth Halliwell, who had then committed suicide. The 'marriages' at the end bestow upon the film more of a black comedy appearance than it actually possesses as a whole, and when the BBFC received the completed film in February 1970, it was viewed by Trevelyan, senior examiner Frank Crofts and examiner Audrey Field, all of whom expressed concern about the convincing homosexual element, even though homosexuality between adults had been legal since 1967. Despite the comedy material, the BBFC wished the film's release date to be deferred until the new 'X' certificate, limiting audiences to eighteen-year-olds and over, came into force later in the year. In any event a cut would have to be made in a sequence where Kath sprawls open her legs and Sloane is seen mounting her, followed by shots of his upwards and downwards movements. The company protested, but Trevelyan was adamant and he personally viewed the edited version on 20 February at the Canterbury premises before finally granting the 'X' certificate. Even then, he asked the distributors to hold back the general release, but not the West End opening scheduled for April, until the revamped 'X' certificate came into effect.

Accordingly *Entertaining Mr Sloane* opened at the Carlton cinema in April 1970 to mixed reviews, but what seemed fresh in 1964, especially the vulgar dialogue, had become close to outdated in the six-year interim. Since 1970 little has been seen of the film, but on 31 December 1988 the BBFC allowed a video version with the 1970 cuts restored, while the Arts Theatre revived the play in January 2001.

The Killing of Sister George

In August 1964 the Royal Court Theatre forwarded to the LCO John Osborne's *A Patriot for Me*, which deals with the Colonel Redl espionage and homosexual scandal in the pre-1914 Austro-Hungarian army. Lord Cobbold, the Lord Chamberlain, was prepared to allow the play only if two scenes were removed. These were one with men in bed together and one of a homosexual ball in which some of the male participants were dressed as women, one portraying Lady Godiva clad merely in a gold jockstrap. Cobbold evidently felt that such material was corrupting and would come within the 1959 Obscene Publications Act's 'tending to deprave and corrupt, taken as a whole' obscenity test. But Osborne refused to budge, and the Royal Court went ahead with the play with private club conditions so wide that these Sunday performances were in effect public. This dispute was never settled before theatre censorship was abolished in 1968.

The influence of this impasse was initially felt at the LCO when the Theatre Royal in Bristol submitted Frank Marcus's lesbian tale, *The Killing of Sister George*, in March 1965. The plot involves two women, ageing actress June Buckridge and Alice 'Childie' McNaught, who live together as lesbians. June is under contract to the BBC and is currently playing the role of district nurse Sister George in a very popular radio series. As the play opens June harbours suspicions that the BBC intends to dispense with her character. These suspicions prove to be well founded when she is visited by Mrs Mercy Croft, a BBC executive, who first reprimands June for a drunken episode, during which she had entered a taxi already occupied by two nuns, and then confirms that, due to a fall in the number of listeners to the series, the role of Sister George is to be killed off.

On the day when Sister George's funeral is to be transmitted, the flat where June and 'Childie' live is filled with floral tributes. Although the loss of the part of Sister George represents a heavy blow to her career, June does her best to face up to the situation until Mercy Croft calls with expressions of sympathy and an offer of a leading role, that of a cow, in a *Children's Hour* serial. June becomes violently abusive and takes to heavy drinking to get her through the day, but meanwhile 'Childie' confides to Mercy the difficulties of living with her exceedingly dominant partner. Mercy is very sympathetic and wins the confidence and affection of 'Childie', who agrees to leave June for Mercy. The play ends with the deserted June in front of her radio listening to Sister George's funeral service and plaintively rehearsing the cow sounds she will presumably be making in her new part.

Ifor Kyrle Fletcher, Reader of Plays at the LCO from 1964 to 1968, noted that a lesbian atmosphere permeated the entire play. However, once this was accepted, there was no dialogue to which the Lord Chamberlain could take exception, although there were one or two episodes, both arising from the masochism of 'Childie', who was the highly submissive partner in her relationship with June, which aroused concern. The first, early in the play, was June forcing 'Childie' down on her knees to eat the butt of June's cigar, and the second was June, enraged because her world was collapsing on two fronts simultaneously, demanding that 'Childie' be punished and should drink June's dirty bath water.[20]

Fletcher referred the play to his immediate superior, Charles Heriot, who pointed out that all the characters were lesbians living in a private world as well defined and as populous as, for example, the perverts in *A Patriot for Me*, a significant comparison, as his comments show.

> This leads me to suggest, I hope without fantasy, that the present play may well be a trap for the Lord Chamberlain. Three of the four characters in the play are going to a 'drag' ball. It is clear that this occasion is entirely lesbian. Sister George and her 'wife' appear in costume as Laurel and Hardy, which gives the former a further chance to reveal her domination and the other woman's masochistic pleasure in being humiliated – at any rate during the first half of the piece. Now, if the Lord Chamberlain licenses this play, I can easily imagine the cries of righteous indignation in some quarters that a play clearly about lesbians is permitted while a play not entirely about perverts is *not*.

Heriot favoured a ban, although his line of reasoning failed to point out that lesbianism was legal whereas homosexuality remained illegal, but John Johnston, the Assistant Comptroller at the LCO from 1964 to 1987, was doubtful about a ban on the grounds that there was nothing in the action of the play that could be considered corrupting. Furthermore, although June and 'Childie' were dressed as men before the party, the party itself was not seen and the lesbian partners were never seen in bed together.

Figure 7 Beryl Reid dressed as Oliver Hardy and Susannah York dressed as Stan Laurel in *The Killing of Sister George* (USA, 1969). Palomar/The Kobal Collection

All the same Johnston conceded that it might be dangerous to allow a play with such a theme and referred the matter to Lord Cobbold, who held a meeting with Johnston and the two play readers before finally deciding to allow the play without amendment in spite of his continuing refusal to sanction *A Patriot for Me*.

Accordingly the Bristol run went ahead from 20 April 1965, and the play was later produced at the Duke of York's Theatre in London and on Broadway, with Beryl Reid as June, Eileen Atkins as 'Childie' and Lally Bowers as Mercy. The reviews were excellent, and film director Robert Aldrich saw it twice in both venues. In 1968 he converted it into a film, shooting mostly in Hollywood, although some sequences were filmed by a second unit in London, including one at the private lesbian Gateways Club. Beryl Reid repeats her stage part, while Susannah York plays 'Childie' and Coral Browne plays Mercy. The film received a certain amount of sensationalist pre-release publicity in Britain during the second half of 1968, even before its American release in October. Afterwards, owing to some unfavourable American reaction, that publicity intensified during mid-December, leading to a review by Ian Christie in the *Daily Express* of 17 December headed, 'It's not the sex I object to – it's the rest of the film.' Another review, by Margaret Hinxman, in the *Sunday Telegraph* of 22 December appeared under the headline of 'Mucking Up Sister George'. These comments were understandable, for Aldrich had cast aside almost all of the play's moving comedy touches and made his film as a heavy-handed tearjerker. Worst of all, he added an unnecessary seduction scene between 'Childie' and Mercy, the cause of much of the American criticism. It was this extra material which aroused BBFC apprehensions when the film was submitted towards the end of January 1969. Senior examiner Frank Crofts required several cuts even for the 'X' certificate. These were the deletion of two lines of June's dialogue, namely 'with 50 c.c. buzzing away between your legs' and 'Go screw yourself, or better still, why don't you try Mrs Croft?', and of the entire lesbian seduction scene towards the end of the film.[21]

However, examiner Ken Penry took a different view. He declared,

(a) Although the theme may be distasteful for many audiences, I consider it acceptable. (b) The dialogue is acceptable except for the words 'piss off'. (c) The cigar chewing scene . . . although unpleasant, is acceptable in the sense in which it is portrayed. (d) The penultimate scene between Coral Browne and Susannah York has obviously been added for sensationalism and . . . is not dramatically necessary. The development of the relationship between the two women has not been developed sufficiently to justify a detailed lesbian scene and I consider that it should be cut from the point where Coral Browne places her hands on Susannah York's breasts, outside her dress, until the entrance of Beryl Reid at the door.

On the general point of whether or not a detailed lesbian scene is yet acceptable, my own view is that although I do not consider that it would corrupt, I feel that public opinion would be shocked to a degree that could prove adverse to the liberalism of film censorship.

The distributors were asked to amend the lesbian scene along the lines that Penry had recommended. However, the press had learned of what was intended, for an article by noted anti-censorship critic Alexander Walker in the *Evening Standard* of 12 February 1969 headed 'Sister George has Censor Trouble' quoted Trevelyan as stating that the BBFC was taking a second look to see if cuts were needed. This was misleading, but Trevelyan went on to explain, more accurately,

It is the length and explicitness of the love-making scene that is causing concern. This section of the film aroused some extreme reactions in America. British critics are generally more liberal when it comes to sex on the screen – but one must be very careful about possible effects the film might have. I gather that the scene lasts for several minutes. But it is unaccompanied by music or dialogue. This would facilitate any cuts the censor felt compelled to ask for.

In Walker's article a spokesman for director Robert Aldrich stated that cuts would be resisted. With the press on its track and a dispute with Aldrich in the offing, the BBFC was anxious to resolve the matter as speedily as possible. Consequently Trevelyan met the head of distributors Cinerama, Robert Lee, on 14 February while the BBFC was still considering how it was going to deal with the amended version of the film that Cinerama had submitted. This was seen by Trevelyan, Audrey Field and examiner Newton Branch, all of whom thought that the love scene had not been sufficiently reduced. Eventually, following two further viewings, Trevelyan decided to remove the scene entirely, as Crofts had advocated in the first place. When Cinerama was informed of Trevelyan's decision, it would not accept it, but Trevelyan replied to Cinerama's protest,

This scene is by far the most explicit scene of lesbian physical love that has ever been submitted to us, and it goes further than any similar scene in this context, although we have, of course, accepted passionate scenes of this kind, with nudity, but only when the relationship was heterosexual. Also, as you will know, we are not ungenerous to scenes of female nudity . . . but it is a totally different matter when the context is one of lesbian physical love.

This correspondence dragged on without result for a further week until Cinerama decided to submit the film directly to the local authorities, starting with the Greater London Council. The BBFC-authorised version had reduced the footage from 12,586 to 12,112 – a cut of some five minutes and thirty seconds – but the Greater London Council gave the film the 'X' certificate and reduced the footage only to 12,402, cutting approximately two minutes' running time from the disputed scene. Thus much of this remained for London cinemagoers, Cinerama accompanying the council's decision with a press announcement to this effect and highlighting the BBFC's total objection to a scene that was allegedly the whole point of the story.

The film duly opened at the Prince Charles cinema in Leicester Place on 25 March 1969, by which time the *Daily Telegraph* of twelve days earlier had reported that a judge in Boston, Massachusetts, had found the film lewd and obscene, and that the cinema manager concerned had been jailed for six months and fined $1,000. Such pre-publicity probably did the film no harm at the box office, but the critics were unenthusiastic, some charging it with tedium and most referring to the love scene and the cuts. Penelope Huston in a belated review for the *Spectator* on 14 April summed up the general verdict when she dubbed the film 'a curious case of grievous bodily harm inflicted on an unprotesting play'. Nevertheless the publicity was welcome to Cinerama, which went on to submit the film to other local authorities, with a variety of outcomes. Many passed it as 'X' in either the BBFC or Greater London Council versions, but one, the city of Chester, banned it to youngsters under eighteen, while more than thirty authorities banned it outright. This process extended into 1970, but by July 1969 Cinerama had successfully applied to a sufficient number of local authorities to feel itself in a strong enough position to ask the BBFC to reconsider its decision. This request was passed to BBFC President Lord Harlech, who rejected it even though it is unclear whether he actually ever saw the film. In January 1970 the new 'X' category, forbidding 'X' films to those under eighteen, was announced, although it was not due to come into operation until well into the year. This development prompted Cinerama in April 1970 to ask the BBFC again for the lesbian seduction scene to be reconsidered, initially without success.

However, Cinerama's persistence paid off to the extent that early in July 1970 Trevelyan notified the company in writing that the BBFC would not pass the contentious scene in full or even in the Greater London Council-approved version but would now pass it up to the point where 'Childie' begins to writhe and gasp orgasmically. This proved acceptable to Cinerama, which some weeks later promised Trevelyan that the only version to be distributed in future would be this most recent BBFC-certificated one. This exchange opened up a long exercise, carried out in phases, of BBFC notification to those local authorities which had supported the first BBFC decision. A variety of responses emerged, with many local authorities again falling in with the Board's lead, some deciding for a total ban and only a very few allowing the uncut version. The entire episode was something of a storm in a teacup, as the lack of a single public complaint to the BBFC showed. The BBFC passed the full version on video in mid-1996.

Notes

1. See, for instance, *The Times*, 13 February 1947.
2. Lord Chamberlain's Plays Correspondence Files, *Now Barabbas . . .* 1947/ 7860. Play reader's report, 17 February 1947. All references hereafter come from this file.
3. Lord Chamberlain's Plays Correspondence Files, *Tea and Sympathy* 1958/1459. Nugent to Hugh Beaumont, 17 November 1953. All references hereafter come from this file.

4. BBFC file on *Tea and Sympathy*. Reader's report, 26 April 1954. All references hereafter come from this file.

5. Philip Oakes, *Evening Standard*, 3 October 1957.

6. *Films and Filming*, August 1957, p. 23.

7. *The Times*, 27 May 1935.

8. Lord Chamberlain's Plays Correspondence Files, *Oscar Wilde* 1946/164A. Play reader's report, 1 July 1946. All references hereafter come from this file.

9. Merlin Holland, 'Now, I feel I can love you, Oscar', *Sunday Telegraph* review, 29 October 2000.

10. BBFC file on *Oscar Wilde*. Reader's report, 13 January 1952. All references hereafter come from this file.

11. Lord Chamberlain's Plays Correspondence Files, *Oscar Wilde* LR 1954/1. Play reader's report, 3 April 1954.

12. BBFC file on *The Trials of Oscar Wilde*. Reader's report, 31 March 1960. All references hereafter come from this file.

13. *Monthly Film Bulletin*, June 1960, p. 93.

14. See, especially, Harold Conway, *Daily Sketch*, 20 May 1960.

15. Lord Chamberlain's Plays Correspondence Files, *Oscar Wilde* WB 1961/1. Play reader's report, 4 January 1961.

16. Lord Chamberlain's Plays Correspondence Files, *The Servant* 1956/9011. Play reader's report, 16 March 1956.

17. BBFC file on *The Servant*. Losey to Trevelyan, 11 January 1963. All references hereafter come from this file.

18. Lord Chamberlain's Plays Correspondence Files, *Entertaining Mr Sloane* 1964/4267. Play reader's report, 2 June 1964. All references hereafter come from this file.

19. BBFC file on *Entertaining Mr Sloane*. Trevelyan to Canterbury Film Productions, 12 June 1969. All references hereafter come from this file.

20. Lord Chamberlain's Plays Correspondence Files, *The Killing of Sister George* 1965/4869. Play reader's report, 18 March 1965. All references hereafter come from this file.

21. BBFC file on *The Killing of Sister George*. Note by Crofts, 3 February 1969. All references hereafter come from this file.

CHAPTER 7

From the 'Angry' Fifties to the 'Swinging' Sixties

' "Cultural revolution" seems not a bad description' is Arthur Marwick's apt summary comment on the sea changes in British society between the 1950s and 1960s. 'The key acts of the period,' he continues, 'were not part of some political blueprint for society but resulted from pressures generated from within society.' Hence, there was the Betting and Gaming Act in 1960 – acknowledging gambling habits across the board; in 1967, the Abortion Act, National Health Service (Family Planning) Act, and the Sexual Offences Act – legalising homosexual acts in private between two consenting adults; the Theatres Act in 1968 – abolishing stage censorship; the Representation of the People Act – reducing the voting age to eighteen – and Divorce Reform Act of 1969; and, in 1970, the Matrimonial Property Act – recognising a wife's work in the home or elsewhere as an equal contribution to family life in the event of divorce, the Equal Pay Act, albeit not immediately effective, and the Chronic Sick and Disabled Persons Act, which ratified the problems of the disabled. 'Acts of Parliament must never be mistaken for the reality of social change,' he cautions, but 'in fact the reality of change was palpable in the archaeology of everyday life, in attitudes, behaviour and artefacts.' Although he takes great care not to underestimate the undoubted 'sources of tension and deprivation – race relations and high-rise housing for instance,' Marwick maintains the 1960s were, if not quite 'a golden age', still 'a time of release and change'.[1]

Nowhere was there more evidence of release and change than in the realms of censorship. The 'great liberation for printed literature', to borrow John Sutherland's words, occurred on 21 July 1959, when the Obscene Publications Act (sponsored by then Labour backbencher, Roy Jenkins) passed into law. This opened the gates. But real freedom from censorship for literature – 'the crucial blow for the freedom of literature and publishing alike' – was decisively won in November 1960 when a jury of three women and nine men returned a verdict of 'not guilty' in the prosecution of Penguin Books for publication of the unexpurgated version of D. H. Lawrence's novel, *Lady Chatterley's Lover*, thereby making it 'available for the first time to the public in the United Kingdom'. Decensorship, Sutherland argues, played a significant part in the transformations of the 1960s. 'The 1960s released all sorts of new energies and dissidence. Television, stage and film chafed against restriction,' he goes on. Furthermore, 'As Roy Jenkins put it in a phrase which the *Daily Telegraph* will throw back in his face for ever more – the permissive society was the civilised society. Liberalisation was fought every inch, but its tide in the 1960s was irresistible'.[2]

So, too, the theatre and film censors appeared to agree. Sir Norman Gwatkin, the Lord Chamberlain's Comptroller, highlighted what he viewed as a grim situation for theatre:

> The Lord Chamberlain cannot, even if he wished to do so, for ever travel in a horse carriage; he is now in a motor car and many people are trying to force him into a spaceship . . . You would probably be surprised to know how much we cut out in words and how much we warn about business, but since the evidence at the trial of *Lady Chatterley* I am beginning to wonder who one is trying to protect.

John Trevelyan, Secretary at the BBFC from 1958, adopted a more upbeat tone for the epigram of the book he wrote after his retirement in 1971: 'Times change and we change with them.'[3]

Gwatkin need not have worried unduly. There were sufficient numbers of people who felt sure they continued to require some form of urgent protection and his office received a regular postbag from 'disgruntled' members of the public, protesting at the 'filth' they witnessed for themselves on the stage and seeking its immediate removal. They did not wish to see any loss in steering power and sought instead increased control of the wheel. That much is evident from the reaction afforded two key stage vehicles of the 1950s and 1960s, *Look Back in Anger* and *Alfie*, both of which were turned into films. In the portrayal of their iconic male characters, Jimmy Porter and Alfie Elkins, moreover, both had a lot to say about the changing representation of masculinity in British theatre and cinema between the moment of the 'angry young man' and the advent of 'swinging' London.

Look Back in Anger

John Osborne was no stranger to controversy by the time the film script of his stage play, *Look Back in Anger*, arrived for pre-production scrutiny at the BBFC in late August 1958. When first presented by the English Stage Company at the Royal Court Theatre, on 8 May 1956, the play had received a welcome and enthusiastic reception in some quarters, notably from Kenneth Tynan, but a lukewarm and occasionally hostile response in others. Most critics agreed, however, that Osborne was a dramatist to watch, if nothing else. Though not an instant box-office hit, the play's prospects revived after the Royal Court press officer dubbed him 'a very angry young man' and the chance remark was then turned into a catch-phrase by the press. Osborne was subsequently interviewed by Malcolm Muggeridge for BBC's *Panorama*, on 9 July, and on 16 October the BBC broadcast of an excerpt from the play was watched by nearly five million people, thereby stimulating further interest. A Granada production of the full play was networked by ITV on 28 November. This exposure, coupled with Fleet Street's increasing tendency to report or embellish Osborne's every comment, added to his notoriety. He was 'the first spokesman in the London theatre' for a generation of 'angry young men'. *Look Back in Anger* undoubtedly marked the breakthrough of 'the new drama' and 'arguably the biggest shock to the system of British theatre since the advent of Shaw'. Osborne 'the rebel' had arrived, and his play was 'the sensation of 1956'.[4]

In fact, Osborne's play had already proved the source of much debate at the Lord Chamberlain's Office when the English Stage Company first submitted it for licence earlier in the year, on 27 February. Charles Heriot, the script examiner, summarised his essentially jaundiced reaction to *Look Back in Anger* in a hastily produced report of 1 March 1956:[5]

> This impressive and depressing play breaks new psychological ground, dealing with a type of man I believed had vanished twenty years ago, but which must be generally recognisable enough to write plays about. It is about the kind of intellectual that threshed about passionately looking for a cause. It usually married girls of good family, quarrelled with all their relations, and bore them off to squalor in Pimlico or Poplar where they had babies and spent all their spare time barracking Fascist meetings. In this play the venue is a large provincial town where Jimmy and Alison, his wife, share frowsty digs with Cliff, Jimmy's friend. The men run a sweet stall in the market place – both having been at a university.
>
> Cliff is platonically loving to Alison. But Jimmy, torn by his secret daemons – his sense of social and intellectual inferiority, his passionate 'feeling' that the old order is, in some way, responsible for the general bloodiness of the world today, his determination to *épater le bourgeois* at all costs and his unrealised mother fixation for the kindly, charitable mother of one of his friends (a charwoman who married an artist, completely uneducated so that Jimmy can, quite unconsciously, patronise her while he praises her goodness) – foams at Alison, insulting her parents, teasing her about her background in an angry way and generally indulging in a grand display of tantrums that only differ from those of the nursery in having an adult sexual flavour.

'The play's interest,' Heriot concluded, 'lies in its careful observation of an anteroom of hell.' Though he recommended the play for licence, he appended a list of nine specific references to be cut or altered. Once the play and Heriot's report had been read by both the Lord Chamberlain, the Earl of Scarbrough, and his then Assistant Comptroller, Brigadier Sir Norman

Gwatkin, six of his suggestions were endorsed and communicated to the Royal Court on 2 March 1956.

Tony Richardson, the play's director and assistant director of the English Stage Company, responded with Osborne's revisions. Some problems were easily, albeit reluctantly, overcome. 'Short-arsed' was changed to 'sawn off' and the line 'There's a smokescreen in my pubic hair' was altered to 'You can quit waiting at my counter, Mildred, 'cos you'll find my position closed.' Similarly, the offending couplet in one of Jimmy Porter's songs – 'I could try inversion/But I'd yawn with aversion' – was amended and expanded:

> This perpetual whoring
> Gets quite dull and boring
> So avoid the python coil
> And pass me the celibate oil.

It was a significant addition because the 'python image' was related to a key speech which they had already been requested to 'tone down'. While the new-found rhyme was allowed, the proposed amendment to Jimmy's highly vituperative attack on his wife over 'the great pleasure of lovemaking' was not. In particular, the examiners objected to continued talk of Alison as she 'lies back afterwards like a puffed-out python to sleep it off' and to 'the peaceful coil of that innocent-looking belly'. 'No' was their private 'blue pencil' comment: 'This is too much the same.' Richardson was duly informed of the approved revisions and the remaining reservations.

Since the premiere of the play was less than six weeks away and rehearsals were in progress, Tony Richardson tried another attempt to win the day:

> Naturally we are very disappointed that you cannot agree to the alterations we sub-mitted. What, however, is absolutely vital to the play, and I would ask you most urgently to try and help us over this, is that the 'python image' – which is central to the whole thought of the play – should be retained, though of course I appreciate the necessity for softening it a little. I am sending you therefore the following possible amendments.
>
> For: 'Oh, it's not that she hasn't her own kind of passion. She has that. She just devours me whole every time as if I were some over-large rabbit and lies back after-wards like a puffed out python to sleep it off'.
>
> Read: 'Oh, it's not that she hasn't her own kind of passion. She has. The passion of a python. She just devours me whole every time as if I were some over-large rabbit.'
>
> We would be most grateful if you could help us over this.

Three possible alternatives were also offered instead of the troublesome line 'the peaceful coil of that innocent-looking belly'. They were: 'That inno-cent-looking belly', 'That peaceful-looking coil', or 'That peaceful-looking belly'. Two of them were obvious attempts at circumvention and the Lord Chamberlain was not deceived. The reformulated 'python' paaragraph was allowed, dropping the allusion to Alison's post-coital state. And reference to 'That peaceful-looking coil' was permitted but with no mention of a 'belly'. Apart from a further, final revision initiated by Richardson and Osborne, for a change, which recommended dispensing with 'You little existentialist' and replacing it by 'Blimey, you ought to be Prime Minister' – which was easily approved – the final manuscript was granted a licence on 28 March, and *Look Back in Anger* was given its premiere on 8 May 1956.

Though the Lord Chamberlain's Office was ostensibly finished with this play, they had not heard the last of it. A letter was written by an irate member of the public to R. A. Butler in October 1957 urging the Home Secretary to use his 'power and influence to have the play *Look Back in Anger* by John Osborne withdrawn both from stage and (I understand) screen'. What rankled was the fact that the New Malvern Players were staging it at the local Torquay Pavilion that week. 'Surely the complete dialogue of this production could not have been passed by the censor?', the enquirer demanded, given that 'It is the conception of a deceased and depraved mentality and the outpourings of a cesspool mind.' 'I am indeed at a loss to understand how this play should reach the English stage,' he stated, as he implored finally: 'I beg of you in the interests of what is left of sanctity and sanity to give this matter your immediate and earnest attention.' 'Treat officially,' noted Butler's private secretary, before passing the letter over to the Lord Chamberlain's Office for a formal reply. The Assistant Comptroller took over the task. After pointing out that 'The Lord Chamberlain, of course, is only responsible for stage plays and censorship of the films is done by the British Board of Film Censors,' Brigadier Sir Norman Gwatkin added, sympathetically:

> The play to which you refer was submitted here some time ago and a considerable number of amendments required. When these were made the Lord Chamberlain felt that, unpleasant though the play was in many ways, it was not one that he could rightly ban in 1956. However the Lord Chamberlain is grateful to you for having troubled to write as it helps him very much in his difficult task to hear what the public reactions are.

'Tormented' of Torquay was plainly not enamoured of Mr Osborne's work. Nor, indeed, were the theatre censors exactly pleased with his efforts. Though his reputation as a new and dynamic playwright soared on the basis of *Look Back in Anger*, the examiners lamented the trend he had started for 'realistic plays'. Despite the intermittent public and occasional private criticism, by the end of 1957 Osborne had enjoyed considerable success with both *Look Back in Anger* and its follow-up, *The Entertainer*. The dramatist was very much in demand and inevitably attracted the attention of many a film producer eager to adapt his material for the cinema. Several factors contrived, however, to prevent the likelihood of any speedy transfer from stage to screen. Though Osborne had immediately been approached with several offers for the film rights to *Look Back in Anger*, for instance, including one from John and James Woolf of Romulus Films in the autumn of 1956, he was keen on retaining a close working relationship with Tony Richardson, who had brought him such notoriety and success.

Life for both of them, furthermore, was nothing if not exceptionally busy. *Look Back in Anger* transferred from the Royal Court to the Lyric Theatre, Hammersmith, on 5 November 1956, and was then taken back to the Court on 11 March 1957, each occasion involving extensive cast changes and further rehearsal time. *The Entertainer* transferred to the Palace Theatre, again with cast changes. Meanwhile, the original Royal Court cast of *Look Back in Anger* was reassembled by Tony Richardson for an American production and all decisions on film matters were postponed until after its Broadway premiere on 1 October 1957.

The acclaim which greeted the Broadway presentation of *Look Back in Anger* not only confirmed Osborne's reputation as a playwright of note but also produced an 'angel' for their film plans in the form of Harry Saltzman. Saltzman, a Quebec-born North American and 'a natural entrepreneur', capitalised on the play's new-found international reputation and Richard Burton's reported interest in playing the part of Jimmy Porter, to extract a budget of between £200,000 and £250,000 from Warner Brothers and Associated British-Pathé. Saltzman, Osborne and Richardson formed Woodfall Films to ensure they retained artistic control and a measure of independence. Given their inexperience of feature-film production, however, some compromises were inevitable at the outset. Of the original cast, for example, only Mary Ure was retained for the role of Alison, and Claire Bloom, who like Burton had a cinema following, was brought in for the part of Helena. Nigel Kneale, an accomplished writer for film and television and author of BBC TV's 1953 sensational science-fiction serial, *The Quatermass Experiment*, was engaged to adapt Osborne's play for the screen. Osborne provided 'additional dialogue' and received his share in the sale of the film rights of his play. Richardson, for his part, got nothing by way of a fee for directing.[6]

Kneale's draft film script of *Look Back in Anger* consciously opened the play out and located several sequences outside the immediate confines of the Porters' claustrophobic flat. In particular, he added more business

Figure 8 Richard Burton and Claire Bloom star in Tony Richardson's screen version of John Osborne's play *Look Book in Anger* (GB, 1959). Woodfall/Associated British/The Kobal Collection

showing Jimmy and Cliff as they run their market stall, as well as a scene in which Alison visits a doctor to confirm her pregnancy and enquires, 'Is it too late to do anything?' (In the play, this dialogue about a possible abortion is presented as a confidential chat between Cliff and Alison.) Some things were sacrificed, notably Jimmy's important speech about there being 'no good brave causes left' to fight for. To make up for that omission, in particular, the script introduced a new character – an Indian stall-holder who, when threatened with racist taunts and pressure, is championed by Jimmy but finally evicted from the market place. Jimmy's jazz background was elaborated and his relationship with Ma Tanner, the mother of his old friend, fleshed out by presenting her in person (as played by Edith Evans). For all the changes, however, Tony Richardson's purpose was clear: 'It is absolutely vital to get into British films the same sort of impact and sense of life that what you can loosely call the Angry Young Man cult has had in the theatre and literary worlds.' 'It is,' he maintained, 'a desperate need.'[7]

The point was not lost on the BBFC's readers when Kneale's film script of Osborne's play was presented for their consideration at the end of August

1958. They were no more happy with it than the Lord Chamberlain's Office had been with the original stage play. Audrey Field commented:[8]

> This sounds dull – and for a very good reason. It *is* dull. Class consciousness is a very common failing. But it has been chewed over enough, and *more* than enough, in the last few years. And all the chewing only makes people worse in this respect than they were before. I saw the play on television and I thought then that it was very mediocre, though good acting did a lot to make it seem better than it was. The film script is even less good, missing no opportunity of dragging in tendentious and irrelevant stuff about white people bullying Indians, etc. It packs less punch than the play and I find it difficult to assess from the censorship point of view. The story is basically 'A' but is adorned with gross and violent language which serves to make it sound like an 'X'. The proper course for the company to take would be to modify the dialogue with a view to getting an 'A' certificate. But I do not think they would do this. In default of this, we could throw our previous standards overboard and give an 'A' to the film without asking for any verbal changes. But I do not think we would do this, and I hope we would not.
>
> We have sometimes been too mealy-mouthed in the past but there is a limit to what we ought to sanction for children. And I think the limit is exceeded in certain passages of this film. The other possibility would be to allow the film uncut for 'X' and perhaps this would be politic, as many people who ought to know think John Osborne's work beyond criticism.

A long list of offending words and phrases was appended with notice of the fact that 'The bloodies are not spared in this script and are usually ugly in the context.' Field took particular exception to the mention of a possible abortion and reacted to Jimmy's 'great pleasure of lovemaking speech' in precisely the same way the theatre censors had responded to it from the outset, highlighting the 'python' reference as a potential problem. This was no great surprise, perhaps, given that talk of Alison's post-coital reaction – 'she lies back afterwards like a puffed-out python to sleep it off' – had been cannily reinserted. Jimmy's continual vilification of his wife was frowned upon, once again, not least his lines: 'I want to see you grovel. I want to see your face rubbed in the mud.' 'This element of sado-masochism' clearly justified an 'X' certificate, Field felt, especially 'when coupled with some fairly frank love stuff.' 'Perhaps I am off beam in even thinking it a bad "X",' she pondered, before suggesting an instant remedy for Jimmy Porter's ills: 'It's just that it seems to me such a wearisome fuss about nothing that couldn't be cured by hard manual labour or going off to the Dominions out of reach of the in-laws.'

A second BBFC script reader, Frank Crofts, shared many of Field's misgivings and clearly felt Jimmy Porter's masochistic streak extended beyond the bounds of his private and personal relationship with Alison:

> It is astonishing that anyone should consider this anything but trite and dreary rubbish. One can imagine Jimmy up to a point though I think he is rather a caricature. But one

cannot have sympathy with him, with his self-pity, his love-hate silliness, his bullying and his masochistic wish not to take advantage of his education. As for Alison and Helena, they are unreal. Alison married Jimmy because he was sun-burnt when she first saw him and because her family (naturally) didn't like him. Helena actively disliked him till she suddenly seduced him. One simply cannot believe a well educated, reasonable girl falling for a seedy little twerp like him. One can put up with his boorishness, his cruelty and his stupidity, but not with his being such a bore.

Having served for a lengthy spell in the Indian civil service before joining the BBFC in 1948, Crofts was particularly upset that the script's references to India were frequently wrong when mentioning Alison's father, Colonel Redfern. 'No one from India brings a household of Indian furniture back with them,' he continued, and 'Gurkhas don't have daggers but very heavy sharp knives known as khukris.' At the last, however, for all his reservations, Crofts differed from Field in concluding: 'I don't think this is really "X". I think it should be passed for "A".'

John Trevelyan, then, had to deal with a conflict of opinion among his readers. Whereas one basically felt the completed film should be given an 'X' certificate, the other believed it would probably pass for the 'A' category. His dilemma was compounded by other matters which required serious attention given that the prospect of a film based on a John Osborne play clearly posed additional problems of note. Osborne, plainly, was perceived as the spearhead of a new movement, in both theatre and literature, which threatened to invade the domain of the cinema and could hardly be treated lightly. Not that Trevelyan intended doing anything of the sort. He had, after all, his own good reasons for wanting to establish where the angry young men would fall in the canon of film censorship, and these lay largely in his overall wish to promote 'adult' films of 'quality' and his desire to lend greater respectability to the 'X' category. *Look Back in Anger*, like *Room at the Top*, which Trevelyan was dealing with concurrently, had just the right credentials – literary pedigree and 'realist' concerns – to accommodate such ambitions. It presented yet another opportunity to settle the critical consensus that Trevelyan wanted to see established for the 'X' certificate.[9]

Trevelyan, therefore, marshalled all the arguments he could possibly muster when seeking to persuade the film-makers of the value in accepting an 'X' on this occasion. He began by inviting Frederick Gotfurt, the scenario editor at Associated British, to his office for a discussion on the BBFC's reservations over the script, following it up the next day with a letter summarising the major points at issue:

This script presents us with a rather unusual problem. The story is basically one which would be eligible for the 'A' category but the dialogue is not suitable for this category. The question then arises whether we work on the basis that the film will have an 'X' certificate, in which case I think we could accept this script virtually unaltered, or whether we work on the basis that the film will have an 'A' certificate, in which case there would, I think, have to be quite a number of alterations to the dialogue. I personally would be most reluctant to alter the dialogue to any extent since I think it will be difficult to establish the character of Jimmy Porter if his language is toned down. In any case this is an important play and people who have seen the play in London will expect the dialogue and characterisations to be roughly the same.

I hope therefore that the company will be prepared to accept an 'X' certificate. But I realise that they may feel that an 'X' certificate will attract not only a smaller audience but an audience which would include some who will be disappointed not to find what is all too frequently shown in this category. As I explained to you, it has always been our intention and hope that the films in the 'X' category would be largely those with adult themes and adult treatment, but I have to admit that it has not always worked out this way except in the case of certain films. I think one can claim that, although the story is one which would be suitable for the 'A' category, the theme behind the story is really adult.

Trevelyan proceeded to outline an extensive list comprising no less than twenty-four significant items which gave rise for concern. Though he welcomed a further meeting to elaborate these matters, if required, his preferred course of action was made abundantly clear – they should agree to take an 'X' certificate. The incentives he offered in that regard, and the probable pitfalls, were plain to see:

I would of course be prepared to discuss these points in detail, one by one, and we might not insist on all of those that I have listed, but I think I have given enough to show you that we would probably require a number of dialogue alterations. I am somewhat influenced in my opinion that this would be better as an 'X' film by the fact that you have a really good cast, and I think that Richard Burton's performance as Jimmy will have a considerable impact which will heighten his sado–masochistic treatment of Alison.

Gotfurt returned for another discussion two weeks later, this time bringing Harry Saltzman with him. Obviously, they were both worried about the prospect of an 'X' certificate and its likely effect on the box-office potential of their film. Trevelyan reiterated his fears about 'the forthright language used' and Jimmy's sado-masochistic treatment of Alison. It was decided they would definitely omit the word 'Christ' – 'a word that we prefer not to have even in the "X" category' – and seek substitutes for 'bitch', 'virgin' and 'bastard'. In addition, they would carefully consider the 'implied references to abortion' so as to render them 'intelligible to adults and unintelligible to children'. Trevelyan, for his part, conceded that 'scripts are apt to be misleading' and that 'some of the dialogue which appears offensive on paper may well sound less offensive in the completed film'. After hearing

Saltzman's ideas regarding their production plans, he was willing to accept that 'the important scenes will be treated with sincerity and restraint'. 'When we see the film,' he promised finally, 'we will give fair consideration to your request that it should have an "A" category.' 'I cannot of course,' he concluded, 'commit the Board to a category at this stage.'

One can only speculate about Saltzman's reactions to the meeting: whether he believed they could provide sufficient 'sincerity and restraint' to merit an 'A'; whether he was more impressed by Trevelyan's persuasive arguments that they should settle for an 'X'; or whether, quite simply, he was determined most of all upon bringing the film to fruition in a fashion that best pleased its makers. Whatever the reasons, only five of Trevelyan's list of twenty-four suggested amendments had been made when the film was completed and presented for award of a certificate in the spring of 1959. In particular, the passing reference to abortion was left precisely as intended in the original version. But by the start of 1959, of course, Trevelyan had already dealt with the finished film of *Room at the Top* and had pretty much resolved, to his own satisfaction at least, the thorny problem of what constituted 'adult' films and 'quality' cinema. *Look Back in Anger* was therefore given the 'X' rating it had been virtually guaranteed at the outset, and no cuts were required.

Alfie

Bill Naughton's stage play of *Alfie* was based on his radio play, *Alfie Elkins and his Little Life*, which was first presented on the BBC's *Third Programme* from 9.10 p.m. to 10.25 p.m. on 7 January 1962 in a production by Douglas Cleverdon. The radio play was much shorter than the later stage version, and a key abortion scene, depicting a successful termination of pregnancy, was also briefly dealt with and discreetly placed towards the end of the drama. Nonetheless, audience research revealed that some listeners found it 'difficult to stomach' and there were criticisms from a minority of the sample that the programme was 'really too sordid for words'. 'Time was,' one listener complained, 'when the BBC would not have considered broadcasting anything so revolting.' Another maintained it was 'not so much kitchen sink as kitchen garbage tin', while a schoolmaster who had enjoyed previous Bill Naughton plays wrote that 'after the first half-hour it became progressively more nauseating; only curiosity as to whether it could get any worse kept me listening after the revolting abortion scene'. 'We know Mr Naughton's gift for portraying working-class life,' he concluded, but 'I regret he should have become so tasteless – what happened to his sense of humour?'

But most listeners claimed to have enjoyed the broadcast, thereby producing 'an appreciation index of 73, well above the current average (63) for *Third Programme* features.' Furthermore, audience reaction among the sample listening public who heard all or most of the play was decidedly favourable:

A large majority of the sample had a high opinion of the programme and had evidently been completely absorbed, even fascinated; it was a memorable piece, some said, which still haunted them. Bill Naughton who continued to be 'a miraculous observer' had produced a brilliant and 'painfully acute' portrait of Alfie, a Cockney character almost impervious to all interests save hard cash and women. It seemed, many listeners said, completely authentic, a moving, spell-binding, disturbing portrayal of an immature man to whom cold self-interest had become the one value he recognised but in whom still survived (bewildering to himself) better impulses which tried to struggle to the surface. Much of what Alfie Elkins said and did was 'appalling', but yet they could not wholly dislike him, listeners sometimes said; his candour and lack of hypocrisy were redeeming features. This 'pithy analysis' was commended as unsentimental ('I liked the unemotional almost documentary slant'); neither did the author indulge in tedious 'moralising'. 'Richly comic' in places, the programme trod the dividing line between comedy and sordid tragedy with complete assurance. It was colourful throughout and the dialogue delighted many listeners by its realism and authenticity ('astonishingly accurate'). Criticisms of any aspect of the production were few indeed. The vivid way in which Alfie and his life had been communicated to the listener was often warmly praised and Bill Owen [as Alfie] was frequently spoken of in the highest terms.

Given the undoubted popularity the play had enjoyed, it was little wonder the BBC chose to repeat the broadcast. It was repeated twice on the *Third Programme* during 1962, in fact, at 6.30 p.m. on 3 February and at 8 p.m. on 11 September. On 16 September, moreover, it was reviewed by *The Critics* including Stephen Potter, Dilys Powell, and Edward Lucie-Smith, where once again it was favourably received and highly praised. It was agreed that the play 'did have a very strong moral basis' though reservations were expressed about the abortion scene, which some found 'excessive'.[10]

Clearly, Bill Naughton must have heard enough to convince him the play was well worth expanding and adapting for full stage presentation, which he duly did. Since he was already contracted to the Mermaid Theatre for a production in March 1963 of his play *All in Good Time*, it made sense to add *Alfie* to Bernard Miles's programme as part of a short Naughton season, with a first night planned for the latter on 19 June 1963. Neither play, of course, escaped the strictures of the Lord Chamberlain's Office.

Initially, at least, *All in Good Time* engendered something of a hostile reaction as far as the Lord Chamberlain's play reader, Maurice Coles, was concerned. Plainly perturbed at the likelihood of a play which he felt would probably give offence in some quarters – for its chosen theme, as well as its mode of expression – his reservations were expressed on both fronts in a long and jaundiced report of 18 January 1963, which began:

> Whether or not you decide to license this play depends upon the overall policy of the Lord Chamberlain. The subject of the play is male impotence. Most of the play is concerned with the inability of the bridegroom, Arthur Fitton, to consummate his marriage to Violet; with the effect this knowledge has on his parents – Ezra and Lucy Fitton – and on his bride's parents – Mr and Mrs Piper; and with the reasons for Arthur's impotence. Both families are working class, so the subject is discussed from every possible angle in language which is often crude. In the course of the play it is suggested, among other things, that Ezra Fitton has – or had – homosexual tendencies, had himself been impotent with his wife throughout his married life, and that Arthur is in fact the result of an affair between Lucy Fitton and Ezra's best friend (to whom Ezra was unnaturally attracted), who disappeared after he had seduced Lucy.

Coles proceeded to outline in detail no less than twenty-two passages which he felt required to be further and carefully scrutinised. Five of them were deemed especially troublesome: a crude joke about the first-night prank done to a newly married couple in which 'fine crystals' were put between the sheets of their bed; Ezra's cursing when he cannot find a bedroom chamber-pot and his recourse to the colloquialism 'sod'; a fleeting reference to 'the safe period system' of contraception; and, in the realms of 'language', once again, use of the phrase 'beggar off'. A warning was also issued against the proposed bit of stage 'business' in which Arthur 'slowly edges her [his bride] to the bed and brings her down on it'.[11]

When passed on afterwards to the Lord Chamberlain for summary comment on the play's worth, however, matters soon took a decided turn for the better. Although it was agreed that the five highlighted areas of key concern should certainly be changed or cut out altogether – not least, the occasional words such as 'sod' or 'beggar off', and the promised stage 'business' on the bed – Lord Scarbrough, for his part, approved of allowing the play to progress into production. He was less certain whether *All in Good Time* would turn out to be widely popular or generally appealing in the eyes of theatregoers. But he was sure that it hardly merited substantial revision for all that, and the play even merited a modicum of praise in Scarbrough's opinion:

> I have read this through. It is not obscene. The question to be decided is whether the main subject presents too much embarrassment. I think the present generation can take it quite easily. It seems to me rather well put together. Whether an audience wider than the present generation – i.e. including older people – will take to it, must await their judgment. It may be licensed.

Further comment was forthcoming from the Assistant Comptroller, Eric Penn, who also decided 'There is nothing disgusting in it.' 'This play is entirely about a newly-married couple not being able to sleep with each other. There are long discussions on the reason why and every encouragement given to them by both sets of parents,' he added, but 'Victory is achieved in the end.' Albeit clearly determined to introduce a doleful note into the deliberations, as ever, when raising the question 'Is this the sort of discussion that one wishes to hear in a theatre?', Penn, too, was grudgingly resigned to let the play pass, and concluded: 'I suppose it is acceptable in 1963.' In the event, however, the Lord Chamberlain's Office still considered that *All in Good Time* required to be carefully watched and followed up in view of the possibility, especially, that new-found stage business might be introduced during the course of rehearsals. Thus, while pre-production scrutiny of the play script had done its job well enough, other measures were available to be utilised in the cause of continued censorship vigilance. Post-production review of the final stage presentation, in effect, was one further course of action that was often employed (and also rigorously applied in the case of *Alfie*).

Given that the script had already received the nod of approval from the Lord Chamberlain himself, Penn enquired whether the usual stipulation that 'plays that may give cause for complaint be checked three days after the first performance' would need to be applied in the case of Naughton's *All in Good Time*, and he queried whether it should be done on this occasion. 'Much as I dislike having to say so,' the Assistant Secretary replied, 'I think there is too much bedroom [business] and that the action *does* want a check.' His note was accompanied by the cynical, if perhaps pragmatic, comment: 'I don't trust any manager these days.' On viewing the play for himself, at last, Eric Penn was reassured that all was well and he confirmed the now widely held opinion among the examiners that 'it is not disgusting but very funny'.[12]

So it proved as far as many theatre audiences were concerned, moreover, thereby further enhancing the play's commercial prospects and virtually guaranteeing its certain adaptation for the cinema. Unlike Naughton's companion-piece of *Alfie*, however, the transition from stage to screen for *All in Good Time* followed a smoothly transacted and easily negotiated path. In the event, the BBFC found no more to worry about the Boulting brothers' retitled film of *The Family Way*, in 1966, than the Lord Chamberlain's men had some years previously, in 1963, with *All in Good Time*[13]. And that, principally, was because the BBFC took its lead from the Lord Chamberlain's Office. *Alfie*, by contrast, encountered innumerable problems with the theatre examiners. It required substantial discussions and revisions – a process which was endured in large measure over again when the screenplay was eventually tendered by director Lewis Gilbert for pre-production scrutiny at the BBFC.

With a first night planned for 19 June 1963, the script of Bill Naughton's play, *Alfie*, was sent for licence to the Lord Chamberlain's Office on 20 January 1963, two days after *All in Good Time* had come up for scrutiny. Its origins as a radio play were evident in some of the dramatic techniques contemplated for the stage Moreover, the import of the abortion scene, now much elaborated, could not be missed. The play reader, Maurice Coles, reported his comments on the same day, as follows:

> This is the study of the sexual adventures of a Cockney wide boy, Alfie Elkins. Alfie himself is the narrator and fairly long sections of the play are narrative soliloquies as Alfie tells his story to the audience. According to him, his sex life is one long struggle against his better nature, against his yearnings for domesticity – but habit dies hard and the end of the play sees him without a woman once again but looking forward to the next one.
>
> The play is well in the fashionable rut of sordid realism – the more sordid the better – includes an abortion on stage (though behind a screen) complete with groans and cries of pain which I cannot think can be allowed and to which I have drawn attention in the list of possible deletions and alterations below . . . This is the abortion scene, involving Lily, Alfie and the abortionist. The abortion takes place on stage, behind a screen, and little is left to the imagination. There is even a description of the foetus and Alfie's disposal of it by flushing it down the lavatory. Just how much, if any, of this scene is to be allowed I leave to you . . . It is perhaps worth mentioning that this play is by the same author as *All in Good Time* which deals with male impotence and which I returned to you a day or so ago. It seems that *Alfie* is to follow the play at the Mermaid. Is there to be a third, forming a sort of trilogy of the sex life of the mole?

'Cut. Cut it all,' was the Assistant Comptroller's response to the reader's query as to how much of the abortion scene might be allowed. Eric Penn was also unhappy with the play generally, and said as much in a memorandum to the Lord Chamberlain: '*Alfie* is a dull and horrid play.' 'Its only merits are the Cockney language of the script', he continued, 'and possibly the representation of life in the East End.' In that regard he was willing to concede that 'many questionable bits of language have been let go in our recommendations'. However, his unease was evident all the same and even concessions over language were grudgingly given. 'This play is rougher than *All in Good Time*', he stated, and 'If this is really considered entertainment in 1963, perhaps it should be allowed; if so it will be interesting to see the reaction.' The abortion scene, however, simply could not be allowed. The Lord Chamberlain agreed and required that it be 'altered or omitted altogether'.[14]

Since they were plainly determined not to be beaten in the matter of the abortion scene, if nothing else, the Mermaid Theatre marshalled its arguments and forces accordingly. 'In view of the fact that this play was presented on the *Third Programme* and received magnificent press,' Bernard Miles wrote in reply, 'may I bring the author and Mr Ide [the theatre administrator] along to discuss the matter in person?' So, indeed, he did. Plainly, the Lord Chamberlain's men were open to discussion, at least. But while they proved malleable on some matters, they were intransigent on others and the resulting discussions were not wholly to the visitors' liking:

> At their request, Bernard Miles and Bill Naughton were interviewed by Col. Penn and Mr Hill [assistant secretary]. The cuts in this piece were agreed by them without question, except for the abortion scene, which is indeed a climacteric in Alfie's life. Our opposition to this scene was influenced by the fact that a scene revolving around the preparations for and after effects of an abortion were all in *I Am a Camera* in 1954. Mild though these were they did give offence.
>
> It was explained to the visitors that it was accepted by the Lord Chamberlain that the play was a moral rather than an immoral one, and that it was realised that the basic facts of life were nowadays discussed freely in any company; but that in our opinion some of the clinical and practical detail in the play was of such a disgusting nature in the literal sense of the word that it was felt that to sanction it would give a precedent for action and properties which could end by blunting the sensibilities of and indeed brutalising the audience. Our viewpoint was accepted at least as a tenable one and Mr Miles read through the abortion scene which was reviewed from that aspect.

If the extraordinary read-through which followed there and then, on the spot, extracted one notable concession, it also highlighted a host of potential problems. The abortion scene might just be allowed, it seemed, but 'the operation ought to be conducted off-stage', thereby also necessitating the removal of large amounts of vital dialogue and associated business. There should be no 'jingle of instruments' nor talk of 'scrubbing away' on the abortionist's part; and no 'cries', 'groans', 'sudden pain and winces' from Lily. 'Remember, the bed is to be off-stage,' it was stated, and the abortionist should 'leave the stage instead of going behind the screen'. Finally, and equally important, most references to disposal of the aborted foetus should be deleted.

Though Bernard Miles and Bill Naughton expressed a willingness to operate within these constraints and to produce a rewritten abortion scene which incorporated the new proposals, they understandably wanted some 'assurance' they would not be 'wasting their time' on the revisions. They sought, in short, advance approval for their efforts since that would provide 'sufficient basis upon which to undertake the additional work'. It was a shrewd and clever move but never likely to win the day. Inevitably, no such assurance was forthcoming. Still, the examiners were more hopeful of a successful outcome to everybody's endeavours:

> It is felt that the scene even when rewritten will be a strong one and will inevitably give offence particularly to some ladies. Nevertheless the play is a straightforward depiction of what is unfortunately a real type, the facts of the play tend to social not anti-social ends, and the acceptance by most people these days of any subject for discussion – VD, homosexuality, etc. – make the scene in our opinion acceptable if not eminently desirable.

In the final analysis, of course, the key decision on revisions to the script rested with the Lord Chamberlain. Moreover, the Lord Chamberlain had just changed. When *Alfie* first landed on the play reader's desk, Lord Scarbrough had been in charge. Now it was Lord Cobbold. However, he was no more inclined to give advance approval than his predecessor had been. Once he had been apprised of the situation by his Assistant Comptroller, and done his homework appropriately, Cobbold endorsed everything the Mermaid representatives had already been told:

> I have read this play and attached papers and also the relevant sections of *I Am a Camera*. The latter seem to be innocuous and not to set too much of a precedent for this scene. I agree that the modifications of the abortion scene proposed at your meeting with Mr Miles and the author make it a lot less objectionable: in particular I am sure that all action relating to the abortion must take place off-stage. But my present feeling is that the scene, even if rewritten on the lines of the interview with Mr Miles, would still be likely to give offence to a lot of people.
>
> I cannot give a definite decision without seeing a rewrite. Nor can I give any commitment not to ask for further alteration. If Mr Miles and the author think it worthwhile to have another shot at it on this understanding, I shall of course be very willing to look at it.

'The Lord Chamberlain is still disturbed about the possible effects of this [abortion] scene', Bernard Miles was told emphatically, and 'feels very dubious about the whole of it'. 'Even with the modification which we agreed provisionally between us,' it was reiterated, 'he is still not prepared to give an unqualified assurance that the scene will be allowed.'

The ball, quite simply, was back in Miles's and Naughton's court. A new script was produced on 3 May 1963. It was, they promised, 'entirely revised and rewritten'. In truth, it was nothing of the sort. If their reaction was predictable as far as the abortion scene was concerned, which was suitably toned down to meet the theatre examiners' needs, they now proved less than willing to accommodate the other demands made of them. Hoping, perhaps, that arguments over the abortion scene had taken the new Lord Chamberlain's mind off everything else required by the readers,

Naughton had quietly proceeded to forget about them. If one battle had been lost, the war was still engaged. But some examiners were ever alert. The reader of the rewritten script – Maurice Coles, once again – commented on 20 May 1963:

> The play has been considerably revised though the general outline of the plot remains unchanged. I have studied the correspondence and memoranda relating to the play and although a lot has been done to tone down the abortion scene, with the operation itself taking place off-stage, some objectionable matter remains. I notice also that no notice has been taken of the other cuts or amendments, outside the abortion scene, called for in your letter of 25 January.

Although the Assistant Comptroller also admitted that the new edition had been 'considerably tidied up from the original', not least regarding the abortion, he too felt prompted to remind the Mermaid Theatre of what had previously been required by way of exceptions generally. For good measure, he added a list of exceptions to material which appeared for the first time in the revised script. Once everything had been dealt with, and not before, the play would be granted a licence. A long, carefully detailed reply from the Mermaid management on 30 May, with further revisions, finally put paid to all the Lord Chamberlain's objections, and *Alfie* was given a licence on 5 June 1963, exactly two weeks to the day before its opening night destined for 19 June. Lest they be taken by surprise, however, plans were made at the Lord Chamberlain's Office on 17 June to ensure the finished production also met with approval. 'I see that this play by Bill Naughton containing the abortion scene etc., etc., is being presented at the Mermaid for the first time on Wednesday 19 June,' Eric Penn recorded. 'In view of the contents of this play, I think that this should be inspected very early on and may arrangements therefore be made for this to happen either on the first or second night.'

The assistant secretary, Ronald Hill, was duly dispatched to watch the play on the second night of presentation and the results of his 'incognito inspection' were immediately forthcoming. While he was clearly satisfied with the staging of the abortion scene – and, indeed, noted the producers had done more than required of them – he plainly had reservations regarding other bits of stage 'business', not to mention a profound distaste for the play, generally, as he reported on 21 June 1963:

> I went last night to the Mermaid Theatre to see *Alfie*. I occupied stall no. D23 and I enclose the programme. The play reads better than it acts and I thought the acting, with the exception of John Neville, so bad that at times the piece instead of being tragi-comedy came perilously close to bathos. Generally speaking, and for these days, there was nothing to which real exception could be taken . . .

1. Reference to 'putting your knee on the steering wheel' – still there which was prohibited.

2. A piece of 'business' – 'Alfie throws back the girl's draws' – surprised we had allowed.

3. Unscripted 'business' with Alfie showing there was no hot water bottle in bed, therefore no intercourse tonight.

4. In several respects the producer has modified what the Lord Chamberlain has allowed – the reference to Lily and Alfie not taking precautions is dropped, and so is all 'business' of a clinical sort connected with the abortion. The practioner merely calls and goes out with Lily to another room, and she comes back in a dressing gown.

5. 'Breast squeezing' . . . 'business' with Ruby in 'house coat and undies'.

We have in our strait-laced past always forbidden breast squeezing and if you admit even a short squeeze you lose complete control: lengthened squeezes, other actions, and greater degrees of breast nudity then follow and short of seeing every performance it is impossible to decide what is really impermissible and what is mildly objectionable. Personally, I would stop this act completely.

If the assistant secretary was not impressed by the play or the cast, apart from John Neville – which included Glenda Jackson and Gemma Jones in leading roles – a good many people were. The Mermaid was doing considerable business. And 'breast squeezing', inevitably, was sufficient cause for concern to the censors in itself. To settle his mind on that score, once and for all, the Assistant Comptroller dutifully trooped along to see the play as well. While the assistant secretary's viewing had been done 'incognito' though still 'official', however, the Assistant Comptroller's visit was 'open' and acknowledged by all parties. Penn responded on 27 June:

> We discussed this play this morning as a result of Hill's official visit (incognito) on the 20 June and my own open visit on 26 June. I phoned Bernard Miles this morning and have explained the Lord Chamberlain's rule that breasts may not be touched. I explained the reason for this is the difficulty in establishing a dividing line between brushing gently against the bosom and gripping them. Bernard Miles said that he appreciated this and will have any touching or handling of the breasts of Ruby immediately stopped. I accepted his suggestion that Alfie could outline the shape of Ruby's bosom with the hand at a safe distance away and he said that if anyone from the Lord Chamberlain's office wished to come and see this new arrangement, he hoped they would do so . . .

It was, of course, hardly necessary. No more visits were required – 'incognito', 'official', open or otherwise. The Lord Chamberlain's Office had done its job well enough. Not that everybody was satisfied. The Stage Plays Sub-Committee of the Public Morality Council, for example, sent its own 'reporter' along to view *Alfie* and felt certain some things had been slipped in after submission with regard to the abortion scene, especially. It noted in a letter to the Lord Chamberlain of 12 September:

> [We] discussed this play which came under severe criticism embodying as it does seduction, abortion, adultery and in the view of the Committee was thoroughly objectionable, despite the skill demonstrated by Mr John Neville in the chief part. The penultimate scene seemed so bad to our reporter as to cause him to wonder whether it had been in fact added after submission to your Lordship for licensing. Whatever the facts are, my Committee would request some word from your Lordship as to the reasons which influenced you in granting a licence for a play of this deplorable character.

The Lord Chamberlain was particularly well placed to respond on this occasion, given the extent of scrutiny afforded *Alfie* at both the pre-production and post-production stages, and did so just two weeks later, on 25 September:

> The scene was not allowed in its original form and at my request the author modified it radically. To be sure the scene was played in an acceptable manner, by modern standards, I arranged for it to be inspected and was informed that the producer had conformed entirely to my directions. The play certainly deals with unpleasant subjects and may not be to everybody's taste. But I hope that your Committee would agree that this is not of itself sufficient reason for banning the play. My endeavour is to form a judgement, admittedly not easy, as to whether such subjects are treated seriously or otherwise, whether the production would normally be regarded as an incitement or a deterrent to immorality, and whether particular scenes or words would, in the present broad state of public opinion, cause general offence to the theatregoing public. The present production (after considerable cuts and alterations at my request) seemed to justify a licence. I think, if I may say so, without disrespect to your Committee, that the attitude of responsible critics and of the general theatregoing public towards the production confirms my judgement.

Norman Gwatkin, the Comptroller, added by way of a cryptic, if strictly confidential comment to the Lord Chamberlain's letter: 'I particularly like this last sentence and I hope they will appreciate the word "responsible". They make occasional sallies in order that they may say that they have done so in the book being produced now and again to wheedle subscriptions from gullible old ladies.' In the event, however, the Lord Chamberlain did not get off entirely on this occasion. Another letter from the Public Morality Council, on 9 October 1963, made it abundantly clear it did not agree with the Lord Chamberlain's point of view:

> I am to suggest that the claims of 'broad-mindedness' should not be accorded too ready an acceptance by your Lordship. Broad-mindedness, in fact, is generally a euphemism for departures from what are generally recognised as decencies of life and it would be reassuring to my Council if you could possibly indicate how far in the direction of broad-mindedness you are prepared to go in licensing plays for

public performance. The line must be drawn between decency and indecency and my Committee feels strongly that in much of modern entertainment (so called) that line is receding dangerously. My Committee makes this point with respect and would add that the play *Alfie* certainly did not seem to our visitors to treat seriously the important matters with which the play deals and hence came under criticism accordingly.

By the time, then, that the film script for *Alfie* landed in the BBFC's lap, in April 1965, it had been through the censorship treadmill already and shorn of several vital elements. While Bill Naughton undoubtedly grasped the opportunity offered by the prospect of a film production to reinsert some of his earlier material – generally lines of dialogue which he had clearly always treasured – the plain fact of the matter is that his script stayed within the limits of what the theatre censors had allowed. Crucially, he chose not to overstep the mark when broaching contentious issues such as abortion. Changes were made, to be sure, to accommodate the demands of working on film as much as anything else. New characters and outside locations were added by director Lewis Gilbert to flesh out the proceedings. But they were hardly substantial changes for all that. Some matters previously consigned off-stage during the abortion scene, for instance, now moved inevitably into the foreground and within view of the camera, with the abortionist plainly on show for one thing. It was done cautiously, however, without graphic or explicit depiction of any controversial aspects, and the abortion itself still took place behind a curtain. The film depended essentially upon the ingredients which had accounted for its stage success – dialogue and characterisation. Most of all, Alfie's key speech about the aborted foetus of his child remained essentially as Naughton had fashioned it to meet the Lord Chamberlain's requirements. The film-makers stayed within the confines of what had already been permitted. It is no surprise therefore, in short, that the BBFC permitted an abortion scene and concluded, moreover, that it was 'the most moral' script they had encountered in some while. Nobody had ever doubted Naughton's 'moral' intent – the BBC critics had agreed it was evident in his original radio play and the theatre examiners had conceded it was present as well. The Lord Chamberlain's Office had, though, added considerably to the realisation of his 'moral' purpose. The BBFC, for its part, merely sought to do more of the same.

It had still to be an 'X', the script reader thought, 'because of the abortion and the grossness of some of the sex talk'. But 'We really do not feel that the sex is dragged in to titillate the idle mind,' Audrey Field concluded on 28 April, and 'I think there is a case for being as lenient as possible.' John Trevelyan concurred and informed Paramount British Pictures on 4 May

1965 that 'Obviously the film could be considered only for the "X" category.' 'It is, however, a basically moral theme,' he continued, 'and if it is made with integrity, as I have every reason to think that it will be, it should not give us much trouble.' As ever, his comments on precise detail ranged high and low:[15]

We would not object to seeing dogs sniffing each other, but there might be trouble if the behaviour of the dogs was a close parallel of what was going on in the car. We are a bit concerned about the script direction '. . . adjusts his trousers and generally makes himself less uncomfortable'. Discretion should be used here. The same applies to Siddie '. . . hitching up her skirt and tidying herself up'.

We think that you should omit the shot of Alfie taking the pair of panties from his pocket and tossing them across to Siddie with his line '. . . 'Ere mind you don't catch cold'. This is more suggestive than we would like.

Although this is not a censorship point, I am doubtful whether you can get a train from Waterloo Station to Forest Hill Station. I would have thought that Victoria was more likely.

Siddie's line 'So long as you don't have to give it to him', and Alfie's reply 'I would if I were built that way', may pass, but I think that you should shoot this scene in a way that would enable these lines to be removed if necessary.

The same applies to the explicit references to menstruation. They may pass, but you should provide for the possibility that they may not.

Here Alfie 'makes a sign' which appears to be a visual illustration of the fact that he has made his girl pregnant. I have no idea what sign is intended, but obviously care should be taken.

I do not know whether the choice of a banana in this scene is intended to have any visual significance or not. Since it might possibly give this impression I suggest that you might well substitute an apple or something of this kind.

I would have thought that there was no need for nudity in this scene. This kind of thing has become a cliché. It will certainly be cut if nudity is clearly visible, and at most only a backview would be accepted. I hope, however, that you will omit this entirely.

Ruby's costume should be adequate and not transparent.

I think the whole of this dialogue should be modified. As it stands it is descriptive of ardent love-making, and I think it would probably be cut if shot as it stands.

The script description reads 'Alfie and Ruby embrace with some extravagant love-making preamble'. It should not be too extravagant. We are not too happy about the phrase 'lust-box'. If you make use of this I think that you should have an alternative available.

These are strong scenes, but they will probably be acceptable in the context, since they do make a valid point against abortion. We would not want any really harrowing moans and screams.

These could be very moving scenes. Obviously we shall not see what Alfie sees in the bathroom.

We are not sure about the lines 'What, you doin' it with groups now then?' and 'Don't be disgusting'. These should be shot in a way that would enable them to be removed without difficulty if necessary.

I have one other general point. I think that the phrase 'having it off with', which is used from time to time, will probably be acceptable, but here again you might have an alternative for post-synching if it should not be.

So it went on. A bit of give and take as usual along carefully laid-down and well-formulated, if ever-evolving, lines. It is no wonder that John Trevelyan once described film censorship in terms of 'a curious arrangement' and, as he aptly added, 'rather typically British in some ways'.[16] When it finally reached the screen, on 24 March 1966, *Alfie* had been through a lengthy and arduous, if sometimes fruitful, process of censorship negotiation, something which contributed substantially to its emergence as a 'basically moral' film. Moreover, it turned out to be a considerable box-office hit in both Britain and America, thereby consolidating the 'cultural revolution' which had taken root in the UK since the turn of the 1960s and cementing the success on both sides of the Atlantic during the previous few years of rock groups like the Beatles and the Rolling Stones, not to mention films like *Dr No*, *Tom Jones* and *A Hard Day's Night*. British popular culture was riding the crest of a wave.

Apart from bringing instant critical acclaim for Michael Caine in its leading role, moreover, *Alfie* won plaudits galore for a host of supporting actors including Jane Asher, Shirley Anne Field, Julia Foster, Millicent Martin, Vivien Merchant, Shelley Winters and Denholm Elliott. The film of Bill Naughton's play was followed a year later by the 1967 Abortion Act, and within two years, yet again, by the 1968 Theatres Act, which proceeded to abolish the Lord Chamberlain's powers of theatre censorship. While social change was plainly taking place in some key areas, in short, it was still lacking in others and in some respects, arguably, matters appeared hardly to have changed. Film censorship as exercised by the BBFC, after all, continues to survive.

Notes

1. Arthur Marwick's case for a 'cultural revolution' is argued extensively and persuasively in numerous publications but his key book on the period remains *The Sixties* (Oxford: Oxford University Press, 1998).
2. John Sutherland, *Offensive Literature: Decensorship in Britain, 1960–1982* (London: Junction Books, 1982), p. 2.
3. Gwatkin is quoted in John Johnston, *The Lord Chamberlain's Blue Pencil* (London: Hodder and Stoughton, 1990), pp. 164–5; John Trevelyan's autobiographical account of his career is found in *What the Censor Saw* (London: Michael Joseph, 1973).
4. The critical and public reception afforded Osborne's first play to reach the London stage is discussed in John Russell Taylor (ed.), *John Osborne: Look Back in Anger, A Casebook* (Basingstoke: Macmillan, 1968), pp. 16–21, and Harry Ritchie, *Success Stories: Literature and the Media in England, 1950–1959* (London: Faber and Faber, 1988), pp. 25–31.
5. LCP Correspondence, *Look Back in Anger*, 1956/8932. Play reader's report, 1 March 1956, and all further memoranda related to same.
6. The events surrounding the transfer from stage to screen were outlined in a radio interview with Tony Richardson for *Frankly Speaking*, 12 December 1962, the script for which is held in the BBC Written Archives, Caversham. See also, 'Unwanted play starts a battle,' *Daily Mail*, 8 December 1956; 'Osborne sells for £35,000,' *Sunday Dispatch*, 13 October 1957; and Alexander Walker, *Hollywood, England: The British Film Industry in the Sixties* (London: Michael Joseph, 1974), pp. 56–60. For Nigel Kneale's career in television, see George W. Brandt (ed.), *British Television Drama* (Cambridge: Cambridge University Press, 1981), pp. 14 and 33. Saltzman, of course, later teamed up with Albert 'Cubby' Broccoli to produce *Dr No* (1962) and several other films in the immensely popular James Bond series.
7. Tony Richardson, 'The Man Behind an Angry-Young-Man,' *Films and Filming* (February 1959), p. 9. Penelope Houston observed Richardson at work on *Look Back in Anger* for *Sight and Sound*, 28/1 (1958/59), pp. 31–3. Osborne provided his own autobiographical account of events in *Almost a Gentleman* (London: Faber and Faber, 1991) and Richardson in *Long Distance Runner* (London: Faber and Faber, 1993).
8. BBFC file, *Look Back in Anger*. Reader's report, 28 August 1958. Remaining BBFC references come from this file.
9. Note also Ian Christie's apposite comment on the notion of 'quality' cinema: 'Above all, it reflects the deep-rooted British cultural bias towards some form of "realism", and the belief that cinema can only be judged by its literary pedigree', in *Arrows of Desire* (London: Waterstone, 1985), p. 102.
10. BBC Written Archives Caversham: *Alfie Elkins and his Little Life*, Audience Research Report, 30 January 1962 112/62/58; *The Critics*, 16 September 1962, transcript. The original radio play was repeated by the BBC yet again,

during 1992, as part of a tribute to Bill Naughton, following his death on 9 January, which comprised a short season of his plays.

11. LCP, Correspondence, *All in Good Time*, 1963/3181. Play reader's report, 18 January 1963. All references hereafter come from this file.

The play reader's reference about Ezra's 'homosexual tendencies' towards his best friend who disappeared, Billy Stringfellow, bears interesting comparison with much later gay readings of the Boulting Brothers' film version of Naughton's play. See, in particular, Vito Russo, *The Celluloid Closet: Homosexuality in the Movies* (New York: Harper and Row, 1981), pp. 147–9; and Stephen Bourne, *Brief Encounters: Lesbians and Gays in the British Cinema 1930–1971* (London: Cassell, 1996), pp. 195–9. At the time of release of *The Family Way* in 1966, however, few critics saw fit to mention it.

Patrick Gibbs raised the question of 'a homosexual relationship' between Ezra and Billy in his review for the *Daily Telegraph* on 23 December 1966, but did not pursue the issue at all. Gibbs wondered 'Indeed, whether any of the men we see function properly', and cited various instances to advance his argument: the distinct hints of an extramarital affair between Ezra's wife and Billy before the latter's sudden departure – thereby 'appearing to be a better friend than even the husband thought' – as well as the seeming fixation evident in the girl's father for his daughter ('or was it just her plaits?'), and the matter of 'the only other wife given prominence telling her husband in a moment of anger that for years the milkman has been doing his job'. In view of the widespread 'Freudian gloss' which he felt overlaid Naughton's basic story line, in short, Gibbs clearly considered that the quesion of homosexuality was no more (or less) important than the other questions raised in the body of the film at large.

12. The Lord Chamberlain's Office had to contend with a lone dissenting voice from an irate member of the public in Poole, however, who complained that *All in Good Time* was 'a particularly indecent play which never ought to have been passed by the censor. I can only think it has escaped your notice or you would never have allowed it.' 'It is most disgusting and thoroughly indecent, as it exposes a *most* delicate subject, and is a disgrace to the British stage,' the letter continued, before concluding in forthright fashion: 'So please ban it immediately.' A reply by Eric Penn of 8 April pointed out: 'The Lord Chamberlain has the task of deciding upon what will do real harm as opposed to that which is vulgar, tasteless, or no more likely to lead to immorality or misconduct than the contributions to this end of other mediums, such as television, books, newspapers, etc.' Apart from noting that 'The views of responsible theatregoers are of great value to him in assessing the state of public opinion', Penn soon put paid to the matter by reiterating the Lord Chamberlain's judgement that 'In the form in which it has been allowed, it is felt that the play in question is acceptable.'

13. Indeed, so far as one can judge, the only film censorship applied to *The Family Way* was forthcoming when the film was banned from the Cunard Company's cruise liners in view of its 'X'-rated certificate and because 'children would

be able to see it'. The film was invested with a degree of notoriety, in short, which it hardly deserved or scarcely merited, doubtless because of a somewhat demure nude scene in which Hayley Mills is glimpsed fleetingly on emerging from a tin bath. Given that the twenty-year-old Hayley Mills, hitherto invariably treated by the press as something of 'a royal princess', was seen to be 'parted at last from her Disneyland image', to borrow Felix Barker's phrase, this was sufficient to merit considerable press headlines and much publicity for the film. It did exceptionally well in the box-office stakes, thereafter, in both Britain and the United States, where it garnered plaudits from Bosley Crowther of the *New York Times* and where its distribution rights were sold to Warner Bros for a then record initial payment of £625,000, to be followed by 35 per cent of the film's subsequent earnings – an appreciable profit on a production which had cost £400,000 to make.

But there is scant documentation of substance in the BBFC's files relating to *The Family Way* – always a sign, in itself, of the trouble-free passage which a film was afforded – to believe the film censors felt they had much to worry about with it. Moreover, a comparison of the play script with the screenplay and the completed film, and, not least, the fruits of numerous interviews conducted with the director, Roy Boulting, confirms how little was changed because of censorship strictures during the course of transition from stage to screen of *The Family Way*.

14. LCP Correspondence, *Alfie*, 1963/3492. Play reader's report, 20 January 1963, and handwritten amendments to same by E. Penn, Assistant Comptroller, along with all further memoranda related to file.

15. BBFC file, *Alfie*: reader's report, 28 April 1965, and Trevelyan's letter to Paramount British Pictures, 4 May 1965. All other BBFC references to the film come from this file.

In fact, Michael Caine did some post-synching of the dialogue soundtrack, comprising 125 new sound loops. This was done not for censorship purposes but to render his character's 'very thick cockney accent' into 'clearer English' for strictly American consumption and the US edition of the film. For which, see the details contained in his useful autobiography, *What's It All About?* (London: Century, 1972). Clearly, lessons had been learned here by the film producers from the decided lack of success that greeted the Broadway presentation of the stage play of *Alfie*, starring Terence Stamp, when it opened at the Morosco Theatre on 17 December 1964 and ran for just twenty-one performances. Stamp maintains the play's notable failure resulted from 'A devout Catholic critic who was reputedly offended by the abortion scene, but too smart to mention the fact, found other ways of making the play seem unwatchable.' See Terence Stamp, *Double Feature* (London: Grafton, 1988), p. 147. Jean Shrimpton, Stamp's then partner, is probably as close to the truth when pointing out that 'The audience did not understand the Cockney rhyming slang; in fact they did not understand the play at all.' 'Terry was dynamic enough,' she continues, 'but this near-monologue from him in an

East End accent was baffling to the audience.' See her *An Autobiography* (London: Sphere, 1991), p. 127. By contrast, of course, the screen version of *Alfie* was a huge hit in America, as in Britain, with even Stephen Farber, the critic of the scholarly Berkeley journal, *Film Quarterly*, maintaining that 'its wit and its stubborn humanity make it seem a giant of a film today'. See *Film Quarterly*, 20/3 (1967), pp. 42–6.

16. The comment was actually made by Trevelyan in a letter to Warwickshire County Council on 8 February 1961, in regard to their continued intransigence over granting a certificate for *Saturday Night and Sunday Morning*, but it serves usefully to summarise his overall and distinctly pragmatic attitude to film censorship as exercised by the BBFC.

CHAPTER 8

Sundry Genres

Dracula/The Black Cat

The 1909 Joint Parliamentary Select Committee recommendations made
no mention of horror as such, but this could arguably be banned on the
grounds of either indecency or religious irreverence. Possibly as a result
the BBFC's published reasons for rejections prior to the early 1930s did
not include horror, but all the same in December 1922 the BBFC rejected
Wilhelm (F. W.) Murnau's classic *Nosferatu* (1922) under the title of
Dracula. This was almost certainly because the widow of the famous 1897
novel's author, Bram Stoker, who had died in 1912, had won a German
court case against the film for breach of copyright.[1] Mrs Stoker's objection
to *Nosferatu* did not seemingly extend to stage adaptations of her
husband's work, for in March 1924 the LCO received a script for a British
play by Hamilton Deane on the same theme for performances at the Grand
Theatre in Derby beginning on 15 May. Whereas the BBFC appears not
to have been unduly concerned about *Nosferatu*'s horror content, this was
by contrast the Lord Chamberlain's principal consideration in 1924.
Reader of Plays George Street commented that the details in the script
were too disgusting for the stage and justified his attitude by explaining,

> There is a great difference between reading horrors and seeing them done . . . the
> whole thing is full of grisly (though silly) horror, and is simply a series of attacks on
> the nerves. It may be a strong measure to forbid the production, as a play, of a once
> popular novel which has of course nothing whatever immoral in it, in the ordinary
> sense, or it might also be thought that the thing was too silly to notice. But holding
> the view that 'horrors', for the mere sake of horror, might fitly be banned by the cen-
> sorship, I suggest for my part that this is an extremely disgusting instance . . .[2]

Accordingly he plumped for a ban, but the Grand Theatre then submitted an amended script, which removed the stage death of Count
Dracula as well as the sight of his blood-sucking a female victim. Even so,
Lord Cromer, the Lord Chamberlain, proved reluctant to allow the play,
but, aware that he might be on shaky legal ground with an outright ban,
he decided to consult his five Advisory Board members, none of whom

favoured this course of action. Cromer awarded the play a licence on 6 May 1924, and the production in Derby went ahead as planned without any public controversy.

In February 1927 Deane added to his licensed 1924 script a brief scene between Dracula and a maidservant before resubmitting the play for a London presentation. This was approved, and the play in this slightly amended form was performed in mid-February 1927 at the Little Theatre with Raymond Huntley as a young and very unlikely Count Dracula and Deane himself as Van Helsing. The reviewer in *The Times* of 15 February saw in the production little of Stoker's novel but occasional scary moments, through noisy sound effects, but on the whole he, like other critics, was unimpressed. Nevertheless the play went on to run in the West End at various theatres for all but a year. There were also licensed productions on the same theme in provincial theatres later in 1927 and again in 1930. Through all this Cromer remained unmoved, writing in September 1927 that *Dracula* was a disgusting play in any version, which he regretted had ever been staged.

The 1927 revivals might well have been the result of *Nosferatu* showings in Paris that year as well as of an earlier abortive Film Society attempt in London to include Murnau's film in its announced 1925-6 programme. Mrs Stoker had been able to frustrate the latter, but the two 1927 stage adaptations enabled the society to screen the film at last on 16 December 1928, when it was known that the Universal film studio had already purchased both the copyright and film production rights to the novel. Universal made its own film version in 1930 at a time when major studio interest in horror as cinematic fare was gathering momentum and talking features were well on the way to dominating the industry in both Britain and the United States.

Tod Browning's *Dracula* is based in part upon Hamilton Deane's play and stars Hungarian Bela Lugosi, whose eerie presence afforded the film much of its appeal. It arrived in Britain in February 1931, when the BBFC allowed it uncut in a version which the studio evidently trimmed by some seven minutes' running time. Later in 1931 Universal made James Whale's *Frankenstein*, with Boris Karloff as the now legendary monster, the film reaching Britain in December and again being passed uncut in a studio-shortened version. Both films fared well at the box office in Britain, but *Frankenstein* gave rise to protests from individual members of the general public to the Home Office after its release early in 1932. From then onwards both the BBFC and the Lord Chamberlain had to take account of possible public distaste for horror themes.

It was in this climate that G. H. Samuelson in early June 1932 submitted Edgar Allan Poe's short story *The Black Cat* to the LCO for production as a play at the Duke of York's Theatre the very next week. This blatant endeavour to cash in on the contemporary horror-film fad at a time when the great trading slump was approaching its zenith in Britain begins in a cellar, where a crazed drunkard is disturbed by his black cat's green eyes. His wife joins him, and after he has raved at her, he attacks the cat and gouges out one of its eyes. He then takes the cat to a bench and tries to kill it with an axe. His wife intervenes with sufficient effect to prevent him, but he unintentionally kills her while the cat manages to escape. The man plasters up his wife's body behind a wall in the cellar. Three days later the police arrive to search for her, eventually tear down the plaster and find the wife's corpse behind the wall with the live cat sitting on her hand. This last scene is explicitly presented on stage, which partly led Street to write, 'An unpleasant horror . . . It is Poe at his worst. Still, it is Poe and for that reason I hesitate to advise its banning.'[3]

As already seen, Cromer had scant patience with the stage horror genre before the early 1930s. This time, without even consulting his Advisory Board, he had no hesitation in deciding upon a ban, tersely minuting, 'Poe or not, this horror goes too far. Licence refused.' Despite the popularity of *Dracula* and *Frankenstein* in the cinema, Samuelson did not challenge the ban and the play was never produced in Britain, while a later Universal film directed by Edgar G. Ulmer in 1934 states in its credits that the story was suggested by the Poe tale. However, although a black cat as the indestructible symbol of evil is gratuitously introduced into the plot, the film has nothing in common with the Poe tale beyond the title. It was allowed by the BBFC, but the title in Britain became *The House of Doom*, a possibly significant change in the light of the Lord Chamberlain's ban on the Poe play. Another film entitled *The Black Cat*, directed by Albert S. Rogell in 1941, also had no connection with Poe. This too the BBFC allowed.

The Green Pastures

Under the 1909 recommendations the Lord Chamberlain should ban any play which violated religious reverence. For this reason the Lord Chamberlain's censorship was always highly vigilant about religious matters and about any material on the stage which smacked of blasphemy, itself illegal. An example is the fate of *East of Eden*, a 1929 play by Christopher Morley. According to Reader of Plays George Street, this play treated God as a joke and would surely shock many people. He recommended a ban, to which Lord Cromer, the Lord Chamberlain, agreed, remarking, 'I agree this whole play turning Genesis to ridicule will not do. It would give great offence.'[4]

Such inflexibility towards perceived religious irreverence was faced with a much greater dilemma over *The Green Pastures*, a 1929 American play by Marc Connelly which presents Old Testament stories as viewed by ill-educated American blacks through the teachings of De Lawd, the black preacher leading his impoverished flock. The Broadway production was highly successful, and moves were shortly afoot to bring the play to Britain, as the *Daily News* of 3 April 1930 reported. Cromer was soon made aware that religious opinion was astir, for he was urged to ban the play by the London Brotherhood Federation on the very day that the news of a possible British production first appeared in the national press. At that time the LCO had received no script, but, while the Broadway run remained in progress, the Haymarket Theatre in London and eminent impresario Charles B. Cochran forwarded a scenario at the end of May 1930, without either an envisaged production date or an intended venue. After 1910 the LCO had interpreted the depiction of God on stage as a violation of religious reverence, but arguably this did not apply to *The Green Pastures*, since God himself does not appear, only De Lawd's vision of what he might look like. On the other hand, the LCO also forbade plays adapted from the Scriptures, and *The Green Pastures* might be regarded as falling within this category.

Reader of Plays George Street took full account of these pressures when he reported,

The question of a licence for this play is interesting as well as extremely difficult. It endeavours to give an account of the Creation and the chief events of the Pentateuch, with a glance at the Redemption, as seen in the mind of a Negro preacher . . . [He] is instructing his Sunday School and his teaching is thrown into dramatic form, with a few interruptions, in a darkened light, of direct narration. It begins in Heaven before the Creation. The angels enjoy a 'fish fry', and God is presented as an idealised Negro preacher in dress and habits, genially accepting a cigar and so on. The Earth and Man are created rather casually and we follow the course of Genesis, God intervening when the conduct of mankind deserves. The stories of Noah and Moses in Egypt are especially elaborated. In Heaven He interviews people in his private office. At the end the infantile simplicity of the play is exchanged for a touch of mysticism in regard to the suffering of God and the Crucifixion is being enacted on earth.

There is of course no irreverence intended. There is merely an extreme degree of anthropmorphism [sic], and that in some degree is common to all forms of religion. There is no more irreverence in a Negro preacher's imagining God as smoking a cigar than there is in the author of Genesis making Him walk in the garden. That is understood in America, where the mentality of the Negro is familiar to most people, and the play has received there the approval of religious opinion of various shades. It is otherwise here, where people generally are not interested in negroes. Twenty years ago I should have had no doubt that this presentment of God would excite widespread horror and indignation. I am not so sure now; there is a better chance of audiences being introduced beforehand and taking the play in the right spirit. But there is still a grave risk that they, or the greatest part of them, might take the play as a joke and therefore a blasphemous joke . . . I confess I think the beauty and pathos of the play have been overrated, though there is something of both and fine acting might increase it . . . It is only if I could be sure of audiences taking the play with understanding that I could recommend a licence.

Cromer was similarly in doubt and decided to consult the Archbishop of Canterbury, Cosmo Lang, who read the script and favoured a ban. Consequently Cromer refused a licence on 13 June, but nevertheless, most exceptionally, ten days later he passed the script on to King George V. The king read it and approved of Cromer's decision, but shortly afterwards the Director-General of the BBC, Sir John Reith, sought the opinions of both Cromer and Lang about a radio version of the play, which, however, was allowed to proceed. In May 1933 two representatives of Marc Connelly met Cromer to discuss possible amendments to the play to make it acceptable for British audiences, but of course they were unaware that Cromer would not go against the king's wishes. In fact Cromer passed his responsibility elsewhere by informing the two men that he could not sanction the play in any version without the approval of British ecclesiastical opinion. In June 1935 another prominent impresario, Sir Oswald Stoll, had a try without knowing the nature of the obstacles he was up against, and he proved no more successful in budging Cromer than his predecessors.

Early in 1936 Warner Bros filmed *The Green Pastures*, top-class if nowadays dated entertainment. It contains snappy direction from Connelly himself and William Keighley, a towering performance from Rex Ingram as De Lawd, an extremely high-calibre black supporting cast, Hal Mohr's excellent cinematography and an apt musical score by Erich Wolfgang Korngold. On 9 June 1936 the film reached the BBFC, which, doubtless very conscious of a likely controversy whatever decision it made, prevaricated for the best part of three months before making contact with the LCO, itself in difficulties over *Parnell* during this period (see next section). On 1 September the LCO forwarded its entire file on the play in confidence to Tyrrell, ennobled in 1929 and BBFC President since November 1935, and to Wilkinson. By this time King George V was dead, but even so on 14 October a meeting took place between the two most senior BBFC staff and Cromer, who was anxious that the BBFC should reject the film. To this end, he suggested that the BBFC should consult Archbishop Lang, which it duly did before the end of October. Tyrrell and Wilkinson were already inclined to allow the film but had delayed doing so for so long only on account of the Lord Chamberlain's ban, for Tyrrell, a Roman Catholic, informed Archbishop Lang that although he had approached the film with a bias against it, this proved unsustainable once he had actually seen it. Lang subsequently viewed it at the BBFC and approved of it. This outcome was not what Lord Cromer had been expecting, but, as Lang informed Cromer, he continued to support a ban on the play even though the differing censorship treatment of film and play could not logically be justified. On 11 November the BBFC passed the film with cuts amounting to 211 feet, but it is no longer possible to reconstruct from the BBFC records the precise cuts that were carried out. *The Green Pastures* opened at the New Gallery in Regent Street in late November to favourable reviews, so that Wilkinson in early December felt able to write to the LCO to point out that although the BBFC was continuing to receive complaints from individuals who had not seen the film, not one single objection to date had arrived from anyone who had actually seen it. Wilkinson anticipated that most of the criticism would vanish after the film had been generally released.

This prediction proved to be accurate, and if Connelly had followed up the film's British release with a further application to the LCO, Cromer would have experienced extreme difficulty in defending a continued ban. But in the event the next licence applications were delayed until after the Second World War – in October 1948, September 1950 and May 1951 – by which time the play was becoming outdated. On each occasion a licence was refused because of opposition from the Archbishop of Canterbury. The Lord Chamberlain's ban on the play was never to be overturned, although three private performances took place, in July 1955 at Sidcup in Kent, in July 1963 at Nottingham and in May–June 1964 at Hazelmere in Surrey.

The Lord Chamberlain's protracted ban on *The Green Pastures* constituted a blot on the record of stage censorship, especially after the release of the film, when many more people saw it than were ever likely to see the play. Even as early as 1930, Cromer's predecessor as Lord Chamberlain, Lord Atholl, had urged him to pass it. Admittedly the BBFC did not have to reckon with opposition from the Archbishop of Canterbury, as Cromer and his successors did, but no effort was made to sound out wider Anglican opinion, still less ecclesiastical views beyond the Church of England. Moreover, none of the Lord Chamberlains concerned recognised that their rule banning the portrayal of God on stage was merely the LCO's interpretation of the 1909 parliamentary recommendation for a ban upon religious irreverence, which did not itself carry the force of law and in any case was arguably not applicable to *The Green Pastures*. The permanent ban on the play stands as a monument to bureaucratic rigidity, coupled with a tendency behind the scenes to pass responsibility elsewhere for the decision.

Parnell

Charles Stewart Parnell (1846–91) rose to prominence in the late 1870s as the fiery young leader of the Irish Nationalists in the House of Commons. His aim was Irish Home Rule, to achieve which he launched in 1877 a persistent campaign of procedural obstruction in the House. His opponents also suspected him of being the master mind behind the constant agrarian violence in Ireland, and by 1886 William Ewart Gladstone, the Liberal Prime Minister, had been converted to the cause of Irish Home Rule. However, his Irish Home Rule bill was defeated in the Commons, Gladstone resigned and the Conservatives won the ensuing general election. This result put an end to Irish hopes of Home Rule for the foreseeable future, given that the Conservatives were implacably opposed to it. The alliance between Gladstone and Parnell was shattered in 1889, when it emerged publicly that the Irish leader had long been conducting an affair with Mrs Katherine O'Shea, the wife of Liberal MP Captain William O'Shea. This liaison had been carried out secretly because of Mrs O'Shea's elderly aunt, from whom a substantial legacy was expected when she died. After her death and the following disclosure of the affair, O'Shea successfully sued his wife for divorce on the grounds of adultery with Parnell. Parnell then married his former mistress, but the scandal badly loosened his grip over his party and cost him Gladstone's support. In 1891, with Parnell still struggling to assert his authority over his Irish MPs, he died unexpectedly.

Historically there were two main points of controversy. The first was whether O'Shea had known of, and in effect condoned, his wife's adultery well before the scandal erupted. The second was whether Gladstone too had known all about it and turned a blind eye until it became public knowledge, after which he virtually demanded that Parnell give up the leadership of the Irish Nationalist MPs as his price for continued Liberal support of Irish Home Rule.

Britain's failure to retain all of Ireland within the United Kingdom in 1921, when the territorial extent of the British Empire was at its zenith, rankled with many among the upper classes on the other side of the Irish Sea until well after the Second World War. In this climate memories of Parnell constituted a painful reminder that if Irish Home Rule had come about in 1886 or in the years immediately before 1914, the partition of Ireland might have been averted. Consequently the prospects for any play dealing seriously with Parnell's life, and particularly the scandal, were far from rosy even after his widow died in 1921. However, in October 1934 the Shilling Theatre in Fulham applied for a licence to present *Parnell*, a drama by Dr W. M. Crofton which had already been performed in Dublin. In this play O'Shea is depicted as something close to a common black-mailer when he asks his wife, after he has ceased to live with her, to pay his election expenses. If she refuses, he threatens to expose the affair with Parnell. O'Shea is also shown as conspiring with *The Times* to link Parnell with revolutionary activity in Ireland and postponing the divorce proceedings involving Parnell until after the rich aunt had died. During the divorce proceedings Parnell alleges that *The Times* had bribed O'Shea, while both sides in the case agree that Gladstone had long known about the liaison.

Reader of Plays George Street observed that although much of the play had been taken from press reports and was therefore not censorable, it was wrong to represent O'Shea, who had died in 1905, as a complete scoundrel while his children and other relatives remained alive. In any case, Street continued, this presentation of events that had occurred only just over forty years before, such as the accusations that *The Times* had bribed him and that Gladstone had prior knowledge of Parnell's adultery, was undesirable.[6] He advised against a licence, a course of action which Lord Cromer endorsed, and the likely O'Shea family objections were conveyed to Crofton two days before Cromer actually received an appeal directly from the niece of Katherine O'Shea not to allow the play. Although the LCO documentation might be interpreted as a piece of pro-Establishment political censorship cloaked with family considerations, the latter were all too real and Crofton accepted the situation.

This matter seemed to be settled, but, unfortunately for Cromer, American playwright Mrs Elsie T. Schauffler had written a play along much the same lines, which was staged on Broadway towards the end of 1934 with well-known British stage actress Margaret Rawlings in the part of Katherine O'Shea. Elsie Schauffler had died two days into rehearsals, but the play went on to become a notable success, and, as a tribute to the late playwright, Margaret Rawlings wished to play the same role in London if possible. The play, also entitled *Parnell*, attracted the attention of two British theatre managements, and a submission to the LCO was made in February 1935, when the play was due to be performed at the Globe Theatre in Shaftesbury Avenue starring Marie Tempest and John Gielgud. Cromer rejected this application on the same grounds as the Crofton drama, but more than a year later independent director/producer Norman Marshall decided to stage the play privately at the Gate Theatre in Villiers Street on 23 April 1936. Marshall's production had Margaret Rawlings repeating her Broadway performance, Wyndham Goldie as Parnell, Maude Vanne as the elderly aunt, Arthur Young as Gladstone and James Mason as O'Shea. Marshall invited a LCO representative to see the play early in its three-week run, a visit which took place towards the end of April. The LCO staff member concerned was Reader of Plays Henry Game, who concluded that although he could see no reason to object to the portrayals of Parnell, Katherine O'Shea or Gladstone, he drew the line at the unsympathetic presentation of O'Shea, whose son was still alive in 1925. There were also two illegitimate daughters of the Parnell–Mrs O'Shea adultery, while Game's postscript added that the O'Shea marriage had produced a son born in 1870 as well as two younger daughters.[7]

Once *Parnell* had opened at the Gate Theatre, the press reviews were favourable and some of these included criticism of Cromer, culminating in *The Times* leading article of 29 April which argued strongly that the ban on the play should be lifted. O'Shea's son, Captain Gerard O'Shea, had seen the play on the previous day, and on the same day as *The Times* editorial he wrote to Cromer asking him to withhold a licence because of the distress that would be caused to him, his sisters and the wider family, including several of his cousins. On 2 May, Cromer adopted the highly unusual course of writing privately to Geoffrey Dawson, the editor of *The Times*, to point out that it was the Lord Chamberlain's duty to protect individuals from attacks upon their forebears in the theatre where reasonably possible, since the libel laws protected only the living. If such protection was withdrawn, Cromer argued, no family whose ancestors had been involved in a public scandal in moderately recent times would have any redress against unscrupulous playwrights. Cromer went to state that he took as his general guideline a fifty-year period, within which he would require from theatre managements, in cases of recent historical plays, an assurance that the family involved would be unlikely to clamour for a licence to be withdrawn after a play had actually been performed in public, as had already happened on two occasions. What Cromer's letter had omitted to state was that the 1909 Joint Parliamentary Select Committee's recommendations had never defined 'recent', and that there was nothing in them about protecting a depicted dead person's relatives. From the perspective of some seventy years later, fifty years seems arbitrary and excessive as a benchmark, but in the 1930s government documents were kept secret for the same period at the very least. Within that framework the LCO's adopted guideline was logical, although the protection of relatives' feelings appears to have been the LCO's own idea.

In his letter to Geoffrey Dawson, Cromer further objected to the assumption in *The Times* leader that the core of the ban was the portrayal of Gladstone because the writer did not expect the Gladstone family to complain, whereas in fact Gerard O'Shea had already complained. Moreover, if the Schauffler play was allowed, other plays about Parnell would also have to be allowed as of right when the degrees of family objections might vary. Cromer was fearful that press agitation on behalf of the Schauffler play might undermine the Lord Chamberlain's censorship altogether, for two days after he had written to Dawson he also wrote to Tyrrell at the BBFC asking for a meeting between the two men to co-ordinate policy over films and plays dealing with recent history. This is a rare documented example, along with that on *The Green Pastures*, of direct collaboration between the two censorship agencies. That same day a cousin of Gerard O'Shea, Colonel Evelyn Wood, relying upon others' description of the play, pressed Cromer for a ban, while a second letter from Cromer to Dawson avidly protested that Charles Morgan, the dramatic critic of *The Times*, had implied that the public interest should take precedence over the Lord Chamberlain's policy of protecting individuals against a perceived slander of their ancestors. Cromer ended this letter by remarking that surely Britain had not yet reached the stage of adopting the Nazi doctrine that minorities not only suffer, but must be made to suffer, in the so-called 'public interest,' presumably a reference to the Jewish persecution then proceeding in Germany.

Cromer's meeting with Tyrrell and Wilkinson was held on 13 May, before which the controversy had been kept in the public eye by Gerard O'Shea's open letter to the press giving his reasons for objecting to the play. A reply from Marshall, the producer, published on 11 May, had been to the effect that he had offered to meet O'Shea to discuss suitable amendments, but O'Shea had declined to meet him. From this Marshall had concluded that O'Shea intended to veto the play in any form so long as Cromer permitted him to do so. At Cromer's meeting with Tyrrell and Wilkinson, *Parnell* dominated the discussion, the BBFC representatives being informed that an O'Shea family member had taken grave exception to the subject matter of the play. Wilkinson thereupon suggested that this was perhaps the case because none of the family was to receive any money from the performances of the play. This cynical but realistic observation emanated from Wilkinson's knowledge of a projected film, with O'Shea's involvement in the pre-production preparations, because a mere six days after the meeting with Cromer the BBFC received a pre-production scenario for *Parnell* from Metro-Goldwyn-Mayer (MGM). The BBFC examiners were divided as to whether the theme was acceptable, but on 5 June the BBFC notified MGM that the Lord Chamberlain's ban would also apply to the film unless O'Shea family objections could be overcome. MGM then officially admitted that O'Shea was involved in the preparation for a revised scenario.[8]

Meanwhile, with Charles Morgan acting as mediator, Marshall had negotiated throughout much of June with O'Shea and his cousin, but it appeared to Morgan that O'Shea was consistently obstructive and petty over details in Marshall's amended script. Towards the end of June, Morgan had lost patience with O'Shea and informed Cromer that O'Shea was not negotiating seriously. Morgan accordingly requested that Cromer should now assume responsibility. Cromer took action, asking Marshall to supply him with a revised script and stating that if Marshall and O'Shea failed to agree, then he would meet them both together. Of the revised version it was considered that O'Shea continued to have grounds for complaint about the portrayal of his father, though less so than earlier; that O'Shea's objection to the subject as being too recent as history remained; that the previous LCO assumptions about non-objections from Gladstone's descendants might not be correct; that Morgan's view was not necessarily typical of critical opinion in the theatre world; and that if the play was allowed, other plays on the same subject would follow, an oblique reference to the already banned Crofton play. The LCO was unaware of O'Shea's adverse reaction to Marshall's amended script when O'Shea and his cousin met Cromer on 7 July. By this time Cromer suspected that O'Shea's obstructionism was linked to a possible Hollywood contract, for at this meeting, under pressure from Cromer, O'Shea admitted that he had been offered a contract to go to Hollywood to assist in the scenario prep-arations for *Parnell* in return for a fee and expenses. Cromer pointed out that if O'Shea signed this contract, he would be inconsistent, a veiled warning that the play would be allowed under such circumstances. Eventually O'Shea agreed to read the latest script and to contact Cromer again in the very near future with any remaining objections. Within a week O'Shea had left for Hollywood, and Cromer noted that this action effectively removed the objection that the play was dealing with history that was too recent.

O'Shea left for Hollywood on 15 July and was absent from Britain for approximately two months. During this time Marshall had commissioned yet another script to meet O'Shea's remaining stated objections, but even in this O'Shea's father was depicted as guilty of an act of adultery of which he had never been accused in a court of law. However, by this time Cromer had lost faith in O'Shea's integrity owing to the film contract and con-sidered his approval as no longer necessary, while in any case he questioned whether public interest in the play remained at the same level as when the Gate Theatre run had opened some four months earlier. Cromer notified O'Shea's cousin, Colonel Evelyn Wood, that the play would now be given a licence, and although Wood attempted to delay matters until the latest film script became available and O'Shea returned home, Cromer was having none of this. On 24 September the press reported that the ban on

Parnell had after all been reversed, while another leader in *The Times* of the same day welcomed Cromer's retreat but also supported the retention of the Lord Chamberlain's theatre censorship.

The licence was issued on 16 October to the New Theatre in St Martin's Lane, O'Shea publicly announcing six days later that the play did not have his approval. What turned out to be a three-month run started at the New Theatre in early November, with Glen Byam Shaw replacing James Mason in the part of William O'Shea as the solitary change from the Gate Theatre cast. The reviews were exceedingly favourable, and when Cromer had awarded this licence, he had done so in the knowledge that Crofton would probably resubmit his play. However, embarrassingly for Cromer and without his awareness, one of Gladstone's descendants had seen the play at the Gate Theatre and taken strong exception to the portrayal of the late Prime Minister, but had refrained from taking action, relying instead upon Cromer's publicly announced ban. Cromer learned of this development only after the press had reported his decision to allow the Schauffler play but before Crofton resubmitted his drama. After all the protracted controversy over the former, Cromer could scarcely reverse his decision again. Nor could he admit to Crofton that the decision to allow the Schauffler play had been taken in ignorance of a Gladstone family objection in case this was leaked to the press. As a result, Crofton was told that his play could be considered for a licence only if it was accompanied by an assurance from both the Gladstone and O'Shea families that they held no objections. As Cromer well knew, this condition amounted to a ban, and the understandably perplexed Crofton responded in acid but principled tones,

[H]ow astonishing it seems to me that speeches delivered in Parliament reported to the whole nation at the time in newspapers and now to be read in Hansard and biographies, must not be said on the stage because they are unpalatable to some one or other descendant . . . Has [the Lord Chamberlain] not obligations to dramatic art, to the public, to authors as well as to a handful of individuals who care for none of these things but who wish to draw a veil over deeds of their ancestors they appear to be ashamed of, a veil over a past that ought to be recalled in the interests of justice and the instruction of future generations?

When considered against the background of awarding a licence to the Schauffler play, Crofton's arguments were of course unanswerable. Not surprisingly, Cromer failed to reply to them in writing but instead offered Crofton the opportunity of a personal meeting with him. Crofton declined, doubtless concluding that the reason for Cromer's inconsistency was his play's Irish provenance. In the event the ban was never rescinded, which left the unfortunate Crofton with every reason to feel aggrieved.

MGM's film arrived at the BBFC in June 1937. It starred Clark Gable as Parnell, Myrna Loy as Katherine O'Shea, Edmund Gwenn as O'Shea, Montagu Love as Gladstone and Edna May Oliver as the elderly rich aunt. Although Parnell's aim of Irish Home Rule and his view that English rule in Ireland was oppressive are made clear, the political world at Westminster is firmly subordinated to the love story, while the integrity of neither O'Shea nor Gladstone is called into question, as it was in the Schauffler play. These glaring omissions were presumably due to Gerard O'Shea's influence on the script, and they robbed the film of whatever interest it might otherwise have possessed. After the play's West End performances and the omission from the film of the contentious material, the BBFC was left with little option but to allow it uncut. However, with the two American leads fundamentally miscast, it failed dismally in both Britain and the United States.

I Want to Live!

As was the case with *Now Barabbas . . .*, anti-capital punishment propaganda on stage was acceptable to the LCO in 1947, although not necessarily as a main theme. In April 1948 the Commons voted to suspend the death penalty for a trial period of five years, and although the Lords soon nullified this decision, capital punishment had been placed on the political agenda. In the late 1940s probably only a small minority of people were convinced abolitionists, but debate on the question intensified during the first half of the 1950s on account of three controversial murder cases.

The first of these was the Christopher Craig–Derek Bentley affair, already described in regard to *Cosh Boy*. In January 1953 this culminated in the refusal of Conservative Home Secretary Sir David Maxwell-Fyfe to grant Bentley a reprieve and his resulting execution amidst much parliamentary and public disquiet. Doubts about Bentley's guilt had arisen owing to sections of the trial testimony, triggering a fierce public debate which was lingering on when in March and April 1953 John Reginald Halliday Christie was arrested and charged with the murder of several women, including his wife. It eventually transpired that Christie had killed at least seven women since 1944, and he was duly found guilty and hanged without controversy in July 1953. However, Christie had been the principal prosecution witness in 1950 against Timothy Evans, who had been hanged for his wife's murder in the same house, 10 Rillington Place in Notting Hill, when Christie had been a lodger there and the Christie murders had taken place. Inevitably, the Christie case had given rise to doubts about Evans's guilt, and although a government tribunal concluded just before Christie's execution that the Evans verdict had been correct, this judgement was passionately disputed by many, most notably Michael Eddowes in his 1955 book *The Man on Your Conscience*.

In 1955 Ruth Ellis was sent for trial accused of murdering her lover, David Blakely. In this crime of passion the main facts and Ellis's guilt were not in question, but it was widely expected that, because she was young and thought unlikely to repeat her offence, Home Secretary Gwilym Lloyd George would reprieve her. In the event he did not and she was hanged in July 1955, the last woman to suffer the death penalty in Britain. There was widespread sympathy for her, some suspecting that she, like Bentley before her, had been the sacrificial victim of the Conservative government's hard-line law and order policy in the face of perceived rising crime.

Together these three cases had challenged the use of the automatic death penalty for murder, and as early as July 1953, some six months after Bentley's execution, there was an abortive attempt in the Commons to abolish it. Although the issue was not one between the two major political parties, in practice most Conservative MPs favoured capital punishment and many Labour MPs opposed it. This gave it the appearance of a party lines controversy, and for the BBFC this meant that contentious screen material on the subject was best avoided at a time when British film-makers wished to exploit the situation. Late in 1953 the BBFC had removed from *Eight O'Clock Walk*, Lance Comfort's run-of-the-mill mixture of murder mystery and courtroom drama, snatches of dialogue expressing the view that jury verdicts were sometimes mistaken. In February 1956 J. Lee-Thompson's *Yield to the Night*, starring Diana Dors, was plainly based upon the Ruth Ellis case and received an unenthusiastic BBFC reception. Although the film was not cut, the director failed to persuade Watkins to award it an 'A' certificate rather than the more restrictive 'X'. Rightly or wrongly, and probably rightly, Lee-Thompson believed that the BBFC had regarded his film, with its story of a young woman in the condemned cell recalling the events that had landed her there, bearing a marked resemblance to Ruth Ellis's premeditated shooting of her lover, David Blakely, as thinly veiled anti-capital punishment propaganda.

Directed by Robert Wise and produced by Walter Wanger for United Artists in 1958, *I Want to Live!* was an altogether different film. It deals with the case of Barbara Graham (Susan Hayward in an Oscar-winning Best Actress role), a woman of dubious character and morals involved in petty crime who at the age of thirty-two was executed for murder in San Quentin prison under Californian law in June 1955. Unlike Ruth Ellis, Barbara Graham's guilt was extremely doubtful, with suggestions that the police had framed her when it was known that she was in fact innocent.

Tabor Rawson's book on the matter was due to be published in Britain in February 1959 to coincide with the film's planned British release, and United Artists accordingly submitted it to the BBFC in good time, in mid-October 1958. Sir Sidney Harris, Trevelyan, senior examiner Frank Crofts and examiner Newton Branch viewed the film, both Harris's and Trevelyan's presence at an initial viewing indicating there might be potential problems with the film. In the event all four men were relaxed about most of the content, perhaps because of the American setting. For much of its running time the film is a simple story of injustice, but the long, climactic and detailed execution sequence transforms it into a harangue against capital punishment, then facing increased criticism within the United States as well.

Yield to the Night contains no execution scene, which explains why the BBFC had allowed it unscathed, but by contrast the gas-chamber preparation and execution scenes in *I Want to Live!* are intended to shock, so much so that at the BBFC viewing both Harris and Crofts favoured their complete removal. However, Trevelyan and Branch doubted whether such drastic action was necessary and argued for only the removal of shots of Barbara Graham in the gas chamber as well as some of the execution preparations. They also wanted one of the BBFC's female examiners to see the cut version, presumably because the executed person was female, before a final decision was taken. The cuts Trevelyan required were extensive and basically involved the deletion of all shots of the victim while in the gas chamber and of any indication of what actually happened at a real gas-chamber execution.[9] Trevelyan conveyed these cuts to United Artists in London on 16 and 21 October, but the company's representatives would not act without first securing Wanger's approval. At a meeting of 17 November 1958, United Artists made it clear to the BBFC that Wanger was opposed to any cuts at all and wanted the film to be shown at the forthcoming Edinburgh Film Festival to enable the critics to judge the full version. Other United Artists staff had talked him out of this notion but suggested either that Susan Hayward should come to London to ventilate the issue at a press conference or that the film should be submitted directly to local authorities. This attempt to bypass the BBFC did not go down well, no agreement was reached and the issue was shelved until Trevelyan could meet Joseph L. Mankiewicz, the famous Hollywood producer deeply interested in the film because his nephew was one of the scriptwriters, on the understanding that the BBFC would not accept scenes showing Barbara Graham's death in the gas chamber, and that only a few of the BBFC cuts might be reconsidered.

United Artists continued to drag its feet, and Trevelyan's planned meeting with Mankiewicz did not take place until 8 May 1959. In consequence

I Want to Live!'s scheduled February 1959 opening had had to be postponed, but even before that the press had latched on to the impasse between Wanger and the BBFC. On 4 January, Roderick Mann of the *Sunday Express* and then Robert Robinson in the *Sunday Graphic* of 25 January had accurately reported the BBFC's gas-chamber objections but had simultaneously created the impression that the BBFC might reject the film. This was unfounded journalistic speculation, but Anthony Carthew in the *Daily Herald* of 16 February, after the announcement of the film's delayed opening, raised the stakes by advocating that it should be shown in Britain uncut and then highlighting the reasons for the doubts about Barbara Graham's guilt. However, while Wanger continued to contest the BBFC cuts, there was more publicity in the British national press and Susan Hayward had won her Oscar. The *News Chronicle* of 9 April even went so far as to devote a leader to the subject, questioning the need for any cuts, while H. O. Ward in the *Reynolds News* of 12 April took the trouble to travel to Amsterdam to see the full version. He concluded that this should be shown in Britain, a view which received reinforcement a few days later when the Republic of Ireland's censors passed the film uncut.

Through all this Trevelyan remained intransigent until he at last met Mankiewicz, when he explained the full extent of the required cuts and the reasoning behind them. Under the impression that more extensive cuts had been requested, Mankiewicz proved amenable, himself supervised the cuts while he was in London and saw to it that when the cuts had been carried out, the film was resubmitted to the BBFC. This speed suggests that before the meeting Mankiewicz had managed to persuade Wanger that the film's British release had been delayed for too long, and that further delay would adversely affect its commercial prospects. Almost three weeks after his meeting with Mankiewicz, Trevelyan went through the cuts with the film's editor, William Hornbeck, and found them satisfactory even though a scene in which a doctor comes to the death cell with a stethoscope and fits this on to Barbara Graham was retained. As Trevelyan commented, there were subsequent shots of her with a length of tube protruding from the front of her dress, which would be unaccounted for if the stethoscope scene was missing. With the other cuts having already been carried out, totalling some four minutes' running time, the stethoscope scene was considered less important, In this version, after Harris and examiner Mary Glasgow had viewed the film again, the BBFC awarded it the 'X' certificate on 28 May 1959.

I Want to Live! was at last released in the West End of London in late July 1959. For the most part the critics found it impeccably made but harrowing, while Nina Hibben in the *Daily Worker* of 25 July and Derek Hill in the *Tribune* of 31 July criticised the BBFC cuts. Moreover, some weeks later Gerald Kaufman, writing in *Forward* on 21 August, fiercely attacked the cuts and accused the BBFC of having acted as pro-capital punishment propagandists. In an unpublished letter to Kaufman, Trevelyan maintained that the BBFC cuts had no connection with the capital punishment debate in Britain. His official line was that the BBFC had never allowed the details of any execution and would never do so lest scenes of this type attracted people with a morbid curiosity. In his view, even with the cuts, the film's abolitionist message remained powerful.

While this was valid, the fact remains that Trevelyan had proved to be uncharacteristically inflexible over *I Want to Live!* at a time when the film was being exhibited uncut throughout Western Europe. Perhaps inadvertently, he revealed in his first interview with a journalist about the film that there was more to it, for he was quoted by Roderick Mann in the *Sunday Express* of 4 January 1959 as saying that allowing execution details in a film would create an undesirable precedent and 'the next thing we know there will be a camera going into Wandsworth to show a chap being swung.' This hints that, despite the American setting, the British controversy over the death penalty was not far from the forefront of Trevelyan's mind. Although personally sympathetic to the abolition of capital punishment, his remark to Mann is an indication that the BBFC cuts to *I Want to Live!* were not entirely unrelated to the contemporary British capital punishment controversy. In the event the British abolitionists carried the day in 1965, since when *I Want to Live!* has remained in a relative British cinematic backwater, although the BBFC cuts were restored in the video version allowed during 1998.

The Devils

This John Whiting play, based upon the 1952 Aldous Huxley novel *The Devils of Loudon*, is set in Loudon in France during the early seventeenth century, when the local priest, Urbain Grandier, opposes King Louis XIII's plan to demolish the village's fortress tower. The high-minded Grandier is a habitual womaniser who conducts an affair with a widow parishioner and seduces a young girl committed to his care, actions which arouse his bishop's strong disapproval, even though Grandier later marries the young girl, and lead to his downfall. The Ursuline abbess, Sister Jeanne des Anges, is a hunchback whose suppressed carnal desire for Grandier leads her into a frantic display of supposed demonic possession and accusations against Grandier of also being possessed by devils and of stimulating her sexual desire for him. This event is seized upon by the bishop and

Figure 9 Vanessa Redgrave as Sister Jeanne des Anges in *The Devils* (GB, 1971). Warner Bros/The Kobal Collection

two other priests, Fathers Barré and Regnier, as a chance to bring about the ruination of Grandier, whom they all hate.

Eventually a member of the royal family, Prince de Condé, is sent to Loudon to investigate the situation. By then Sister Jeanne's hysterical out-pourings are abating through an exorcism by enema, but they have been followed by similar behaviour from the nuns in her charge. Barré and Regnier persuade the nuns to renew their hysteria before Condé's arrival, but nonetheless Condé reports that Grandier is innocent of the accus-ations. However, Louis XIII and his chief minister, Cardinal Richelieu, overrule him, grasping the opportunity to destroy resistance to the demo-lition of the village's defences. Grandier is consequently brought to trial for dealing with Satan and is condemned to death by burning after being tortured for the extraction of a confession which will weaken Grandier's support among the villagers. But, even when finally facing death at the stake, he refuses to acknowledge his guilt.

The Shakespeare Memorial Theatre forwarded the play to the LCO on 14 August 1960 for production at the Aldwych Theatre in the

West End during the following December. Reader of Plays Troubridge reported,

> To the basic Huxleyan scientific anti-clericalism are added many instances of the ignorance, spitefulness and superstition of human nature, somewhat irradiated by the courage and religious philosophy of the falsely accused priest, Grandier. As the main action relates to the supposed demonic possession of four nuns, there are some lewdnesses . . . [which] will want careful sorting out. There is also a prolonged torture scene that is objectionable and much general blasphemy . . . The torture, much of which we see, is what is called in Scotland the Boot, the crushing of the bones of the feet and legs by wedges.[10]

Troubridge recommended eighteen possible changes involving blasphemous and sexual dialogue as well as scenes of the confessional, a Mass and the enema. He also drily observed that torture scenes were usually played off-stage. Lord Chamberlain Scarbrough agreed with much of this, although he did permit one of two confessional scenes. His decisions were conveyed to the Shakespeare theatre company on 30 August, which formed the prelude to a meeting on 16 September between Whiting and the LCO Comptroller, Sir Eric Penn. Their discussion concentrated upon five points: (1) allegedly joke dialogue drawing a parallel between men kneeling in church and their kneeling to enter a woman, (2) dialogue in a speech by Grandier regarded as blasphemous, (3) the line 'all of you' indicating Grandier's entire body as he is being shaved before the burning, which was seen as a reference to his pubic area, (4) the enema scene, particularly the sight of a syringe and (5) the torture scene. Whiting undertook to rewrite the last two scenes with fresh stage directions and to amend the offending dialogue, but this was not completed and resubmitted to the LCO until 23 December 1960. Meanwhile the production had been delayed, and the question of the torture scene remained outstanding.

On 3 January 1961 Troubridge regarded the resubmitted script as a singularly half-hearted attempt to comply with the Lord Chamberlain's instructions, with new objectionable lines, while the ordered deletions too often remained in truncated form. Lord Scarbrough was adamant that the latter should be either altered or removed, although he allowed one or two and retained an open mind on several main points for the moment. These were: (1) whether or not the syringe should be visible in the enema scene, (2) a new scene in which Grandier conducts his own marriage service with the girl he has seduced, (3) the torture scene and (4) the translation into Latin of the blasphemous words in Grandier's speech.

Eventually Scarbrough insisted upon several more dialogue cuts, the removal of a scene with Grandier and the girl he married in bed together and no references or 'business' indicating the enema or noises of the 'devil's' coitus. He would allow the torture scene only if the torture chamber was blacked out on stage when the wedges were being inserted and hammered home. Whiting and the play's director, Peter Wood, were notified of all this on 14 January, which led to a further meeting between Penn and the theatre management on 2 February. At this meeting all the outstanding matters, except the torture scene, were finally resolved, but four days later the theatre's intentions on this were communicated to the LCO in minute detail.

The stage was to be divided into three sections. The torture would occur in the centre, while Grandier's young wife would appear on the right. A lattice-work grill was to be positioned across the front of the whole centre section, and when Grandier was about to be tortured, a low table was to be brought in and placed in the middle of the centre section, while the torture box was to be placed on the low table. Grandier was then to be forced into the box, at which point the lights would be adjusted so that the table, the box and Grandier himself would all be plunged into darkness. Then two beam lights from either side of the stage were to send a horizontal channel of light across the centre section to show merely the heads and shoulders of the tor-turers in the scene. When the three wedges were about to be hammered into the box to break Grandier's legs, the same procedure was to be adopted each time, when one of the torturers was to hold the wedge pointing downwards and move it downwards towards the box, which was to remain in darkness. Another torturer would raise the hammer over his shoulder, seen in the beam of light, and bring it down so that it passed out of the beam before he hit the wedge in the darkness. Grandier's screams were to be heard from the darkness, while his wife was to continue in full light throughout the pro-ceedings. Her reactions to the torture and resulting screams of pain were to be visible, which meant that she would indirectly communicate the horror to the audience. After the third wedge had been hammered into the box, the lights were to go up in the centre section, when Grandier would be taken out of the box with his legs covered by a blanket.

This was perhaps the first time a torture scene on stage had ever been allowed, which explains the LCO's supervision of it in such depth. Lord Scarbrough sanctioned the scene with these stage directions, and *The Devils* received a licence in February 1961. When the play opened at the Aldwych Theatre, with Richard Johnson as Grandier and Dorothy Tutin as Sister Jeanne, the critics were enraptured more by the acting than the play. However, the public was more receptive, and the cast was revised from 18 May, when Virginia McKenna replaced Dorothy Tutin. The play closed in December 1961 and was the subject of only one public complaint to the LCO from a married woman living in Shropshire, who had seen the play in mid-June in the company of her daughter, an almoner in a London hospital. This letter was couched in very strong terms indeed, the play being described as 'pornographic filth' and 'not only unclean, but blasphemous'. The writer declared that she came away from the theatre feeling that what she most needed was a bath, as she had always understood that he who touches pitch is defiled, and she felt she had been liberally besmirched with pitch of the deepest dye. This lady was highly articulate and understood the workings of theatre censorship very well, but not perhaps the spirit of the changing times. In his reply Penn stated that the Lord Chamberlain did not believe the play to be blasphemous since it represented historical fact. He also felt it was not corrupting and a ban would therefore not have been justified. Nonetheless Lord Scarbrough sent LCO staff to see the play, and they reported that it had been staged without the exaggerations mentioned in the press, which a producer intent on stage obscenity might have carried out.

The lady's letter to the LCO, which bore out the LCO's view that only intelligent people would be likely to see *The Devils*, was possibly rooted in her religious conviction, although she did not refer to religion as such. It proved to be a foretaste of what awaited the film of *The Devils* ten years later. In the interim British 'new wave' cinema had gathered momentum through such films as Basil Dearden's *Victim* (1961), Tony Richardson's *The Loneliness of the Long Distance Runner* (1962) and *Tom Jones* (1962), Lindsay Anderson's *This Sporting Life* (1963) and *If . . .* (1968), Joseph Losey's *The Servant* (1963) and *King and Country* (1964) and Lewis Gilbert's *Alfie* (1966). Some of these, particularly *Tom Jones* and the James Bond cycle beginning with *Dr No* (1962), were successful in the United States, with the result that the major Hollywood studios became ready to finance British films. One such case was *The Devils*, with money provided by Warner Bros. Production on this under the direction of Ken Russell opened at Pinewood Studios during August 1970, with Oliver Reed as Grandier, Gemma Jones as his young wife and Vanessa Redgrave as Sister Jeanne. The names of the lesser characters were sometimes changed, but the plot remained substantially the same as the play, although here and there embellishments were made, and Russell was not the man to overlook the sexploitation opportunities offered by certain aspects of the story.

Political and social conditions were highly untimely for such a film. The unexpected election of Edward Heath's Conservative administration in June 1970 had opened the door to those intent upon a resolute assault against a perceived over-liberal trend in public life generally and the arts in particular. Furthermore, Ken Russell had already acquired a reputation among such folk as a cinematic symbol of the 'permissive society' for his

1969 film *Women in Love*, an adaptation of the D. H. Lawrence novel which included the screen's first nude wrestling scene between two males (Alan Bates, Oliver Reed), shown in full frontal view. In the following year Russell's *The Music Lovers*, an idiosyncratic life of Tchaikovsky (Richard Chamberlain), stresses his homosexuality and depicts his unhappy marriage to a nymphomaniac (Glenda Jackson) in sexually explicit terms. These two films focused attention on Russell as an apostle of the 'permissive society' in the eyes of its opponents, a trend exacerbated by press sensationalism over *The Devils* in the *Daily Mirror* and the *Sunday Mirror* during November and December 1970 before the film was completed.

This sensationalism contained some grains of truth, and the adverse pre-publicity for the film meant that the BBFC could not evaluate it without regard to public opinion. Warner Bros had slashed five minutes from the film before its American release, and it is probable that Trevelyan knew of this, for he saw the film in rough cut sometime early in January 1971 and again with Lord Harlech, the BBFC President, on 27 January at a special private showing which Russell had arranged. In the first of these viewings and also possibly the second the five minutes' cuts which Warner Bros had insisted upon, a climactic scene of a blasphemous orgy, were included. Trevelyan at some stage was adamant that the scene would have to go.[11] Accordingly, when the film was officially submitted to the BBFC on 9 February, this scene had been deleted, the footage being 10,122.

Four examiners viewed this version, in itself an indication that unusually difficult problems were anticipated. The general tone of their reactions was epitomised by Audrey Field,

> [F]or me, the chief impression given is of people who want to make a lot of money by unbridled sex, violence, horror and brutality . . . we would all be very glad if the picture could be left to the local authorities, since we cannot see much possibility of it being toned down sufficiently for us to feel at all happy about it, or for the Board's general standards in regard to sex and brutality not to be at risk in passing the film . . . It may be a good thing to show the film to representatives of the Roman Catholic Church; but if they have no objection, I don't think it should dispose of ours.[12]

Her specific objections were to maggots on a corpse on a wheel; a plague scene; Grandier coming down from Christ's crucifixion cross to copulate with Sister Jeanne (in her fantasy); the huge syringe being applied to Sister Jeanne in the enema sequence; too much nudity, too much masturbation, and sequences of nuns making love together; too much beating of Grandier's feet and legs in the torture scene; and Sister Jeanne using Grandier's charred thigh bone as a phallus.

Two of the other examiners, Newton Branch and Ken Penry, reported in much the same vein, after which Trevelyan held a number of meetings with Russell, the precise course of which is unclear from the confusing BBFC internal records and correspondence. However, over the next few weeks Russell accepted most of the demanded cuts, for by early April he was writing to Trevelyan at some length in an effort to stave off further cuts. A viewing of this cut version took place before the entire examining team, which meant that senior examiner Crofts was seeing the film for the first time. Harlech believed that this version was acceptable, whereas Crofts favoured further cuts, particularly to the torture scene and a prolonged one in which Sister Jeanne is seen masturbating on a bed. Although Crofts was apparently in a minority of one, he stuck to his guns, and either Harlech was sufficiently fair-minded to modify his views upon reflection or Trevelyan supported Crofts without saying so openly at the viewing, for in fact further cuts were demanded. These were: (1) the reduction of the fantasy scene in which Grandier lies on top of Sister Jeanne on the ground, (2) the deletion from the exorcism scene of Sister Jeanne's legs being held apart while the syringe is pushed in the direction of her vagina, (3) the removal from an orgy scene of a naked girl twirling on a chain, and (4) the removal from the torture scene of one of the two final hammer blows into Grandier and the resulting blood on his legs. Russell made these cuts, although for technical reasons he reduced the shot of Grandier's legs to a murky flash. On this basis *The Devils* finally received the 'X' certificate – altogether it had been cut by 132 feet to 9,990 feet, approximately 89 seconds' running time.

Unfortunately for the BBFC, during the three months it had taken to complete the censorship of the film the opponents of permissiveness had mobilised themselves and been supported by some press critics, especially Felix Barker of the *Evening News*. Accordingly, when *The Devils* was released in Britain in July 1971, it immediately encountered a torrent of press criticism, although only a review in *The Sun* of 14 July went so far as to advocate a ban. By this time Trevelyan had retired from the BBFC and had been succeeded by Stephen Murphy, a fifty-year-old whose previous career had been spent with the BBC and the Independent Television Authority. Murphy saw *The Devils* only after its release but totally agreed with Trevelyan's decision, despite the receipt at the BBFC of much hostile correspondence from the general public.

The religious anti-pornographers led by Mrs Mary Whitehouse had formed themselves into an organised body called the Nationwide Festival of Light in mid-1971 and were concentrating their attacks almost exclusively on the mass media. In this context *The Devils* presented an immediate target for the Festival, which sought to keep the issue alive for as long as possible as pre-publicity for a planned mass rally in late September. In consequence the Nationwide Festival of Light asked the Greater London Council (GLC), which had replaced the London County Council in 1964, to view the film in the hope that the council would ban it. However, once the viewing took place, the GLC sided with the BBFC. After this unsuccessful ploy, Councillor Frank Smith of Bromley, a vigorous anti-pornography campaigner, raised the matter again at a full GLC meeting on 12 September, but with no more success. In October, Glasgow became the first local authority to ban the film, while complaints continued to pour into the BBFC from all parts of the British Isles until mid-1972. There is evidence among the BBFC records of orchestration of these protests from Bromley during April and May 1972, doubtless under the influence of Councillor Smith.

Throughout this storm Murphy stood firm in private, in public and in his dealings with the increasingly anxious local authorities. He never wavered in his view that *The Devils* possesses considerable artistic merit, even if he sometimes failed to couch his replies to those who complained in the more diplomatic language favoured by his predecessor. In November 1971 Sam Peckinpah's *Straw Dogs*, which includes a truncated rape scene and a protracted violent sequence with much blood and gore during the siege of a Cornish cottage, was released. The release of Stanley Kubrick's *A Clockwork Orange*, with a very violent rape scene, followed in January 1972. These two features, and the related Nationwide Festival of Light activities against them, both distracted public attention from *The Devils* and simultaneously kept alive local-authority concern about the film. By the end of August 1972 only twelve local authorities had banned it, while an additional five went on to do so. The complete version of the film has never been seen in public in Britain or anywhere else, and it now seems likely that it is no longer extant. The National Film and Television Archive holds no print, while a video version allowed by the BBFC on 3 July 1984 was shorn of six minutes in addition to the original BBFC cuts. This was before the 1984 Video Recordings Act became operative, but the decision was confirmed on 31 January 1988. This version was transmitted on satellite television in March 1990, while the 1971 BBFC-authorised version was shown on Channel 4 on 25 November 2002.

Notes

1. For the full story of *Nosferatu*, see James C. Robertson, *The Hidden Cinema: British Film Censorship in Action, 1913–1972* (London: Routledge, 1989), pp. 19–22.

2. Lord Chamberlain's Plays Correspondence Files, *Dracula* 1924/5485. Play reader's report, 27 March 1924. All references hereafter come from this file.
3. Lord Chamberlain's Plays Correspondence Files, *The Black Cat* LR 1932/6. Play reader's report, 7 June 1932. All references hereafter come from this file.
4. Lord Chamberlain's Plays Correspondence Files, *East of Eden* LR 1929/10. Minute by Cromer, 6 June 1929.
5. Lord Chamberlain's Plays Correspondence Files, *The Green Pastures* LR 1930/4. W. Higton to Cromer, 3 April 1930. All references hereafter come from this file.
6. Lord Chamberlain's Plays Correspondence Files, *Parnell* LR 1934/13. Play reader's report, 25 October 1934. All references hereafter come from this file.
7. Lord Chamberlain's Plays Correspondence Files, *Parnell* 1936/15298A. Play reader's report, 29 April 1936. All references hereafter come from this file.
8. Lord Chamberlain's Plays Correspondence Files, *Parnell* 1936/15298B. All references hereafter come from this file.
9. BBFC file on *I Want to Live!* Examiner's note, 15 October 1958. All references hereafter come from this file.
10. Lord Chamberlain's Plays Correspondence Files, *The Devils* 1961/1425. Play reader's report, 14 August 1960. All references hereafter come from this file.
11. Mark Kermode, 'Raising hell', *Sight and Sound* (December 2002), pp. 28–31.
12. BBFC file on *The Devils*. Examiner's report, 11 February 1971. All references hereafter come from this file.

CHAPTER 9

Conclusion

The recommendations of the Joint Parliamentary Select Committee in 1909 kept significant criticism of the Lord Chamberlain's theatre censorship at bay until after the Second World War, when pressure for its abolition built up by degrees. In 1948 a Parliamentary Question was tabled on the subject in the Commons, while in March 1949 a private member's bill for abolition was passed in the Commons by 76 votes to 37 but fell due to a lack of Commons time before the 1950 general election. However, by the mid-1950s the private theatre clubs, which had proved to be an outlet for plays which the Lord Chamberlain refused to license, were used more and more to undermine censorship.

In 1956 the New Watergate Theatre Club leased a mainstream London theatre, the Comedy, and enrolled some 68,000 members on the basis purely of a mailing list. The club went on to present a number of unlicensed plays, while the Arts Theatre Club booked an annexe in another London theatre and recruited new members on virtually unrestricted terms. Lord Scarbrough, the Lord Chamberlain from 1952 to 1963, was considering whether or not to have the law tested when the New Watergate plan collapsed. This development eased the pressure on theatre censorship for a time, but Scarbrough endeavoured to persuade Home Secretary R. A. 'Rab' Butler to amend the 1843 Theatres Act so that he was empowered to license plays with 'adult' themes, particularly homosexuality. Had Scarbrough succeeded, this would have been the stage counterpart of the BBFC's 'X' certificate, but Butler was reluctant either to initiate this reform or to allow Scarbrough to use the law against the offending theatre clubs. An article in *The Times* of 15 May 1958 by A. V. Cookman, headed 'Blue Pencil in the Wings,' drew attention to the problem, but although Scarbrough decided six months later not to ban homosexual themes as a matter of course, matters drifted on into 1960.

In November of that year, in an obscenity test case under the 1959 Obscene Publications Act, the D. H. Lawrence novel *Lady Chatterley's Lover*, banned in Britain in its unexpurgated form since 1930, was found by a jury not 'to have a tendency to deprave and corrupt when taken as a whole.' This verdict legalised the book and paved the way for the theatre clubs to challenge the Lord Chamberlain's censorship more directly than hitherto, as stage plays had been placed within the orbit of the Obscene Publications Act. Some of these performances were held under such lax club membership conditions that the plays were virtually open to the general public. This forced Scarbrough and his successor in 1963, Lord Cobbold, to issue general warnings to the private theatre clubs concerning a possible prosecution. By the time that Scarbrough relinquished office he had tried to convince the Home Office that theatre censorship was better enforced by other means than through the Lord Chamberlain. Cobbold also held this view, but he was no more successful than Scarbrough had been in persuading the Home Office that change had become necessary until events made themselves felt.

This process began in Parliament during 1962 when the Labour MP Dingle Foot was refused leave to introduce a private member's measure for the abolition of the Lord Chamberlain's censorship and the substitution of a voluntary system similar to that for films. In May 1964 Lord Willis, the author Ted Willis, asked in the Lords whether the government would abolish theatre censorship and received a negative reply. The election of Harold Wilson's Labour administration in October 1964 raised hopes of a different policy, but when Cobbold approached the new Home Secretary, Sir Frank Soskice, on 11 February 1965, the latter was reluctant to contemplate change. However, four months later the Royal Court Theatre, which had been at the forefront of the movement for change, submitted a script for Edward Bond's play *Saved*, which brought matters to a head. Cobbold was prepared to allow it with amendments, but Bond and the Royal Court refused to accept them and went ahead with the production anyway under supposedly private club restrictions. This was close to civil disobedience, which left Cobbold with no alternative but to take action, although he virtually threatened to resign before the Attorney-General and the Director of Public Prosecutions would agree. In January 1966 the latter launched a prosecution against the Royal Court over *Saved*, the case being tried by a magistrate at Bow Street from 14 February to 1 April 1966.

The Royal Court was found guilty of breaching the 1843 Theatres Act but was given a twelve-month suspended sentence, a decision against which the theatre declined to appeal, presumably because political events had taken over. Towards the end of 1965 Roy Jenkins had replaced Soskice at the Home Office and, with the knowledge of the impending prosecution against the Royal Court, Jenkins agreed to a full-scale Lords debate on theatre censorship. This occurred on 17 February 1966, when both Scarbrough and Cobbold defended continued theatre censorship but not by the Lord Chamberlain. However, other Lords had different ideas, including abolition, and finally the government accepted a Joint Parliamentary Select Committee similar to that of 1909. The March 1966 general election then meant that the committee could not be set up until mid-July 1966, the court case against the Royal Court being decided on the day after the election result returning Labour to office. The committee's membership comprised eight peers and eight MPs – seven Labour, five Conservative, two Liberal and two independent.

The committee met on six occasions between 26 July 1966 and 6 June 1967 and unequivocally recommended the abolition of theatre censorship. Jenkins accepted this, but there were later Cabinet delays and the first draft of the necessary bill was not published until 1968. Unlike 1909, there was no opposition to abolition from the monarch. The bill became law in mid-July 1968 and was operative on 1 September 1968. The 1843 Theatres Act was repealed, local authorities rather than the Lord Chamberlain became responsible for the licensing of theatres, and the laws of libel and slander were amended so that the performance of a play legally became a permanent form of publication subject to the 1959 and 1964 Obscene Publications Acts. It became a criminal offence to stir up racial hatred or encourage a breach of the peace in a play, while the Attorney-General's consent was necessary for any private prosecution against a play.

Even those who favoured the retention of theatre censorship did not mount a stern opposition to its abolition, and although a number of plays during the early 1970s tested the public's tolerance of verbal obscenity and nudity on the stage, only one play was actually prosecuted. Moreover, the Attorney-General refused his consent in 1970 to an attempted private prosecution against *Oh! Calcutta* for nudity. In 1982 he again refused his consent to Mary Whitehouse's private prosecution against *The Romans in Britain*, which had to be brought under the 1956 Sexual Offences Act, although the suit was eventually withdrawn. These were isolated incidents, and since 1968 there has been no concerted movement from any quarter to restore theatre censorship.

The government in 1968 acquiesced in abolition because the stage as a medium of communication had been relegated to relative insignificance by films and television. Theatregoing was largely a middle-class leisure pursuit, whereas cinema attendance had always been a mainly working-class activity. As a result, films increasingly figured as the battleground for defenders and opponents of the 'permissive society,' for by the second half of the 1960s films were becoming more explicit in sex and violence, increasingly in combination. As previously noted regarding the film of *The Devils*, this had reached the point where those resisting permissiveness organised themselves in mid-1971 into the Nationwide Festival of Light and campaigned against the BBFC for allowing certain films during the early 1970s. However, by 1973 this aspect of the Festival's agitation had little to show for its efforts and was displaying signs of losing its momentum. Consequently Festival supporters had recourse to private court actions under common law against BBFC-certificated films from late 1973 to 1976, with varying outcomes, until this avenue was blocked on 1 December 1977, when films became subject to the 1959 and 1964 Obscene Publications Acts. During the 1970s, after John Trevelyan's retirement, he was active in the cause of abolishing adult film censorship. This was taken up by some prominent local authorities, especially the Greater London Council for a time, but neither the Home Office nor the film industry favoured such a measure, while there was no clear indication either way from the general public.

The issue was suspended between June 1977 and October 1979 by the deliberations of the Home Office-appointed committee on obscenity and censorship led by Professor Bernard Williams. However, the committee recommended the retention of adult film censorship in principle, and while this particular finding provoked a certain amount of public debate for a time, the government in January 1981 finally rejected the Williams report in full. In consequence the film censorship structure survived intact from its various 1970s challenges, but the film industry and the BBFC were in manifest decline. Adult film censorship would probably have eventually withered away but for the onset of the video cassette recorder on the open market in 1980.

This event produced in Britain the appearance of American and European extreme horror and sex videos of the kind that the BBFC had routinely rejected or severely cut on film during the 1970s. The outcome was the media-induced 'video nasties' moral panic of 1982–3 and the introduction of a state video censorship through the 1984 Video Recordings Act. The BBFC was given the task of implementing the Act, which came into operation by stages from September 1985 to August 1988, since when video has come to dominate the BBFC's work. Video censorship revitalised the BBFC, but under its impact adult film censorship was retained by default and the question of whether it was still necessary has all but disappeared from public debate. This is understandable in that since the mid-1980s the BBFC, renamed the British Board of Film Classification in mid-1985, has rejected only two films and film cuts have gradually become far fewer. Instead the BBFC has been more concerned with classifying films, while the local authorities since the early 1970s have by degrees almost always accepted BBFC film decisions.

Nevertheless the issue flared up again briefly in 1997 when, despite much adverse pre-release media agitation, the BBFC allowed David

Cronenberg's *Crash* (1996), a Canadian film in which a couple (James Spader, Holly Hunter), injured in a car crash, join a group sexually aroused by car crashes. Westminster City Council and a handful of other local authorities banned it, the first time in well over a decade that any local authority had overridden a BBFC ruling. However, as so often in British film censorship history since 1913, once *Crash* had been released, the controversy immediately subsided. What little public argument there was over whether Britain still requires film censorship for adults, as distinct from classification, died away as well and to date has not been revived. Meanwhile video censorship is alive and well, although the number of banned videos has decreased in recent years.

Select Bibliography

Unpublished Sources

British Board of Film Classification, files on *Alfie*, *Cabaret*, *Cosh Boy*, *The Devils*, *Entertaining Mr Sloane*, *The Family Way*, *I Am a Camera*, *I Want to Live!*, *Irma La Douce*, *The Killing of Sister George*, *Look Back in Anger*, *The Moon is Blue*, *Oscar Wilde*, *Serious Charge*, *The Servant*, *Tea and Sympathy*, *The Trials of Oscar Wilde*, *Women of Twilight*.

British Broadcasting Corporation, Written Archives, Caversham. 'Frankly Speaking', radio interview with Tony Richardson, 12 December 1962; 'Alfie Elkins and his Little Life', audience research report, 30 January 1962; 'The Critics', transcript, 16 December 1962.

British Film Institute National Library, British Board of Film Censors pre-production scenarios, 1946 and 1947.

British Library, Department of Manuscripts, Lord Chamberlain's Plays Correspondence files on *Alfie*, *All in Good Time*, *Auction of Souls*, *The Black Cat*, *Cabaret*, *Cosh Boy*, *Damaged Goods*, *Desire Under the Elms*, *The Devils*, *Dracula*, *East of Eden*, *Edith Cavell*, *Edith Cavell: Her Passing in the Image of Christ*, *Entertaining Mr Sloane*, *The Green Pastures*, *I Am a Camera*, *Irma La Douce*, *The Killing of Sister George*, *Look Back in Anger*, *The Moon is Blue*, *Mourning Becomes Electra*, *No Orchids for Miss Blandish*, *Now Barabbas...*, *Oscar Wilde*, *Parnell* (Crofton), *Parnell* (Schauffler), *Pick-Up Girl*, *The Price She Paid*, *Professor Mamlock*, *Serious Charge*, *The Servant*, *The Shanghai Gesture*, *Tea and Sympathy*, *Tobacco Road*, *The Trials of Oscar Wilde*, *Women of Twilight*.

National Archives, Kew. Cabinet Conclusions (minutes) 23/57; Foreign Office papers FO 395/418 and 427; Home Office papers HO 45/10955/312971.

Theatre Museum, London. Miscellaneous files.

Official Documents

House of Commons debates, vols 213 and 214 (1927–8).

Books

Aldgate, Anthony (1995), *Censorship and the Permissive Society: British Cinema and Theatre, 1955–1965*, Oxford: Clarendon Press.

Baxter, John (1971), *The Cinema of Josef von Sternberg*, London and New York: Zwemmer and Barnes.

Bourne, Stephen (1996), *Brief Encounters: Lesbians and Gays in the British Cinema, 1930–1971*, London: Cassell.

Brandt, George W. (ed.) (1981), *British Television Drama*, Cambridge: Cambridge University Press.

Caine, Michael (1972), *What's It All About?*, London: Century.

Chibnall, Steve and Robert Murphy (eds) (1999), *British Crime Cinema*, London: Routledge.

Christie, Ian (1985), *Arrows of Desire*, London: Waterstone.

Davis, John (1990), *Youth and the Condition of Britain*, London: Athlone Press.

De Jongh, Nicholas (1992), *Not in Front of the Audience*, London: Routledge.

De Jongh, Nicholas (2000), *Politics, Prudery and Perversions*, London: Methuen.

Gale, Maggie B. (1996), *West End Women*, London: Routledge.

Johnston, John (1990), *The Lord Chamberlain's Blue Pencil*, London: Hodder and Stoughton.

Lewenstein, Oscar (1994), *Kicking Against the Pricks: A Theatre Producer Looks Back*, London: Nick Hern Books.

MacKillop, Ian and Neil Sinyard (eds) (2003), *British Cinema of the 1950s: A Celebration*, Manchester and New York: Manchester University Press.

Magnus, Philip (1964), *King Edward the Seventh*, London: John Murray.

Marwick, Arthur (1990), *British Society since 1945*, Harmondsworth: Penguin.

Marwick, Arthur (1998), *The Sixties*, Oxford: Oxford University Press.

Mathews, Tom Dewe (1994), *Censored*, London: Chatto and Windus.

Mizejewski, Linda (1992), *Divine Decadence, Fascism, Female Spectacle and the Makings of Sally Bowles*, Princeton, NJ and Oxford: Princeton University Press.

Osborne, John (1991), *Almost a Gentleman*, London: Faber and Faber.

Phelps, Guy (1975), *Film Censorship*, London: Gollancz.

Rayman, Sylvia (1952), *Women of Twilight*, London: Evans.

Rebellato, Dan (1999), *1956 And All That*, London: Routledge.

Richardson, Tony (1993), *Long Distance Runner*, London: Faber and Faber.

Ritchie, Harry (1988), *Success Stories: Literature and the Media in England, 1950–1959*, London: Faber and Faber.

Robertson, James C. (1985), *The British Board of Film Censors: Film Censorship in Britain, 1896–1950*, London: Croom Helm.

Robertson, James C. (1989), *The Hidden Cinema: British Film Censorship in Action, 1913–1972*, London: Routledge.

Russo, Vito (1981), *The Celluloid Closet: Homosexuality in the Movies*, New York: Harper and Row.

Shellard, Dominic (ed.) (2000), *British Theatre in the 1950s*, Sheffield: Sheffield Academic Press.

Shrimpton, Jean (1991), *An Autobiography*, London: Sphere.

Sinfield, Adam (1999), *Out on Stage*, New Haven, CT and London: Yale University Press.

Stamp, Terence (1988), *Double Feature*, London: Grafton.

Sutherland, John (1982), *Offensive Literature: Decensorship in Britain, 1960–1982*, London: Junction Books.

Taylor, John Russell (ed.), (1968), *John Osborne: Look Back in Anger, A Casebook*, Basingstoke, Hampshire: Macmillan.

Thomas, Donald (2003), *An Underworld at War*, London: John Murray.

Travis, Alan (2000), *Bound and Gagged: Secret History of Obscenity in Britain*, London: Profile.

Trevelyan, John (1973), *What the Censor Saw*, London: Michael Joseph.

Walker, Alexander (1974), *Hollywood, England: The British Film Industry in the Sixties*, London: Michael Joseph.

Wilcox, Herbert S. (1967), *25,000 Sunsets*, London: Bodley Head.

Articles

Aldgate, Anthony (1999), '*I Am a Camera*: Film and theatre censorship in 1950s Britain', *Contemporary European History*, 8: 3, 425–38.

Aldgate, Anthony (2000), '*Women of Twilight, Cosh Boy* and the advent of the "X" certificate', *Journal of Popular British Cinema*, 3, 59–68.

Aldgate, Anthony (2000), ' "Obstinate Humanity": the Boultings, the censors and courting controversy in the late 1960s', in A. Burton, T. O'Sullivan and P. Wells (eds), *The Family Way: The Boulting Brothers and British Film Culture*, Trowbridge, Wiltshire: Flicks Books, pp. 238–54.

Aldgate, Anthony (2003), 'From script to screen: *Serious Charge* and film censorship', in Ian MacKillop and Neil Sinyard (eds), *British Cinema of the 1950s: A Celebration*, Manchester and New York: Manchester University Press, pp. 133–42.

Fink, Janet and Holden, Katherine (1999), 'Pictures from the margins of marriage', *Gender and History*, 11: 2, 233–55.

Holland, Mervyn (2000), 'Now, I feel I can love you, Oscar', *Sunday Telegraph* review, 29 October.

Johnson, Kathryn (2000), 'Apart from *Look Back in Anger*, what else was worrying the Lord Chamberlain's office in 1956?', in Dominic Shellard (ed.), *British Theatre in the 1950s*, Sheffield: Sheffield Academic Press, pp. 116–35.

Kermode, Mark (2002), 'Raising hell', *Sight and Sound*, December, 28–31.

Kidd, Kerry (2003), '*Women of Twilight*', in Ian MacKillop and Neil Sinyard (eds), *British Cinema of the 1950s: A Celebration*, Manchester and New York: Manchester University Press.

McFarlane, Brian (1999), '*Outrage: No Orchids for Miss Blandish*', in Steve Chibnall and Robert Murphy (eds), *British Crime Cinema*, London: Routledge, pp. 37–50.

Richardson, Tony (1959), 'The man behind an angry-young-man', *Films and Filming*, February, 9.

Robertson, James C. (1984), '*Dawn*: Edith Cavell and Anglo-German relations', *Historical Journal of Film, Radio and Television*, 4: 1, 15–28.

Index of Personalities

Index of Film Titles

Index of Play Titles